AF531609

Educational Attitude and Skills Progress

Educational Attitude and Skills Progress

Dr. S.K. PANNEER SELVAM
Assistant Professor, Department of Education
Bharathidasan University, Tiruchirappalli, Tamil Nadu

and

Mrs.R.JAYANTHI
Assistant Professo, JJ College of Education
Tiruchirappalli, Tamil Nadu

RANDOM PUBLICATIONS
NEW DELHI (INDIA)

Educational Attitude and Skills Progress

ISBN 978-93-5111-530-4

Published in 2015 in India by

RANDOM PUBLICATIONS

4376-A/4B, Gali Murari Lal, Ansari Road
New Delhi-110 002
Phone : +9111-43580356, 011-43142548, 011-23289044
e-mail : sales@randompublications.com
info@randompublications.com
randomexports@gmail.com

Reprinted 2021

Type Setting by : Shah Computer Graphics, Delhi-110094
Printed at : Replika Press Pvt. Ltd.

Contents

Part 3
Relationship Between Parental Educational and Student Achievement

---

Part 4
Women Empowerment and School Teachers

Part 5
Invariable Fears of Teachers

Part 1

Computer Potentiality For Higher Secondary Students

1

Computer Potentiality For Higher Secondary Students

Introduction

We are living in a society, which is completely drawn into the computer environment. Computer has become an integral part of our life and living. Now, we cannot think a world without computer. The wonderful achievements of computer have glorif ed the modern world and transformed the modern civilization into a computer civilization.

Computer Education can provide training in scientific method and also helps develop a positive attitude by the learner through learning computer are of great value to citizen living in the society hence computer education is now made a compulsory subject in every system of school education right from the elementary stage.

Computer teaching in schools can make a difference in the lives of children and difference should be aimed at the positive side of the educational ladder. Computer achievement is dependent upon the will of the people, their will of decision making citizens to support it and their will as individuals to become scientist. Therefore liberal educated people in a free society should understand the nature of computer enterprise, the social, economic and political factors that affect its development and the personal satisfactions that come to one who pursues a carrier in it.

Computer covers the wide range of knowledge, the learner wonders at the intricacies. The fast changing world is witnessing so many changes in the curriculum, methodology and Students abilities. Amidst such changing scenario, it would be effective if we change the approaches or methods keeping the Students abilities in mind. We should not forget the fact that all Students can not have chance to go into nature, but every learner can get access to visit the Omnipotent Nature by clicking mouse. It is possible under simulated condition. To make it true and real, computer education is the answer for all of us. When such things are realized in the field of education, there is a chance to create an atmosphere, where everybody can have acquaintance with the nature in this simulation process. But other factors are they're achieving this state of affair in computer education.

Education

Education in the largest sense is any act or experience that has a formative effect on the mind, character or physical ability of an individual. In its technical sense, education is the process by which society deliberately transmits its accumulated knowledge, skills and values from one generation to another.

The word education is derived from *educare* (Latin) "bring up", which is related to *educere* "bring out", "bring forth what is within", "bring out potential" and *ducere*, "to lead".

Computer

In today's educational system, computer is emerging as a very important technology. It is being used on a very large scale in the developed countries due to its interactive capabilities, particularly technology. It is being used any computer can store much data, arrange them properly, record anything that are stores, analyzing the responses of the pupils and can arrange various types of learning materials. In spite of all these, instructions can be imparted to the pupils through computer.

Many decisions regarding of educational technology the computer occupies very important place. Computer is used for individualized instruction. It is based on the self-instructional system. The use of computer has increased not only in education but also in business, industry, war, administration; computer has influenced research work, examination system and instructional system. Hence it is also known as 'Electronic Brain'. Instructional are selected by the computer on the basis of learning behavior.

Meaning of Computer

The word "Computer" has been derived from the word "Compute". Initially, these were considered of fast calculating machines. A computer manipulates the number of symbols, which it accepts as input, processes that input and reproduces this as output. Computers are also called "Data Processors" as they store, process and retrieve data.

A Computer is a device made of electronic circuits and wires etc. More precisely, 'a computer is and electronic device which works under the instructions of stored programmes, automatically accepting the supplied data to analyze and process the data to produce information called the result of that processing device used to calculate and store the data at large, excellent and speed which follows the input processing and output sequence'.

The basic function performed by a computer is the execution of a programme. A programme is a sequence of instructions, which operates on data to perform certain tasks.

In modern digital computers, data is represented n binary forms by using two symbols '0' and '1' which are called 'Binary digits' or 'Bits'. In general, computers use eight bits is termed as a 'byte'.

Thus, one byte is used to represent one character internally. This means that to represent any alphabet, numeral or special character (E.g. A, B, C ... or 1, 2, 3...0 etc) one byte is used. Hence, the computer can be defined as 'a device that computers or calculates numbers'.

A computer can edit text, generate pictures or groups, translate language and even play games in short; a computer is an electronic device with the ability to:

1. Accept data supplied by the user.
2. Input, store and execute instructions.
3. Perform mathematical and logical operations.
4. Give results in accordance with user's requirements.

Major Components of Computer

A computer is an electronic machine that takes input from the user, processes the given input and generates output in the form of useful information. A computer accepts input in different forms such as data, programs and user reply. Data refer to the raw details that need to be processed to generate some useful information. A computer includes various devices that function as and integrated system to several tasks. These devices are,

1. **Central Processing Unit (CPU):** It is the processor of the computer that is responsible for controlling and executing instructions in the computer. It is considered as the most significant component of the computer.
2. **Monitor:** It is a screen, which displays information in visual form, after receiving the video signals from the computer.
3. **Keyboard and Mouse:** These are the devices, which are used by the computer for receiving input from the user.

The unique capabilities and characteristics of a computer have made it very popular among its various users, including engineers, managers, accountants, teachers, students, etc.

Characteristics of Computer

The characteristics and capabilities of a modern digital computer include, among others:

1. **Speed:** A computer is a fast electronic device that can solve large and complex problems in few seconds. The speed of a computer generally depends upon its hardware configuration.
2. **Storage capacity:** A computer can store huge amount of data in its different storage components in many different formats. The storage area of a computer system is generally divided in to two categories-main memory and secondary storage.
3. **Accuracy:** A computer carries out calculat ons with great accuracy. The accuracy achieved by a computer depends upon its hardware configuration and the instructions.
4. **Reliability:** A computer produces results without any error. Most of the errors generated in the computer are human errors that are created by the user itself. Therefore, they are very trustworthy machines.
5. **Versatility:** Computers are versatile mach nes. They can perform many different tasks and can be used for many different purposes.
6. **Diligence:** Computers can perform repetitive calculations any number of times with the same accuracy.

Generations of Computer

Over the years, various computing devices were invented that enabled people to solve different types of problems. All these computing devices can be classified into several generations refer to the phases of improvement made to different computing devices. The different phases of improvement made to computing devices resulted in a small, cheap, fast, reliable and productive computer.

The evaluation of the modern computer can be viewed specific 'Generations' which, starting from the early forties cover 4 generations to date and we are in the middle of the 5th generations today.

History of Computer

In ancient times, people used different mechanical devices and methods for performing computing operations. However, these devices and methods used for calculations were not very fast and accurate. This fact led to the invention of a computer. The computer was developed to produce accurate results at a very fast speed. Since its invention, the computer has gone through several phases of technological developments.

Table 1.1 Generation of computers-a snapshot

	First Generation	Second Generation	Third Generation	Fourth Generation	Fifth Generation
Year	1940-1956	1956-1963	1964-1975	1975-1989	1989-till date
Speed	Fastest computing device of its time	Faster than First generation	Faster than Second generation	Faster than third generation	Fastest of all time
Technology	Vacuum tubes	Transistor	IC	VLSI	ULSI
Programming language	Machine level language	Assembly Language	High level language (HLL)	High level language	HLL, integrated
Development Example	EDSAC EDSAC	IBM-1401, IBM-1620	IBM 360, Honey well -6000	IBM pc Series, Apple Series	Laptop, PDA
Disadvantage	Large & Bulky, Difficult to program	High cost, limited to special purpose tasks	Limited storage capacity	Difficult to manufacture	Lack of human like intelligence

Manual Computing Devices

Sand Table: The idea of using stones for representing numbers and putting them at a place for performing simple calculations led to invention of a device called sand table. It is used for the purpose of calculations. Used stones for representing numbers, Stones were arranged in 3 channels, each channel could have maximum 10 stones.

Abacus: The idea of sand table led to the development of a fast calculating device of that time, which was known as abacus. The abacus replaced the sand frame with a wooden frame, the grooves with wires and the stones with beads. The user of an abacus can perform arithmetic operations by sliding the beads on the wires by hand.

Napier Bones: Another complicated manual computing device called Napier Bones was developed by John Napier in the year 1614. This device was specially designed for the multiplication and quotient of numbers.

Automatic Computing Devices

Difference Engine: Charles Babbage, a professor of mathematics at the Cambridge University, made some worthwhile efforts towards automatic computing. He is also considered to be the father of modern computer. In 1822, he presented a working model of his concept with the help of an automatic mechanical computing machine as difference engine.

MARK 1: In 1937, an American mathematician. Howard Aiken designed MARK I was one of the well-known early computers that could perform the multiplication of two numbers of twenty figures in just 6 seconds.

ENIAC: The Electronic Numerical Integrator and Calculator (ENIAC) was another general-purpose electronic digital computer developed by John Eckert, John Mauchly and their team in the year of 1946. This computer also used the vacuum tube technology in constructing the basis circuits. It was a general purpose computer that was capable of solving all types of computing problems.

EDVAC: in 1949, another electronic computer that used the binary number system for representing and processing values was introduced. This computer was known as Electronic Discrete Variable Automatic Computer (EDVAC). EDVAC was also invented by John Eckert and John Mauchly and was considered as the successor of ENIAC. EDVAC was the first computer that worked on the principle of stored program. The stored program computer considers the programs and data stored in the memory as a string of binary numbers.

EDSAC: Electronic Delay Storage Automatic Calculator (EDSAC) was another early British electronic computer developed by Maurice

Wilkes and his team at the University of Cambridge Mathematical Laboratory in 1949. It also used the vacuum tube technology in constructing the basic logic circuits and mercury delay lines for constructing the memory of a computer. The typical input and output unit of this computer system was punch card and teleprinter respectively. These computer systems were only able to carry out 650 instructions per second.

UNIVAC: In 1951, the company invented the first commercial computer that was known as Universal Automatic Computer (UNIVAC). This computer was bulky computer that used 5200 vacuum tube s for constructing the basic logic circuits. The mercury data lines were used to construct the memory for storing data and programs. It was able to process numbers as well as alphabetic characters in an efficient manner. The important feature of UNIVAC-that made it unique among other well-known early computers-was that it provided separate processes for handling input/output and processing functions.

Applications of computer

Today, computers are used in almost every sphere of life such as Education, Communication and Banking. The various application areas of computers are as follows:

1. **Education:** Computers are used in schools are used in schools and colleges to teach students in a better and easy way. The students can get more information about a specific topic or subject using the Internet. Computers help in easy learning by creating presentations on a specific topic. Today, students can fill their application forms and give their exams online that facilitates distance education.

2. **Business:** Computers are used in different types of businesses to store a large amount of information in the form of database. Using computers, business meetings can be held between people sitting at remote locations through web conferencing. Buyers and sellers can conduct business online through the use of computers and Internet.

3. **Communication:** Computers that the connected with each other through Internet can be used to transfer data to and from other computers. In order to establish communication between two users, e-mail is one of the most common mediums that are used. Through e-mail users can send/receive text messages, graphic messages and life attachments.

4. **Science:** Computers are used by various scientists for the purpose of research and development. They generally make use of computer for research analysis of new theories. With the help of computers, scientists are moving towards the possibility of predicting natural disasters such as earthquake and tsunami.

5. **Engineering:** Computers are used by engineers for the creation of complex drawings and designs while working in different fields like automobiles and construction.

6. **Entertainment:** Computers are used in the entertainment industry for creating graphics and animations. There is various free as well as proprietary graphics software available for creating graphics and animations.

7. **Banking:** Now days, computers are being increasingly used for online banking. Through online banking, the users or customers can transfer and receive money by using computers and Internet. Some banks also provide the facility of online bill payment through their websites.

8. **Health:** computers are used by doctors to diagnose various kinds of diseases and ailments. Several analog and digital devices are connected with computers enabling the doctors to monitor the condition of a patient and view the internal organs of the body.

Computer Education

The International Education Commission, 1972 (Learning to be) has rightly reported that in educational systems and establishment's computers are widely used for solving administrative problems such as payment of salaries control of funds invoicing and accounting. They have been found useful in organizing school, transport networks with maximum efficiency in solving complex problems of organization and in planning and building etc. especially when the volume of data involved is massive. Computers can identify, evaluate, collect and classify information in all its complexity and detail and supply them when required.

Computers are greatly used in pedagogic research and experiments. They are found very useful in evaluation and checking schoolwork. They can store and retrieve vast quantities of information about the entire school going population without much time and difficulty. Data profiles on each pupil for the entire school career are prepared and maintained easily with the help of the computer. Computers help Students in developing self-education practices by devising library classification by data selection information on educational and employment facilities.

The computer plays an important role ion life long education and enables Students to acquire knowledge and explore possibilities to solve problems. This develops their decision-making faculties and improves conditions for mutual interaction between the pupil and system. There are also several devices, which use graphics to assist speech training and make it pleasant views, have been developed to help visually handicapped persons read text. Even the totally blind people can learn to use option that translates printed words into tactile signals, received by the reader through the fingertips.

Computer in Education

The computer is now regarded as a super teaching machine, its use in education has been tried as an innovation and it has proved its reaching efficiency in many developed countries. The computer has been helping the teacher in the following areas.

1. Preparation of timetable and schedules.
2. Allocation of learning materials according to individual needs and interests.

3. Provision of direct interaction between pupils and subject matter.
4. Providing information or data for guidance and reference.
5. Engaging Students in tutorial work.
6. Evaluation of Student's performance and classifications of children according to abilities.
7. Maintenance of progress cards efficiently and confidently.
8. Providing immediate feedback to Students for better interaction and motivation.

Advantages of Computers in Education

Computers are very good at searching, sorting and displaying information in a wide variety of forms. Text, number, picture, sound, animated sequences and now even video can be stored and manipulated using a computer. Moreover, because they can do this manipulation very fast. The following are other significant advantages of computers more particularly in an educational system.

1. The computer helps in individualizing instruction.
2. It never gets tired nor loses patience.
3. It can repeat the information as many times as the Students want.
4. It can also be used for the Student evaluation, record keeping and reporting.
5. Computers can perform a large sum of work within a second.
6. Computers can help the learner in storing, retrieving, searching for and collecting relevant information.

Application of Computer Education

The new innovation in the educational technology is the application of computer education. Even though it enters the field of education very late, it plays a very important role in today's education. These days, the modern computers can be classified into the following two categories. This categorization depends on the application of the computers. These are,

Special purpose computers:

These computers are designed for particular job. E.g. Printing Computer, color photo printing computers.

General purpose computers:

Such are designed to meet the need of variety of technical problems. These computers used to prepare pay bills, print sales reports, etc...

Computers are used not only to tabulate and store data, but for different statistical analyses. Besides their simple arithmetic marks, then are used for presenting complex graphs and tables in appealing colors and accurate information. There are computers that can read for blind or low vision learner, software to read aloud for moderate deaf. The entire teaching process at least in higher education level started moving ahead in this way of right use of computers in academic setting.

Computer Managed Instruction (CMI)

In computer managed instruction the role of computer is mainly record keeping and it does not provide any direct instruction to the learner. This type of instruction helps to assess the learner's present level of knowledge weakness or gaps in his learning and remedial action possible.

Computer Based Instructional Simulation (CBIS)

Computer based Instructional Simulation (CBIS) is the most powerful application of computers in instruction as it provides realistic substitutes for real life experiences that might be otherwise impractical, time consuming or even dangerous. CBIS creates a model situation, which imitates some aspect of reality and the simulation model may be static or dynamic, in which conditions are changed as a result of feedback of pupil's actions and responses.

Computer Assisted Instructions (CAI)

A typical CAI installation consists of individual learning booths, each with a console. The Student is seated. Facing him on the console is a television screen for displaying information. Before he starts a programme, the Student checks in which the computer by displaying his identity number. This connects him with his part of the learning programme.

Advantages of CAI

Computer assisted instruction proves better than all other aids in several respects. There is not only saving of time in learning but it also performs miracles in processing the performance data. This later characteristic helps to determine Subsequent activities in the learning situations. The large amount of information stored in the computer is made available to the learner more rapidly than by any other medium. The dynamic interaction between the Student and instructional programme is not possible to source in any other medium. With CAI, we would completely individualize materials.

Before computers can be of any use, they must be carefully programmed to perform desired functions. This requires through planning of every step and prior thinking. Computers are simple minded. They demand instructions spelled out in explicit detail. Human beings are brilliant but rather sloppy thinkers; computers are stupid but accurate.

Instructional Uses Of Computer

Although a computer can be used in many ways in the educational programmes, the following are some of the areas where is proves to be effective in the instructional process.

Drill and Practice

The Student sits at a specially designed electronic typewriter, which is connected to a computer by telephone lines. He identities himself by a code number and his name. The machine types out the first question and the Student responds. Soon the lesson is underway. The computer keeps track of each Student's performance and can 'read back' to the teacher a summation of each Student's work whenever the Student might be referred to a branching type of remedial exercise. As in programmed instruction, the Student moves at his own, gets immediate feed back and receives individual tutoring.

Tutorial dialogue

The subject matter is literally taught by the Computer programme. Explanations are given orally through audiotape and needed visuals presented in Cathode Ray Tube as in Television. The Students responds on a typewriter keyboard or by pointing on the screen with a light pen. The computer reacts to student's responds by 'talking' to him. Student makes further response. A kind of dialogue takes place between Student and machine. The talking typewriter developed in 1996 by *O.K. Moore* also serves a similar purpose.

Simulation and Games

Simulations are realistic imitations. Simulations are frequently planned in the form of competitive games to increase motivation and interest. Organized social simulations are called gaming, as for example, historical games. Simulation may involve simulator trainers or mock ups which are really Three-Dimensional (3D) teaching aids E.g. an aircraft flight simulator. The most obvious uses of simulation are in extending the experience of pupils and in stimulating their interests. Simulation and gaming increase motivation and self-confidence and can accommodate student of different ages and levels of maturity.

Information handling

One area where processing and information handling capacity of the computer is profitably used is counseling and guidance. Computers store complete cumulative records and match them against employment needs and potentialities.

Limitation of Computer

Maintenance of the computer is also expensive especially when the computer is subjected to heavy use. The design and production of computers specifically for instructional purposes has lagged behind than the design and production for other purposes, i.e. the development of computer system cannot be used with another.

Scheduled Tribes

Tribal peoples constitute roughly 8 percent of the nation's total population, nearly 68 million people according to the 1991 census. For the first time after the country became the formulation of National policy on scheduled Tribes. The policy seeks to bring scheduled into the mainstream of society through a multi-pronged approach for their all-round development without disturbing their distinct culture. There are 67.8 million populations of Scheduled Tribe people, constituting 8.08 percent of India's population. Scheduled Tribes are those, which are notified as such by the President of India under Article 342 of the constitution. The first notification was issued in 1950.

Five principles spelt out in 1952, known as Nehruvian Panchasheel, have been guiding the administration of Tribal affairs. They are;

1. Tribes should be allowed to develop according to their own genius.
2. Tribes' rights in land and forest should be respected.
3. Tribal teams should be trained to undertake administration and development without too many outsides being inducted.
4. Tribal development should be undertaken without disturbing tribal socio and cultural institutions.

5. The index of tribal development should be the quality of their life and not the money spent.

National Policies For Education of Tribal Population

The Indian Constitution assigned special status to the Scheduled Tribes (STs). Traditionally referred to as advises, Vanbasis, Tribes, STs constitude about 8% of the Indian population. According to the Indian Education Report 2002, there are 573 Scheduled Tribes living in different parts of the country, having their own languages different the ones mostly spoken in the state where they live. There are more than 270 such languages in India. Realizing that scheduled Tribes are one of the most deprived and marginalized groups with regard to education, a host of programmes and measures were initiated ever since the Independence. Elementary education is apriority area in the Tribal sub-plans from the 5th Five-Year Plan. Education of ST children is considered important, not only due to the Constitutional obligation but also such as a crucial input for total development of Tribal communities.

Another important development in the policy towards education of Tribal population in the National Policy on Education (NPE), 1986. For the improvement in the education among the Tribal people the NPE specified the following things.

1. Priority will be accorded to opening primary schools in tribal areas.
2. There is need to develop curricula and devise instructional material in Tribal language at the initial stages with arrangements for switchover to regional languages.
3. ST youth will be encouraged to take up teaching in tribal areas.
4. Ashram Schools/Residential Schools will be established on a large scale in Tribal areas.
5. Incentive Schemes will be formulated for STs. Keeping in view their special needs and lifestyle.

Formal Education of the Scheduled Tribes

Formal Education is the key to all round human development. Despite several campaigns to promote formal Education ever since Independence, to achieve the objective of reaching the benefit of Education to Tribal the national policy will ensure that.

1. Tribal are included in the national program of Sarva Shiksha Abhiyan run by the ministry of human Resource Development.
2. Education is linked with provision of supplementary nutrition.
3. Emphasis incentives like Text Books, Uniforms, etc...
4. Educated tribal youth as teachers.

The constitution of India ensures equality of opportunity for Education of all levels and also guarantees the educational advancement of the scheduled tribes and scheduled caste become of their backwardness in Education. At the core of different special programmers being implemented by the Central and State Government for the measures for their educational advancement, besides, residential schools run by the welfare department provision of scholarship, reading and writing materials mid-day meals and garments are the other facilities being offered to the ST and SC Students.

Education is the soul of human civilization and development, which is lacking among the tribal. To complete with general communities, it is necessary to equip them educationally. A sizable proportion of the tribal people live in forest areas. The manner in which forest resources are utilized has a great impact on their welfare, collection of forest produce, grazing, meeting everyday requirements for firewood, etc., are daily life or tribal of they suffer from any disease, medical services are also not available in interior places.

In Educational aspect, increasing the number of tribal as teachers can improve the awareness in education, Tribal form a major chunk of India population true, majority of them are remained in isolation.

Yet with the fast give guidance and counseling whenever necessary. We have to implement the skills in arts and crafts and vocational training in the area of bee keeping, basket making, sericulture, spinning and wearing and fruit preservation etc.,

Need and Significance of the Study

1. In order to bring effective improvement in the quality on education. It is necessary to focus attention on the new technologies.
2. One such recent and most dominating technology is computer technology. But when we think about its development in the field of education.
3. It is only in an infant stage. Hence, it is important to study the awareness of Tribal area higher Secondary Students towards computer potentiality.
4. Computer in modern world is an inseparable component of every walk of life. All the fields in general, directly or indirectly make use computers very powerfully that one cannot imagine the future without the use of computer.
5. In this High-tech era, Students would have much opportunity to know the uses of computer in different setting and for different purposes. But they may not use them or influence somebody to use computer for any of their ventures amidst this broadband web society.
6. Education can enable individuals to make personal responsibility for improving their own status and their community and nation. So computer is bringing some exciting innovations to education.
7. It helps the individuals to make over the most the drudgery of schooling. Computer allocates learning resources to individuals and groups.
8. Computer education provides easy access to files of information for reference and guidance. Computer education engages the students in tutorial interacting and dialogue.

9. Hence the investigator made an attempt to study the awareness on computer potentiality among higher secondary students in Tribal areas.

Statement of the Study

Computer Education is a new one in the field of Education. But it turns most of the educationalists towards it. Add now many researches are going on in this field. Many new methods in teaching and learning process adopted by using computers are emerging day by day. In the modern context it is very important to think about computers in the field of Education generally and a special reference must be made on Teacher Education.

Pupils are distributed with different levels of potentialities. They have different attitudes and perceptions about the world around them. Many psychological experiments tell us that individuals differ in their awareness, interest and many other aspects. Tribal Area Higher Secondary School students are not exceptional for this. In this context the investigator attempts to study the awareness of Tribal Area Higher Secondary Students towards computer potentiality and the topic is *"Awareness on Computer potentiality among Higher Secondary Students at Tribal areas in Namakkal District".*

Background of the Study

In view of the increasing importance of the computer, students who are the citizens of the nation and will be employed in various walks of life cannot afford to keep themselves aloof from this potential medium. The government has therefore, decided to provide the computer education by imparting profound technical knowledge and skills developing positive attitude and interests in the computer. Today our educational system is knowledge and examination oriented that test only the rote memory of the students. The effective domain such as attitudes is neglected in our teaching. Thus the children should also be encouraged to develop positive attitude towards computer which is a part of technology and possess application in almost all human activities. Hence the main outcome of the introduction of computer is the in calculation of proper attitude towards it. Therefore, the present investigation has been undertaken with a view to find out how far the awareness of computer potentiality developed among higher secondary students in Tribal area.

Dfinition of the Terms

Awareness: Awareness is the state or ability to perceive to feel, or to be conscious of events, objects or sensory patterns. In this level of consciousness, sense data can be confirmed by an observer without necessarily implying understanding. More broadly, it is the state or quality of being aware of something.

Computer: A Computer is an electronic machine that takes input from the user, processes the given input and generates output in the form of useful information. A computer accepts input indifferent forms such as data, programs and user reply. It is capable of doing any arithmetic and logical work rapidly that does all work given by its master accurately.

Potentiality: Potentiality and potency are translation of the Ancient Greek word Dunamis or dynamic as it is used by Aristotle to contrast with actuality. Its Latin translation is "potential", root of the English word potential and used by some scholars instead of the Greek or English variants. Dynamics is an ordinary Greek for possibility or capability. Depending on context; it could be translated "potency"," potential", "capacity", "ability", "power", "capability", "strength", "possibility", "force" and is the root of modern English words "dynamic", "dynamite", and dynamo.

Secondary school Students: Secondary school is a term used to describe an educational institution where the final stage of schooling, known as secondary education and usually compulsory up to a specified age, takes place. It follows elementary or primary education, and may be followed by university (tertiary) education. There are many different types of secondary school, and the terminology used varies around the world. Students usually transfer to secondary school between the ages of 10 and 16 years, and finish between the ages of 16 and 18 years, though there is considerable variation from country to country.

Tribal area: Many Tribal groups are settled down in forests or hilly forest tracts that areas are called Tribal Area that means where they are living such areas are called Tribal Area. Mostly they are stay in that place to collect forest products for their daily life. So residence is considered as a great component to make an impact mainly on the awareness on the Computer potentiality.

Objectives of the Study

1. To find out the level of awareness on computer potentiality of Higher Secondary Students at Tribal area.
2. To find out the level of significant difference on the awareness of computer potentiality between Male and Female Students in Tribal area.
3. To find out the level of significant difference on the awareness of computer potentiality between Maths and Science group Students in Tribal area.
4. To find out the level of significant difference on the awareness of computer potentiality between Maths and Arts group Students in Tribal Area.
5. To find out the level of significant difference on the awareness of computer potentiality between Science and Arts group Students in Tribal area.
6. To find out the level of significant difference on the awareness of computer potentiality between educated and uneducated parents of Higher Secondary Students.

Null Hypotheses of the Study

1. There is no significant difference on the awareness of computer potentiality between Male and Female Students.
2. There is no significant difference on the awareness of computer potentiality between Maths and Science group Students.
3. There is no significant difference on the awareness of computer

potentiality between Maths and Arts group Students.

4. There is no significant difference on the awareness of computer potentiality between Science and Arts group Students.

5. There is no significant difference on the awareness of computer potentiality between educated and uneducated parents of Higher Secondary Students.

Scope of the Study

The topic is an investigation on the awareness of Tribal are Higher Secondary Students towards Computer potentiality. Since this is the survey study. The investigator attempted to know the awareness of computer potentiality among Higher Secondary Students at Tribal Area. This study will be of great help for the educationists particularly for the teachers since the concept of education has been changing from time to time.

The awareness may differ from person to person one can learn and do anything with involvement only when he had a better awareness towards it. If we compel anybody to do any work in which one does not have good attitude, then it may be the root cause for many problems. It may give a lot mental fatigue to a person. Thus he can't do it effectively. In this context the investigator attempts to study the influence and awareness of computer potentiality among Higher Secondary Students at Tribal area.

Delimitations of the Study

Broadly speaking any study is impossible without limitation. Research studies in general will have limitation due to many factors. This study too has some limitations. It is the responsibility of the researcher to see that the study is conducted with maximum care in order to be reliable. However, the following limitations were unavoidable in the present study,

This present study was primarily concerned with the awareness of Computer potentiality among Higher Secondary Students at Tribal area in Namakkal District of Tamil Nadu. In this present study the investigator analyzed about the awareness of Computer potentiality among the variables such as gender, studying group (Maths, Science, and Arts), literate and illiterate parents.

Organisation of This Study

The report of the thesis will be presented according to the following sequences. The irst chapter gives introduction, definitions of terms, Statement of problem, objectives and delimitations of the study. Second chapter deals with the review of related literature which are done in India and abroad related to this study. Third chapter gives a detailed account of research procedures and methodology used in this study. Fourth chapter deals with the tabulation of analysis and the interpretations of the data in detail. Fifth chapter describe the findings, conclusions and certain recommendations about the study. This is followed by the bibliography and appendices which consist of the tools used for the study and the related matters.

Conclusion

In this chapter, the investigator described the statement of the problem taken for the research study, objectives of the study, delimitations of the study and the need for the study. In the following chapter, a review of related literature and studies conducted in relevant areas will follow.

II

Review of Related Literature

Introduction

As essential aspect of a research of research project is the review of the related literature such a review represents the third set of the scientific method outlined be Dewey and other educational philosophers and the serious student of research will find an exhaustive Survey of what has already been done on the problem an indispensable step in its solution.

Practically all human knowledge can be found in books and libraries. Unlike other animals that must start a new with each generation a man builds upon the accumulated and recorded knowledge of the past. A survey related literature was found necessary to have an idea of what has been done in similar area to scrutinize the methodology used in coordinated study with others to find gaps to avoid duplication and to direct the work along useful lines.

Review of literature is arranged with a view to look into the findings of few researches which were conducted earlier and which are related to the problem of this current study. The analysis of the previous research findings helps the researcher to known how the hypotheses are constructed types of data, tools for research etc...

Need For Review of Related Literature

For any worthwhile study in any field of knowledge, the research worker needs an adequate familiarity with the library and its many resources practically all human knowledge can be found in books and in libraries. A very effective search for specialized knowledge will be possible only with the help of the related literature. This will help in understanding various aspects of the problem. A review of literature would develop the insight of the researcher. The importance of the review is quite obvious in delimiting the research problems and in defining it better. A complete and elaborate survey of literature will largely enable the investigator to overcome the problems in all quarters of his study. It imparts some sort of confidence in the investigator and consequently the investigator would get a clear picture of the area, his investigation is affiliated to.

Purposes of Review of Related Literature

The survey of related research literature is not without purpose. The following are some of the purposes of such a survey.

1. Complete survey of related literature gives to the researcher's necessary insight into the problem. It enables him to put forth vigorously the rationale for the study.
2. It becomes an important part of the introduction of the thesis.
3. It helps to orient the readers with types with types of research that has been conducted in the field previously.
4. It widens the horizon of the researcher.
5. It suggests appropriate methods to tackle the problem under study.
6. It helps avoiding unnecessary duplication of research of the same nature.

7. It provides basis for formulating valuable hypothesis.
8. It helps to locate data that can be used in comparative interpretation of results.

Studies Conducted in India

P. Srinivasan & R. Muthumanickam (2010) conducted a study on "An Innovative Computer-Assisted Instructional Programme". In this study aims at constructing a Computer-Assisted Instruction Programme (CAIP) in the lesion "Learning" (Education Psychology) for the trainees of Diploma in Teacher Education, Tamil Medium, the investigators found that the students who participated in the CAIP not only enjoyed it and were self-motivated but also should higher achievement when taught through CAIP.

Noushad Husain (2010) conducted a study on "Computer-Based Instructional simulations in Education: Why and how. Children construct their own knowledge through experiences gained by observing, exploring and performing in the real world. The constructivist approach to education centers on this claim, Vygotsky's social constructivist also supports the use of tools, which through scaffolding and providing directed points can "enrich and broaden both the scope of activity and the scope of thinking of the child". Through computer-based instructional simulations we can provide a wide variety of learning experiences to the learners. The simulation environment provides learners with the observations and experiences that they must existing knowledge. This present paper describers the role of computer-based instructional simulations in teaching-learning process.

Sibichen, K.K., St. Joseph's Monastery & Annaraja P. (2010) conducted a study on "Teacher Trainees computer competency enhances their Technology Use in Classroom Teaching". The method adopted in the present study was survey. The investigator used stratified random sampling technique for selecting the sample. The sample consists of 75 secondary teacher education students; among them 37 are male students and 38 are female students. In this study aimed at finding out whether teacher trainee's Competency in computer usage helps them to improve their techno-pedagogical skills in the classroom.

K. Saikumari (2010) conducted a study on "Computer Phobia of IX Standard Students and their Attitude towards Educational Usage of Computer". The investigator used random sampling technique for selecting the students from three types of schools, Government, Aided and Private. The sample size was 310. The sample included boys and girls of the age group 13 to 15. The investigator found the factors like gender, locality of the school and types of management of the schools do not influence the computer phobia of IX standard students and their attitude towards computer usage in education.

Devender Bhukya (2010) conducted a study on "Educational provisions for Tribal Children in India". The author says that teachers working in tribal schools should play a key role in imparting education for tribal children and adds that teacher regularity in the school is essential to reduce dropout rate and improve student attendance.

Dr. D. Ushalaya Raj (2010) conducted a study on "Effectiveness of Computer Assisted learning multimedia on Science Achievement". The present investigation was carried out in two Government Higher Secondary Schools in Chennai. The total sample consists of 98 students that include both boys and girls studying class IX under State Board Syllabus. Computer Assisted learning material with Multimedia module was designed and developed for certain science concepts and used as a tool in the teaching-learning process. Achievement test was constructed by the investigator. The findings were, At the post-Test Level the mean values of achievement differs significantly from the pre-test for experimental group for which the learning-experiences have been provided by incorporating the Computer Assisted Learning (CAI) with Multimedia presentation. The results of the study show that the CAL strategy positive influence on the learner's achievement, there is a significant difference in the mean values of achievement, of control and experimental group after experimentation. This shows that Computer Assisted Learning multimedia strategy has facilitated the students to score better Compared to that of Traditional method.

The mean gain scores of achievement differ significantly between High Achievers and Low Achievers of Experiment group. The low-achievers mean gain score is much higher than high achievers. This indicates that CAL strategy is facilitating the performance of all the categories and low-achievers are more attracted and motivated to utilized effectively for the beneficial of low-achievers and to improve their performance.

Dr. Girija. N. Srinivasalu & Dr. S. Vijayalakshmi (2010) conducted a study on "Effectiveness of Computer Multimedia Package (SLM) on Achievement in Social Science, an Experimental Study". The study was experimental in nature and post test single group experimental design was used. The study included those students studying Social Science at Secondary school level. As a sample 104 students of IX standard of Indiranagara, comprising boys and girls were groups i.e. Control and experimental group. Both the groups were equated on the basis of their pre test scores. The findings were 1) a strategy implemented with self learning material of Multimedia techniques brings about improvement in Social Science on the achievement of students of Experimental group. 2) There was a superior performance of experimental group over the traditional group which suggests that SLM (MMP) was found effective. 3) A focused treatment with self learning Material of Multimedia techniques has enhanced the achievement of students of experimental group in Social Sciences. 4) The gender of the students has no influence on the achievement in Social Science of students of Experimental group.

Vimal Kishor & Neha Mahant (2010) conducted a study on "Attitude of Tribal and Non-Tribal High School Students towards Studies". The major purpose of this research was to investigate the attitude towards studies among secondary school tribal and non-tribal students. The data were collected on 120 subjects selected through purposive through S.P Anand Student's Attitude towards studies scale. The collected data were subjected to t-test for large independent groups and means on different dimensions of the scale. The results indicate that the tribal and non-tribal high school students do not vary on most of the dimensions of the 'students' attitude towards studies 'scale. The locale too does not have much effect on the attitudes of the students towards studies. Further, it was also found that the tribal and non-tribal high school students differ significantly on their total attitude towards studies and 'linking for studies' dimension of 'students' attitude towards studies' scale.

Santhosh Kumar Behera (2009) conducted a study on "Attitude of Scheduled Caste and Scheduled Tribe children Towards Education in Kalahandi district of Orissa: A Comparative study. In this study 44 children of 30 SC families and 47 children of 30 ST families (total-91 children both SC and ST families) residing in Kalahandi district of Orissa were taken as representative sample of the whole population. An attitude Scale (Likert-Type) was used for knowing the attitude of the SC and ST children towards education. The findings were, 1) The attitude of SC children towards education is more favorable than that of ST Children. 2) There is significant difference between the attitude of male-and female children belonging to ST group towards education. 3) The attitude of male-children of Sc group towards education is more favourable than that of female-children of ST group. 4) The attitude of female-children of SC group is more favourable than the male-children of ST group towards education. 5) There is significant difference between the attitude of male-children of SC group and male-children of ST group towards education. 6) The attitude of female-children belonging to SC group is more favourable than that of female-children of ST group.

Rafeedali E (2009) conducted a study on "Computer-based Technology and its pedagogical Utility". The investigator used the self developed tool for collection of data (Computer awareness Questionnaire). The objective scoring procedure was adopted for analyzing the questionnaire. The investigator decidec to assign one mark to each "Yes" response and zero mark "No" response. The investigator made a criterion of 50% as the essential minimum percentage to substantiate the hypothesis. The sample selected for the study was 300 teachers of higher secondary schools from the Malappuram district of Kerala. The findings were, 1) Most of the Higher Secondary School teachers have basic computer knowledge. 2) The concept of smart classroom is unfamiliar to most of the Higher Secondary School teachers. 3) Only 12.67% of Higher Secondary

School teachers are able to handle LCD. 4) Computer is a very helpful device for evaluation but only a small percentage of higher secondary school teachers are using computers for evaluation. 5) Among the Higher Secondary School teachers female teachers are using computer more for educational purposes than male teachers. 6) Higher Secondary School teachers are not applying the Information of Higher Secondary School teachers are using PowerPoint presentation in the classroom. 7) Only 11.33 percent of high Secondary School teachers are using LCD. 8) The investigator finds that most of the teachers use computers for educational purpose.

Dr. Anil Ambasana (2009) conducted a study on "Utilization of Computer Technology in Remedial Instruction. In this study purposive sampling was done. Shri Sarvodaya Vidyalaya a secondary school of Rajkot city was chosen for the study. One class out of three classes of grade X was selected randomly. There were forty students in that class. Thus the sample size was of forty. The findings were, computer-Assisted Instruction program in remediation task was found successful as the students were able to overcome the difficult points of the content. They were able to increase their achievement significantly.

Jagannath K. Dange (2008) conducted a study on "Effectiveness of computer Assisted Instruction in the development of Environmental awareness and Environmental attitude". The investigator developed a CAI package on five units pertaining to environment in the syllabus in Science prescribed for 8th Standard in the Karnataka State Syllabus. After administering a pre-test he taught a sample of 30 students for a period of one and a half month these units with the package and conducted a post-test. The results indicate that the CAI package has made for a statistically significant gain in attitude and awareness scores of the sample.

K.B.S. Jyothi (2007) conducted a study on "Impact of Computer-based Learning on students of chemistry". In this study undertaken to prepare a self-instructional module on the topic "chemical Bond" for class IXth students of Chemistry and compare the effectiveness of this self-instruction module with conventional teaching methods, the Investigator finds that the self-instructional module prepared by a teacher through PowerPoint presentation has immense positive impact on learning of chemistry.

B. Vijayalakshmi & T.S. Shri Valli. (2006) conducted a study on Computer Education in High Schools. The investigator used the survey method. A questionnaire was constructed and developed after interviewing heads of the Institutions, high schools computer teachers, taking into consideration the views expressed by the experts in the field of computer and education. The analysis and interpretation of the data are presented under the following heads. (1) Computer education in schools with respect to area of schools. (2) Computer education in schools with respect to type of management.

Sr. Nirmala Sundararaj (2005) conducted a study on "Attitude towards computer Education of the B. Ed Trainees of Tamil Nadu Open University". The investigator has used survey method for studying the problem. Attitude towards computer education scale was developed and validated by the investigator. The sample was 60 B. Ed Trainees of Tamil Nadu Open university are selected at random from St. Ignatius College of Education centre, Palayamkottai. The findings were, 1) There is significant difference between male and female B. Ed Trainees in their attitude towards computer education. 2) That are the female B. Ed trainees are better than the male trainees. 3) There is significant difference between rural and urban B. Ed Trainees in their attitude towards computer education. That is the urban B. Ed trainees have better attitude towards computer education than the rural trainees. 4) There is significant difference between arts and science B. Ed trainees in their attitude towards computer education.

Vaiyapuri (2004) conducted a study on "Attitude of the teacher's towards computer in Cuddalore Educational District". According to this study, the researcher found out the attitude of the teachers, the difference between male and female teachers, difference between Urban and Rural teachers and the difference between Secondary grade and post graduate teachers were analyzed with respect to cognitive attitude towards computer it was found that the gender and subjects of the teachers evinced no significance difference. Also it was found that the gender, locale of the school evinced no significance difference with respect of their affective attitude towards computer.

Bala Ayyappan (2003) conducted a study on "B.Ed student's attitude towards the use of computer". The study showed that gender of students caused significance with respect to their attitude towards the use of computer, but the locale and educational qualification did not cause significance difference with respect to their attitude towards the use of computer.

Rajesh (2003) attempted to examine in the study entitled "A study on the attitude of Teacher training procedures towards computer education in Kottayam district-Kerala", the attitude of teacher training Students towards computer education, to compare the attitude of male and female teacher training students towards computer education, to compare the attitude of rural and urban teacher training students, and to compare the attitude of arts and Science students towards computer education.

S.Rajasekar (2002) conducted a study on "University Students' Attitude towards computer". In the present study, a scale to measure the attitude towards computer, constructed and standardized by kumaran (997) was used. The sample of the study was 294 second year post-graduate students from the Arts and Science faculties of Annamalai University were selected using cluster sampling technique. The present study has shown that gender, the subjects (Arts and Science) and the locale of the university students do not influence their attitude towards computer. Also this study has shown that a large number of (78.91%) University students have a relatively favorable attitude towards computer.

Kumaran, D. and Selvaraju, K. (2001) conducted a study on "A study of cognitive and Affective Computer Attitudes of Teachers". The objectives of the study were (1) To validate the cognitive and affective computer attitude scale using factor analysis. (2) To study the computer attitude of the teachers. (3) To study the cognitive computer attitude of the teachers. (4) To study the affective computer attitude of the teachers. (5) To study whether the teachers differ significantly in computer attitudes, with respect to their personal background and contextual variables.

The sample consisted of 275 teachers, selected through stratified random sampling techniques. The investigators developed the computer attitude scale based on the ideas gained through article authored by Bannom, Marshall and Fluegal (1985) for use in data collection. SD, and 't' were used for the data analysis.

The findings of the study were (1) In general, teachers had more favourable computer attitude. (2) The gender of the teachers had significant influence on effective computer attitude and no significant influence on cognitive computer attitude. (3) Age of the teachers had little influence on computer attitude. (4) Younger teachers had more favourable cognitive computer attitude subscale. (5) Difference in the designation of the teachers had no significant influence on computer attitude. (6) Teachers with post-graduation qualification had more favourable computer attitude. (7) The professional educational qualification of the teachers had no significant influence on computer attitude. (8) The subject of specialization of the teachers had little influence on computer attitude. (9) The teachers belonging to computer attitude. (10) Different types of managements of schools had no significant influence on teacher's computer attitude. (11) The types of schools (Boys, Girls, and Co-education) had little influence on computer attitude. (12) The schools belonging to different boards of education had no significant influence teachers' computers attitude.

Panda, Subhash Chandra and Chaudhury, Jayakrushna (2000) conducted a study on "Effect of Computer Assisted Learning (CAL) in Achieving Higher Cognitive skills". The objectives of the study were (1) To determine the degree of attainment of cognitive skills through computer-assisted learning (CAL) compared to traditional approach to teaching. (2) To compare the effect of CAL on the learning achievement of boys and girls.

The sample consisted of 40 students (23 boys and 17 girls) within the age group 15-17 years from Class XII, selected using cluster sampling. They were further divided equally into two groups as control and experimental group. Standard Raven's Progressive Matrices to measure intelligence and objective based achievement test constructed for the purpose were used. Special objective-based lesson plans on CAL were used for treatment in experimental group. Statistical techniques like 'F' test and chi-square were used to analyze the data.

The findings of this study were (1) Computer assisted learning (CAL) resulted in greater learning achievement in all hierarchies of cognitive domain. (2) Male students were found to be superior to female students in learning physics.

Studies Conducted in Abroad

Ngo, Truyen Kim (2006) conducted a study on "Effectiveness of Computer-assisted Instruction (CAI) uses Odyssey in the High School Chemistry Classroom". The purpose of this study was to compare 2 methods of instruction: traditional and computer-assisted. The unit of instruction concerned molecular polarity and intermolecular forces which is a fundamental concept in high school chemistry and the computer-based application used in this study is a new educational software program called Odyssey. This study will review the effectiveness of computer-assisted instruction (CAI) using the Odyssey software compared to traditional instruction on student achievement among first-year high school chemistry students at Orange Country High School of the Arts (OCHSA). The results of this research study determined that while achievements scores on Molecular Polarity and Intermolecular quiz for CAI group were marginally larger than the traditional group, comparison of improvement scores between groups was not statistically significant. Both CAI and traditional instruction were determined to be effective strategies in improving student learning in chemistry. By understanding the effectiveness of CAI in chemistry education, possible suggestions and implications can be better understood among educators and researchers.

Barnett, Louise B. (2006) conducted a study on "The Effect of Computer-assisted Instruction on the Reading Skills of Emergent

Readers". The purpose of this study was to examine the effect of computer-assisted instruction (CAI) on the reading skills of emergent readers in kindergarten classes at select Reading First schools in the School District of Palm Beach Country, Florida. The reading software analyzed was Destination Reading (Riverdeep, 2001), used during the 2004-2005 school year. Comparisons were made between users of the program who used or did not use it. Another factor analyzed was how teacher attitude toward the computer affected student reading achievement. This was established by survey responses. The measures used to compare treatment and non-treatment schools were the Dynamic Indicators of Basic Early Literacy Skills (DIBELS), which tested letter naming ability, initial sound identification, phoneme segmentation ability, and nonsense word decoding. The Word Recognition and Reading Running Record assessments from the Schools District of Palm Beach country reading Writing Assessments System Grades K-1 protocol booklet tested identification of 25 sight words and ability to read continuous text. Students using destination Reading (Riverdeep, 2001) did not benefit significantly from use of the program compared to nonusers. Only on the letter-naming measure was there a significant advantage for all students in the sample and the English language learner group. The CAI group scored significantly lower on the initial sound fluency measure. Word Recognition and Reading Running Record assessments showed no significant results. ESE students showed no significant advantage in having had supplemental computer-assisted instruction on any measures. Factorial ANOVAs were used to compare DIBELS scores for effectiveness of the treatment, pre- and posttest comparisons, and interaction of treatment with test scores for the CAI compared with the nonuser group. ¯-distributions were used to analyze data from the Reading Running Record and Word Recognition assessments. There were no significant differences between the CAI and comparison schools on these two measures. Teacher attitude toward computers did not affect students' acquisition of reading skills, as survey responses were in the positive range for all participants.

Saleem, Huma (2005) conducted a study on "Antecedents of Computer Self-Efficacy and Behavioral Intention to Use New IT: An investigation of the Role of Personality Traits". Computer self-efficacy has been shown to play and important role in one's decision to use new information technology. While there has been a wealth of relationship with individual characteristics and it is only recently that the role of stable individual traits has gained prevalence. Meanwhile, in the 1990's, researchers converged upon the Five-Factor Model of personality as the premiere framework of personality and uncovered several relationships between these 5 factors of personality and organizational behaviour variables. Due to a needed focus on individual differences as they relate to IT use, in conjunction with the emergence of the five-factor model of personality as a credible tool in psychology, this study aims at investigating the relationships between the five factors of personality and computer self-efficacy. A web-survey of 143 faculty members available at a large Canadian university was conducted. Results suggest that extraversion is positively related to CSE, while neuroticism is negatively related to CSE. Results also indicate a positive relationship between PEOU and behavioral intention to use new IT. The study offers a humanistic viewpoint to the technology adoption literature, adds to research examining the relationship between stable and dynamic individual differences, and to organizational behaviour literature that has shown a renewed interest in the role of personality in organizational contexts. Results are also useful in training and selection processes.

Kohlmyer, Matthew Adam (2005) conducted a study on "Student performance in Computer Modeling and Problem solving in a Modern Introductory Physics Course". Matter and interactions, an innovative introductory physics curriculum developed by Ruth Chabay and Bruce Sherwood, emphasizes computer modeling and fundamental physical principles. Two think-aloud protocol studies were conducted to investigate the performance of students from this curriculum in solving physics problems that require computer modeling. Experiment 1 examined whether Matter and interactions students would, given the choice, use computer modeling to solve difficult problems that required predicting motion, and how their solution approaches differed from those of students from a traditional introductory physics course. Though they did not overwhelmingly choose computer modeling, some M & I students did write computer models successfully or apply the iterative algorithm by hand. The solution approaches of M & I students and traditional course students differed qualitatively in their use of the momentum principle and pre-derived special case formulas. In experiment 2, Matter and Interactions students were observed while they wrote programs in the VPython language in order to examine their difficulties with computer modeling. Areas of difficulty included determining initial conditions, distinguishing between simulated time and the time step, and updating momentum and position especially troublesome for students was the multistep procedure for calculating a force that changes with time. Students' understanding of the structure of a computer model improved by the end of the semester as shown by their performance on a line sorting task. Students with fewer difficulties proceeded through the computer model in amore linear, straightforward fashion. Instruction was revised instruction, had fewer difficulties on the same tasks, though other factors may have been involved in the improvement.

Ahang, Yaw-Dir (2005) conducted a study on "Variables associated with Computer 'Attitudes and Perceived usefulness of Computers in Taiwan". This study investigated the influence of gender, age, computer experience, computer competency, computer usage, computer ownership, computer anxiety, learning style (collaboration), and personality traits on students' computer attitudes and their perceptions of the usefulness of computers. Through the results, teachers can better understand students' needs and thus provide them with appropriate teaching strategies and technologies. Conducted in a private junior college located in the middle of Taiwan, this research used a sample of six hundred students (N=600) with an average age of twenty. All participants were selected by stratified random sampling. To collect data, a questionnaire including demographic information, the Computer Attitudes Scale (CAS), the Perceived Usefulness of Computers, the Computer-Email-Web (CEW) Fluency Scale, the Grash-Riechmann Student Learning Style Scales, and the IPIP (International Personality Item Pool) Five-Factor Personality Inventory was administered to the sample. The multiple regression method was utilized to analyze the collected data. The results indicated that gender; computer usage, computer ownership, computer anxiety, computer competency, learning style (collaboration), openness to experience, and conscientiousness were each found to make significant contributions in predicting computer attitudes. Computer anxiety contributed most to the prediction of computer attitudes. The results also showed that only computer anxiety, computer competency and learning style (collaboration) were each found to make significant contributions to prediction of perceived usefulness of computers of these three, learning style (collaboration) played the most important part in predicting perceived usefulness of computers. The findings provided several implications; that educators should design suitable teaching strategies in order to adequately address the existence of technology gender inequity in the classroom, that school authorities should spare no effort in helping students own a computer, that school authorities should extend the computer labs hours to increase accessibility of computer technologies to students. Besides, in order to improve students' levels of computer competency, educators should set up specific evaluation standards for computer competency and sponsor computer competency contests to encourage student to reach acceptable levels of computer competency. Educators should establish a collaborative learning environment to enhance students' computer attitudes through teaching and learning from each other. Educators also should employ suitable teaching strategies that accommodate different learning styles and personality traits.

Lipinski, Edmund R. (2005) conducted a study on "Using Technology in Higher Education: Differences among Outcomes, Learning Styles, Gender, Computer Self-efficacy, Course Contexts and Ethnicity". The purpose of this investigation was to examine the potential differences between learning outcomes and learning predictors in higher education. Specifically, this research addressed several research hypotheses via a mixed research design, design among learning outcomes and student learning styles, gender, computer self- efficacy, course context and ethnicity. Participants were 192 students taking an Introductory Psychology course at Mesa Community College; learning outcomes were measured by a quiz of Psychological concepts taught in Introduction to Psychology; learning styles Murphy, Coover and Owen's Computer Self-Efficacy Scale measured computer self-efficacy. Results indicated that gender, ethnicity and course contexts were significant contributors to learning outcomes; implications and limitations of these findings were discussed.

Coleman, Bridget K. (2004) conducted a study on "An Examination of Teachers' Self-efficacy in Using Computer Technology for Instruction". This study was designed to examine elementary school teachers' sense of self-efficacy in using computer technology and how it relates to other specific teaching contexts. Of particular interest were teachers' computer self-efficacy beliefs as they relate to student achievement levels and socioeconomic status in schools. Other relevant factors explored were years of teaching experience, subjects and grades taught, technology training, availability of computer technology, frequency of usage and the tasks for which computers are used. One hundred sixty-nine teachers from seventeen elementary schools, eight with the highest student performance levels and nine with the lowest student performance levels, participated by responding to a questionnaire. Teachers reported their perceptions of their abilities to use computers and described contextual factors pertaining to their teaching assignments. Six participants were interviewed following the completion of the questionnaire to provide additional insight into teachers' computer self-efficacy. Although the results did not show a relationship between teachers' computer self-efficacy and school performance levels or socioeconomic status, a relationship was revealed between computer self-efficacy and teaching experience. Newer teachers typically had higher computer self-efficacy than their more experienced colleagues. Teachers' use of computers was generally more for personal tasks than for instructional purpose.

Chi (1994) studied "Computer knowledge interests and uses faculty in two Teachers' Universities in China". This study was designed to assess teachers' current computer knowledge, computer uses, attitudes concerning computers and the factors that affect the integration and application of the computer in the classroom. The study revealed computers are much like those of American teachers. The majority of teachers showed very positive computer attitudes and there is potential to increase computer use among them. The Chinese teachers were seemed to do rather well, but the use of computers in instruction appeared too weak leaving the most room for improvement.

Hamelin (1994) had conducted a study "The effects of personalized software Assignments in computer knowledge and attitudes toward computers in a college level computer literacy course". The objective of this study was to examine one aspect of constructivism: the effects of assignments of projects that were personalized for each student. These findings of the study supported the constructivist position that personalizing encouraged students to find alternative frame works leading to better achievement.

Lioce (1994) conducted a study on "Attitude toward computers of ROC public middle school teachers". The results of data analysis indicated that the instrument had low factors which were labeled as "teacher's positive ness toward computers" and teacher's negative ness toward computers.

Clayton (1993) made a study on "the Relationship between computer Assisted Instruction on selected Student Variables". This study was designed to determine the effectiveness of computer Assisted Instruction on reading and Mathematics achievement, attitude toward reading and mathematics achievement and attitude of low socio-economic students. Findings indicated that CAI improved reading for students at the fourth grade level, and increased positive attitude toward readings for third and fourth grade students in the low socio-economic category.

Schleifer, Neal, (1993) conducted a study on "The effects of using computers in writing instruction on writing apprehension and attitude towards using computers". This study revealed that when possible correlates of writing apprehension tested, only gender was found to be significant.

Harris and Harrison (1993) studied "An evaluation of an innovative use of computers and volunteers in 7th grade Math Instruction". This paper summary a formative evaluation of a developed project designed to maximize the potential use of computers in mathematics instruction through the use of volunteers. The Volunteers determined with mathematics skills each student needed to practice by referring to the student files, determined what software programme would be appropriate for the student and managed all the necessary student data.

Chan and James (1993) have conducted, "A case study of Computer Mediated Educational Experience in an ESC Classroom". This study explored the ways teachers made curricular decisions in selecting and integrated software inter instruction and observed students to understand their experiences with. The results of this study included the NCTE redesign that was intended to promote the quality of teacher education through the articulation of high professional standards and the application of rigorous process of assessment.

Daily and Bonnie (1992) carried out a study on the "Effectiveness of a computer Integrated, Multimedia learning environment of Engineering education". This research has a series of empirical studies conducted on the effectiveness of the Advanced Technology classroom, ATC (a computer integrated multimedia, learning environment). The research findings suggested strong support for the effectiveness of teaching with the ATC in engineering based curriculum.

Wizer (1992) made a study on "Small Croup Instruction with special education and non special education students using microcomputers". The purpose of this study was to determine which types of group process were most helpful and most harmful to small group learning with computers. This study confirmed the findings in the research literature regarding the importance of explanations. The results of this study also indicated that, it was still not known which internal group behaviours relate to achievement for LD Students.

ANALOGY

Out of the total 37 studies identified, majority of the studies belonged to survey studies and few of them are Experimental Studies.

Most of the studies followed Random Sampling Technique in the collection of data and the size of the selected sample ranges from 30 to 600 samples. In majority of the studies data was collected from the School Students and few were collected from the Teachers, Teacher Training Students and College Students.

In majority of the studies the Questionnaire, oppinnarrie, achievement test and rating scale developed by the investigator was utilized as a tool. Since all the reviewed studies were related to high awareness and attitude. Mean, Standard Deviation and 't' test were the Statistical Technique followed in the majority of the studies.

The findings of the studies reported that all are having more Effectiveness of computer and attitude of computer education. The findings of the various studies also revealed high attitude and achievement of computer education. Similar results were obtained, from the studies conducted by the E. Rafeedali, Jagannath, K. Dange, Sr. Nirmala sundararaj, Vaiyapuri, s. Rajasekar.

Conclusion

The study so far conducted mainly on the role of computers, microcomputers in classroom, teacher' awareness towards computer, uses of computers, development of computers and instructions are done. It is felt only a few studies were done on computers and the awareness of higher secondary students in Tribal area towards computer potentiality. So the Investigator wishes to know whether factors like literacy of parents, Gender, Studying Groups... have any influence on the awareness of computer potentiality among Higher Secondary Students in Tribal area.

III

Method and Procedure

Introduction

The main objective of the study was to find out the awareness on Computer potentiality among higher secondary students in Tribal area. The need for the study, objectives and the scope of the study were split out in Chapter-I. An extensive review of related literature covering the awareness on Computer potentiality among higher secondary students in Tribal area and some other related fields were presented in chapter II.

This chapter deals with the design and procedure adopted for the present study. In the simplest way research design is a plan structure and strategy of investigation in order to obtain answer to the research question. "Design is the blue print of the procedures that reaching valid conclusions about relationships between independent and dependent variables" says Best (1978). Hence to the right towards the goal, it is necessary to have a design for the research being carried out at the very beginning. But it is also true that "selection of a particular design", as Best (1978) suggests, "Is based on the purpose of the experiment, the types of variables to be manipulated and the conditions or limiting factors under which it may be conducted". So it is apparent that the designs differ, as the problems differ.

The ultimate aim of such a science is to provide knowledge that will permit the educator to achiever his goals by the most effective methods. Scientific problems can be resolved only on the basis of data, and the major responsibility of the scientist is to set up a research design capable of providing the data necessary to the solution of the problem".

Observed by George J. Mowly (1964) the selection of methods for research work depends upon the nature of the problem selected. Mainly methodology consists of tools, techniques and procedures. The success of investigation depends on the priority of the method and the tools and techniques the researcher uses.

Research methodology is a way to solve the research problem systematically. It is necessary for the researcher to know not only the research methods and techniques but also the methodology.

The methodology varies from problem to problem. The researcher has to specify very clearly what decisions were selected and why he did select them and how they can be evaluated by others. The purpose of study may very from researcher to researcher. But in any form of research the investigator has to follow certain methods.

Research Methods

Research methodology describe the various steps of the plan of attack, to be adopted in solving a research problem, such as the manner in which the problem are formulated, the definition of terms, the choice of subjects for investigation, the validation of data gathering tools, the collection, analysis and interpretation of data, and the processes of inferences and generalizations. Research methods are classified into three main methods.

1. The Historical Method
2. Survey Method
3. Experimental Method

1. The Historical Method

Historical research is the application of the scientific method of inquiry to historical problems. Historical research is one of the most difficult types of investigation to conduct adequately. In historical method the source of data is by direct observation and through indirect observation through documents. It gives the accurate record of past events, interpretations, relationships and evaluation of present day problem and procedures.

2. Survey Method

The word "survey" has been derived from the words "sur" or "ser" and "vecir" or "veidor" which means "over" and "see" respectively that is the term normally implies the determination of normal or typical conditions. The descriptive or normative survey method of educational research is very common. It is that method of investigation which attempts to describe and interpret what exists at present in the form of conditions, practices, processes, trends, effects, attitudes, beliefs etc. It is an organized attempt to analyze, interpret and report the present status of a social institution, group or area.

3. Experimental Method

Experimentation is the most scientifically sophisticated research method. It is defined as observation under controlled conditions. It studies observable changes that take place in order to establish a cause and deliberate and controlled modification of the conditions determining an event and in the observation and interpretation of the changes that occur in the event itself.

Method Adopted in the Present Study

The research method employed by the investigator is the survey method.

George J. Mouly has said "No category of educational research is most status and descriptive research" (Kulbir Singh Sidhu, 1984, P.107). The broad classification comprises a variety of specific techniques and procedures all similar from the stand point of purpose that is, to establish the status of the phenomenon under investigation.

The survey method gathers data from a relatively large number of cases at a particular time. It is concerned with the generalized statistics that result when data are abstracted from particular cases" (P.106). The survey is an important type of study. It involves a clearly defined problem and definite objectives. It requires export and imaginative planning, careful analysis and interpretation of the data gathered and logical and skillful reporting of the findings.

Characteristics of survey method

1. It gathers data from a relatively large number of samples.
2. It involves defined problem and define objectives.
3. It provides information useful to the solution of local problem.
4. It is not concerned with the characteristics of individuals.
5. It does not seek to develop an organized body of scientific principles.

In the present study the investigator intended to measure the Awareness on Computer potentiality among Higher Secondary Students at Tribal area. So this study aims at measuring the activity of leaning. Here normative survey method is the best method for conduction research study.

Design of the Study

Research design is a plan, a structure and a strategy of investigation conceived to obtain awareness to issues in research. The object of research design is to test the research hypothesis. The research design therefore is built in the principle of maximization of the results of study and minimization of variance. A research design however, is not a highly specific plan to be followed without direction. Rather, it is a series of guideposts to keep right direction. Thus research design is the process of planning a research, choosing methods and procedures that can be expected to yield meaning and most interpretable results.

Table: 3.1

Schematic Representation of the Research Design

S.No.	Type	Source
1.	Nature of the Research	Normative Survey Method
2.	Tools Developed	Type of Tool Awareness on Computer potentiality among Higher Secondary Students at Tribal area in Namakkal District.
3.	Variables	1. Gender 2. Studying group 3. Parents Educational status
4.	Sampling Technique	Cluster Sampling Technique
5.	Size of the Sample	Students- 205 (Boys: 102, Girls: 103)
6.	Statistical Techniques	Mean, Standard Deviation, and 't' test

The present study belong to Normative survey Research. The variables used are Gender, group, parent's educational status among higher secondary students at Tribal area. It is developed by the investigator to access the awareness on the computer potentiality among higher secondary students at Tribal area in Namakkal District separately, along with a personal data sheet to know the back ground of the students. In this study Cluster Sampling Techniques was followed, data were collected from 205 students of Tribal area schools of Namakkal district. The statistical techniques Mean, Standard Deviation and 't' test were used.

Objectives of the Study

7. To find out the level of awareness on computer potentiality of Higher Secondary Students at Tribal area.
8. To find out the level of significant difference on the awareness of computer potentiality between Male and Female Students in Tribal area.

9. To find out the level of significant difference on the awareness of computer potentiality between Maths and Science group Students in Tribal area.
10. To find out the level of significant difference on the awareness of computer potentiality between Maths and Arts group Students in Tribal Area.
11. To find out the level of significant difference on the awareness of computer potentiality between Science and Arts group Students in Tribal area.
12. To find out the level of significant difference on the awareness of computer potentiality between educated and uneducated parents of Higher Secondary Students.

Null Hypotheses of the Study

6. There is no significant difference on the awareness of computer potentiality between Male and Female Students.
7. There is no significant difference on the awareness of computer potentiality between Maths and Science group Students.
8. There is no significant difference on the awareness of computer potentiality between Maths and Arts group Students.
9. There is no significant difference on the awareness of computer potentiality between Science and Arts group Students.
10. There is no significant difference on the awareness of computer potentiality between educated and uneducated parents of Higher Secondary Students.

Construction of Tool

The investigator prepared a questionnaire under the guidance of the guide and information from various sources. On the basis of the suggestions given, some questions were dropped, few were modified and some new questions were also added. The investigators framed 60 questions.

Pilot Study

Before finalizing the questionnaire a pilot study was conducted. The draft questionnaire consisting of 60 items was used for the pilot study. The pilot study was conducted on 50 students. The investigator was with the students at the time of administering the questionnaire. The doubts raised by the students were cleared and items concerned were noted down. The items, which were found to be ambiguous, were also noted. After pilot study, the ambiguous questions were modified and rewritten.

Reliability and Validity

Reliability applies to a measure when similar results are obtained over time and across situations. It should be noted that reliability is a necessary condition for validity, but a reliable instrument may not be valid. A reliable but invalid instrument will yield consistently may not be valid. A reliable but invalid instrument will yield consistently inaccurate results. The investigator used the four point rating scale method, the 't' values found in the Rating Scale such as 0.80. Then the tool was accepted as the valid tool for administering in this study.

Personal Data Sheet

The personal data sheet serves to collect personal information, students were asked to write their name, sex, studying groups, and parent's educational status that they studied in Higher Secondary School.

Scoring

The data were collected consolidated codified and used for suitable analysis. Score of the response sheets was done as per the scoring scheme described earlier. The scores were summed up separately and the total of each individual was taken.

The fifty statements in the rating scale offer the following comprehensive view. 50 x 4 =200, 50 x 3 = 150, 50 x 2 =100, 50 x 1 =50 thus all the scores could fell maximum 200 and minimum 50 scores.

Table 3.2

Distribution of Marks for Statement in Tool

S. No	Categories of response	Scores	
		Positive Statement	Negative Statement
1.	Strongly Agree	4	1
2.	Agree	3	2
3.	Disagree	2	3
4.	Strongly Disagree	1	4

Likert Technique

A method of scaling know as summate rating that is known as Likert technique name after Likert is a widely used technique for developing an Computer potentiality scale. The investigator assumed a large number of items relevant to the computer potentiality scale as favorable and unfavorable. This was administrated to subjects; the subjects gave their response to each item.

In this method each proposition usually called for a responded underlying of the four words such as strongly agree (SA), agree (A), Disagree (DA), Strongly Disagree (SDA) as a basis for determine the item to be selected for the final scale. The discriminated value of each item is calculated. This is done by obtaining the difference between the average scores for each item when the total scores are arranged in qualities.

Tools used for the Study

The instruments employed for collecting data are called tools. "Tools employ distinctive ways of describing and qualifying the data". Best 1992.

The tools of research are instruments that provide for the collection of data upon which hypothesis may be tested. There is large number of tools and techniques available for data collection in research from these tools, the researcher selects the most appropriate forms of information that could be most useful. The important tools of educational research should include schedules, questionnaire, opinionative, and observation, checklist, rating scale, interview, psychological test and pentagrams.

By the evaluation of the different data gathering devices used in educational research, the investigator was fully convinced that the development of an awareness tool with help in collecting data.

Table 3.2

Distribution of statements in Awareness on Computer potentiality among Higher Secondary Students

S.No	Students		Total
	Positive Items	Negative Items	**50**
1	1,2,3,5,7,8,11,12,14,15,17, 18, 20,21,22,24,25,26,27, 29,30,36,37,38,39,40,42, 44,45,47,48,50.	4,6,9,10,13,16,19,2 3,16,28,31,32,33, 34,35,43,46,49.	
Total	**32**	**18**	

The above table 3.2 shows the student's opionnaire to access the awareness in Computer potentiality among Higher Secondary School Students at Tribal area in Namakkal District. This tool consists of four point scale with 32 positive and 18 negative statements.

Population and Sample

Population

Population is the aggregate or totality of objects or individuals regarding which inferences are to be made in a sampling study. A population is any group of individuals that have one or more characteristics in common that are of interest to the research. The population of the present study was all the higher secondary school students at Tribal area in Namakkal District.

Sample

A sample is small proportion of a population selected for observation and analysis. "A good sample of a population with great accuracy" (Corwell.1960). By considering here the research which proposes to ascertain what is the normal or typical condition or practice at the present time"(Sukhia, et.al1969). It is the only means through which opinions, attitudes and suggestions for improvement and such other data can be obtained. Survey studies help in contributing to other type of investigations and cover a large number of traits and characteristics of the groups.

Sample in This Study

The present study the cluster sampling method was used. This method presupposes the division of the population in a finite number of divisions and other identifiable groups. For example, a human population might be regarded as composed of individual persons, families or group of persons residing in town or a village. The smallest units into which the population can be described are the elements of the population and groups of elements are called clusters. Cluster sampling consists in forming suitable clusters of units and surveying all the units in some cluster selected according to an appropriate sampling scheme. The clusters of units are formed by grouping neighboring units or those which can be conveniently surveyed together. From the population, the investigator has selected 205 higher secondary school students at Tribal area in Namakkal district by using cluster sampling technique. The names of the schools are listed as following table,

Table 3.3

The Schools Name and Place of the sample

S.No	School Name	Place	Category of Sample	N	Total
1	G.T.R.H.S. School	Mullukurichi	Boys	57	97
			Girls	40	
2	G.T.R.H.S. School	Kollihills	Boys	46	108
			Girls	62	

G.T.R.H.S. School: Government Tribal Residential Higher Secondary School.

The investigator collected the response of all higher secondary school Students of each School.

Table 3.4

The sample are shown according to the following variables

S.No.	Category of the variable		No. of Samples	Percentage	Total
1.	Gender	Boys	102	50 %	205
		Girls	103	50 %	
2.	Studying group	Maths	70	34 %	205
		Science	67	33 %	
		Arts	68	33 %	
3.	Parents Educational	Uneducated	84	41 %	
	status	Educated	121	59 %	205

Collection of Data

The investigator obtained adequate number of copies of the awareness tool scale for the actual collection of data. Selected College of Education was visited and their principal and lecturer were contacted for getting permission and co-operation for the collection of data. The awareness scale was then distributed among the student teachers. Adequate instructions were given for marking the responses. Strict uniform procedures were adopted in the administration of the awareness tool to student teachers of different Colleges. The following steps were invariably followed while administrating the awareness scale.

1. Distribution of the individual awareness tool to each student.
2. Giving directions of how to mark the responses in the awareness tool.
3. Clearing the doubts of the students and giving additional instructions wherever necessary.
4. Giving sufficient time to mark the responses.
5. Strictly enquiring the marking of independent responses.
6. Collecting all distributed awareness tool.

Statistical Techniques used

(a) Mean

Mean is used to measure the entire data by one value. It is obtained by adding to gather all the items and by dividing the total by the number of items.

$$\bar{X} = \mathbf{A} + \frac{\Sigma fd}{N} \times c$$

Where,

C = Class interval

Σfd = Total of the products of each class frequency with the steps

Deviation of the respective class

N = Total frequency$\bar{X}$

$\bar{X}$ = Arithmetic mean

(b) Standard Deviation

The standard deviation concept was introduced by Karl Pearson in 1823. It is used to measure dispersion standard deviation is also known as root of the mean of the square deviation from arithmetic mean.

$$\text{S.D.} = \sqrt{\frac{\Sigma fd^2}{N} - \left(\frac{\Sigma fd}{N}\right)^2} \times c$$

Where,

N = No. of samples

c = class interval

d = $\frac{X-A}{C}$

x = Midpoint of the class interval

A = Assumed mean

Σfd = Total of the products of each class frequency with the steps Deviation of the respective class

Σfd^2 = Total of the products of each class frequency with the square deviation of the respective class.

(3) Techniques used for testing hypotheses

Student 't' test is used to find out the significance of the means of different groups of students. For example are boys and girls. The hypotheses formulated are tested using relevant statistics (ie) 't' test.

The test of significance of the difference between the two means is known as 't' test. 't' is calculated by using the below formula,

$$t = \frac{M_1 - M_2}{\sqrt{\frac{a_1^2}{N_1} + \frac{a_2^2}{N_2}}}$$

Where,

M_1 is mean of the first sample a_2^2
M_2 is mean of the second sample
N_1 is number of cases in first sample
N_2 is number of cases in second sample
a_1^2 is standard deviation of first sample
is standard deviation of second sample

Conclusion

This chapter deals with methodology of the present investigation as enumerated. Thus it gives brief details about selection of sample, pilot study, administration of tool in the study, data collection and statistical technique use in this study. Hawing described the detailed methodology of the study in the chapter analysis and interpretation of the data for the present study is next chapter.

IV

Analysis of Data

Introduction

The analysis of data represents the application of the inductive and deductive logic to the research process. It is a very important step in the total procedure of research. Analysis of (variable or data) means studying the tabular material. It involves breaking down existing complex factor into simple parts and putting the parts together in new arrangements for the purpose of interpretation. Interpretation of calls for a critical examination of the results of one's analysis in the light of all the limitations of this data gathering.

Analysis of data means studying the tabulated material in order to determine the inherent falls or meaning. Data accepted by the investigator got their meanings, when they are chanalized into the process of statistical analysis. It will give the investigator an insight into the problem. It simplifies the masses of number and facts and presents them in an understandable manner. Therefore analysis must lead to interpretation of data.

The purpose of present investigation is to study the awareness of Traffic Rules among student teachers. The data for the study was collected from the students by means for a questionnaire.

The analysis of data was attempted as per the objectives of the study. In the present study, the data are analyzed using mainly the following statistical techniques.

1. Percentage
2. Arithmetic Mean.
3. Standard Deviation
4.' t ' Value

Testing of Hypothesis

After formulating the hypothesis, it is necessary to

1. Deduce its consequence.
2. Selected or develop tools that will determine whether these consequences actually occur and
3. Use the tools there by collecting facts that will confirm the hypothesis.

"A hypothesis is never proved; it is merely sustained (or) rejected"

Table 4.1

The level of awareness on Computer potentiality among higher secondary students

Category	Samples (N)	Mean	S.D
Awareness of Computer potentiality	205	75.7	6.98

The above table 4.1 shows Mean and S.D values of the higher secondary school students at Tribal area. The total number of sample is 205 from higher secondary school students at Tribal area in Namakkal District. An almost homogeneous group of 205 (102 Boys and 103 Girls) was selected for this study.

Table 4.2

Mean and Standard Deviation of Computer Potentiality

S.No	Variable Type	Sample	Mean	Standard Deviation
1	Gender		Boys	75.6 6.9
		Girls	75.79	7.07
2	Group		Maths	77.50 6.46
		Science	74.90	6.89
		Art	74.62	7.22
3	Parents Educational	Educated	75.75	7.21
	Status	Uneducated	75.62	6.66

Table 4.3

Significant difference the awareness of Computer potentiality between Boys and Girls

Variable	N	Mean	SD	't' value	Level of Significance (0.05)
Boys	102	75.6	6.9	0.19	1.97
Girls	103	75.79	7.07		

From the above table 4.2 it shows the calculated 't' value is less than the tabulated 't' value at 0.05 level of significance. So there is no significant difference on the awareness of Computer potentiality between Boys and Girls of higher secondary students at Tribal area.

Table 4.4

Significant difference the awareness of Computer potentiality between Maths and Science group Students.

Variable	N	Mean	SD	't' value	Level of Significance (0.05)
Maths group students	70	77.50	6.46	2.28	1.98
Science group students	67	74.90	6.89		

From the above table 4.2 it shows the calculated 't' value is greater than the tabulated 't' value at 0.05 level of significance. There is significant difference on the awareness of Computer potentiality between Maths and Science group Students.

Table 4.5

Significant difference the awareness of Computer potentiality between Maths and Arts group Students

Variable	N	Mean	SD	't' value	Level of Significance (0.05)
Maths group students	70	77.50	6.46	1.17	1.98
Arts group students	68	74.62	7.22		

From the above table 4.2 it shows the calculated 't' value is less than the tabulated 't' value at 0.05 level of significance. So there is no significant difference on the awareness of Computer potentiality between Maths and Arts group Students.

Table 4.6

The awareness of Computer potentiality between Science and Arts group Students

Variable	N	Mean	SD	't' value	Level of Significance (0.05)
Science group students	67	74.90	6.89	0.23	1.98
Arts group students	68	74.62	7.22		

From the above table 4.2 it shows the calculated 't' value is less than the tabulated 't' value at 0.05 level of significance. So there is no significant difference on the awareness of Computer potentiality between Science and Arts group Students.

From the above table 4.2 it shows the calculated 't' value is less than the tabulated 't' value at 0.05 level of significance. So there is no significant difference on the awareness of Computer potentiality between educated and uneducated parents of Higher Secondary Students.

Table 4.7

The awareness of computer potentiality between Educated and Uneducated parents of Higher Secondary Students

Variable	N	Mean	SD	't' value	Level of Significance (0.05)
Uneducated	84	75.62	6.66	0.414	1.97
Educated	121	75.75	7.21		

4.3 Conclusion

Data analysis is ultimately necessary for any research. The obtained data was subjected to necessary statistical computations. The results thus analyzed in terms of the corresponding table value are interpreted accordingly. The findings were calculated without any researcher's bias, which serve as a recommendation for further study.

V

Findings and Conclusions

Introduction

In this chapter an attempt had been made to consolidate all the findings of the present study, the investigator also made some recommendation, which include the relevant area for this research and lastly the conclusion. The findings are based on the result collected from the awareness tool.

The Study in Retrospect

The aim of the present investigation was to find out the awareness of Computer potentiality.

Methodology in Brief

For the present study normative survey method and cluster sampling technique was adopted. For the study, 205 Higher Secondary Students at Tribal area in Namakkal District were the Samples. The tool used for the collection of data is Awareness Rating Scale.

Statement of the Study

The problem under the study is entitled as "A study on the awareness of Computer potentiality among Higher Secondary Students at Tribal area in Namakkal District".

Major Findings of the Study

From the present study the investigator came to the following findings.

(1) There is no significant difference on the awareness of computer potentiality between Boys and Girls Higher Secondary Students in Tribal area.

(2) There is significant difference on the awareness of computer potentiality between Maths and Science group students.

(3) There is no significant difference on the awareness of Computer potentiality between Maths and Arts group students.

(4) There is no significant difference on the awareness of computer potentiality between Science and Arts group Students.

(5) There is no significant difference on the awareness of computer potentiality between educated and uneducated parents of Higher Secondary Students.

Conclusions Based on Findings

1. On noticing the results with regard to the Tribal area Higher Secondary Students between boys and girls, there is no significant difference on the awareness of computer potentiality. Because the boys and girls having similar awareness about basic knowledge of Computer potentiality. Now a days both are having similar awareness about basic knowledge of computer. Because they are good specialty for accessing computer in their area. Government also provides more specialties in tribal area. So there is no difference between Boys and Girls.

2. On noticing the results with regard to the Tribal area Higher Secondary Students between Maths and Science Group students, there is significant difference on the awareness of computer potentiality. Because the Maths Group students are mostly using computer for solving their problems. So they are having more awareness of basic computer knowledge than Science Group students.
3. On noticing the results with regard to the Tribal area Higher Secondary Students between Maths and Art Group students, there is no significant difference on the awareness of computer potentiality. Now a days the Computer field is provided so many job opportunity. So both are having similar awareness about basic computer knowledge.
4. On noticing the results with regard to the Tribal area Higher Secondary students between Science and Arts Group students, there is no significant difference on the awareness of computer potentiality. Because the Science and Art Group students having similar awareness about basic of computer knowledge.
5. On noticing the results with regard to the Tribal area Higher Secondary Students between educated and uneducated parents of students, there is no significant difference on the awareness about Computer potentiality. Because the Computer potentiality is depends upon the student's individuality not depends on the parent's educational status.

Computer assumes immense importance now-a-day in various fields of human activities, industry, business, traffic control, space travel, evaluation, guidance and counseling, crime direction, sports and games, etc. Communication is one of the important human Endeavour's that lifts achievement and excellence of the human society. Although communication revolution began with printing technology, computers have brought the wealth of information at everyone's fingertips. The electronic data communication has made the information revolution possible.

Areas of Research For the Future

Research is a chain activity. There purpose of any research in education is to find solutions for problems related to teachers, students, learning etc... But investigation on one problem always leaves many related research questions that can be investigated by other researchers; some of the areas for research in the future may be as follows,

1. The present study could be undertaken at various states in India.
2. A study can be conducted on the Primary, Middle and High school teachers.
3. A similar study can be conducted on the professional college students.
4. A comparative study on the awareness of computer potentiality among the students of different categories like Scheduled Tribes and Scheduled Castes students.
5. A critical study on evolving strategies for promoting the awareness of computer potentiality among the Arts and Science students.
6. A study can be conducted on the D.T.Ed trainees.
7. A study can be conducted the Attitude of Tribal and Non-Tribal High School Students towards computer potentiality.

Recommendations

Computers are an inherent part of life today. And all over the world they are making their presence felt in every sphere of life. From launching satellite to shopping for books, teaching any subject to play games. We are at the beginning of the age of computers, which are likely to have a bigger effect on the other products of the scientific revolution.

Not only has the computer made possible calculation either for beyond human capacity, but it is certain to alter radically the whole of our thinking about quantitative methods in calculation. The computer is certainly no substitute for mathematical thought at least not yet. But it could stimulate mathematical thought in new directions. Several modes of approach which were simply not formerly considered, because the calculations involved would have been prohibitively time consuming are now very much within the research of ordinary researchers, thank to the modern high speed computers.

In the modern world, application of computers is receiving a high sense of special effects. For the development of information technology, computers are widely used in every part of the world. Information technology is a vast developing field in industry, communication and transfer of information. The world is coming closer to closer through the development of information technology, the importance of computer application is highly increasing in the field of medicine, agriculture etc... Hence the chances for increasing job opportunities in various fields are widely opening. The Following Recommendations are given for the awareness using Computer potentiality among Higher Secondary Students at Tribal area.

1. Generally the tribal area higher secondary students have favorable awareness towards computer knowledge. So the government schools must provide modern gadgets to the students.
2. CAI must be compulsorily added in the curriculum of teacher training.
3. The teachers must have favorable attitude towards of computer Education.
4. To enhance the quality of teaching computer education is must in school level.
5. The students may be trained to give some activities like quiz, debate, discussion, seminar, workshops etc., on awareness on Computer Education.
6. The teachers may be trained to teach their lesson using Computer.

Conclusion

The planet earth is experiencing the impact of the developments and products of science and technology computer education offers an opportunity to bring elements of practice into the classroom. The limitation of this technology is that the simulated environments are not a complete substitute for the real thing. However, they can provide enough complexity and flexibility to make them a worthwhile vehicle for the practice of many activities which are not possible by the other teaching methods.

Thus computer literacy should help in defining and implementing futuristic, global, intuitive, critical and holistic thinking.

Bibliography

Book References

1. Aggarwal, Y.P. Statistical Methods Concepts Application and Compotation, Sterling Publishers (P) Ltd., New Delhi - 110016.
2. Balagurusamy, E. (2010). Fundamentals of Computing and Programming. New Delhi: McGraw Hill Education private limited.
3. Good, Carter.V. (1959). Introduction of Educational Research, Appleton Century Crafts, IINC, New York.
4. Gupta, C.B. (1972). An Introduction to Statistical Method, Vikas Publishing House, Delhi.
5. Kothari, C.K. (1985). Research Methodology, Wiley Eastern Ltd., New Delhi.
6. Sharma, R.A. (1980). Fundamentals of Educational research, Loyal Book Dept, Meerut.

Journal References

1. Dr. Girija, N. Srinivasalu & Dr. Vijayalakshmi, S. (2010). Effectiveness of Computer Multimedia Package (SLM) on Achievement in Social Science, An Experimental Study. Journal of Educational Research And Extension, Vol.47 (4), 35-48.

2. Jagannath, K. Dange. (2008). Effectiveness of Computer Assisted Instruction in the development of Environmental awareness and Environmental attitude. Experiments in Education, Vol. XXXVI No.2, 9 – 11.

3. Noushad Husain (2010). Computer-Based instructional Simulations in Education: Why and How. EDUTRACKS, Vol.10 - No.3, 22 - 26.

4. Rafeedali, E. (2009). Computer-based Technology and its pedagogical utility. EDUTRACKS, Vol.9 - No.2, 37 - 39.

5. Saikumari, K. (2010). Computer phobia of IX standard students and their Attitude towards Educational usage of Computer. EDUTRACKS, Vol.10 - No.4, 43-45.

6. Sibichen, K.K, St. Joesph's Monastery & Annaraja, P. (2010). Teacher Trainees Computer Competency enhances their Technology Use in Classroom Teaching. EDUTRACKS, Vol.10 - No.4, 33-37.

7. Srinivasan, P. & Muthumanickam, R. (2010). An innovative Computer-Assisted Instructional Programme. EDUTRACKS, Vol.9 - No.12, 33 - 41.

8. Sr. Nirmala Sundararaj. (2005). Attitude towards Computer Education of the B.Ed Trainees of Tamil Nadu Open University. Journal of Educational Research And Extension, Vol.47 (4), 35-48.

9. Vimal kishor & Neha Mahant. (2010). Attitude of Tribal and Non-Tribal High School Students towards Studies. Experiments in Education, Vol. XXXVIII No.2, 25 – 26.

Thesis Reference

1. Dr. Venkateswaran, R. (2005). A study on the Attitude of Female teacher Trainees towards Computer Education, Bharathiar University, Coimbatore.

Part 2

Problems of Commerce Learning Students

1

Problems of Commerce Learning Students

Introduction

Education is an important human activity. It was been with the birth of human race. It will continue to function as long as the human race lives. Its implications are rich and varied. Education may also be consisted as the deliberate and systematic influence exerted by the matured person upon the immature through instruction, discipline and harmonious development of physical, intellectual aesthetic, social and spiritual powers of the human being according to individual and social needs and directed towards the union of the educated with his creator as the final end.

Knowledge in basic skills, academics, technical, discipline, citizenship or is it something else? Our society says only academic basics are important and that is based on collecting knowledge without understanding its value. How about the processing of knowledge, using inspiration, visionary ambitions, creativity, risk, ability to bounce back from failure motivation? Most education institutions don't consider these skills. These skills are associated with understanding the value of knowledge. There is a huge disconnected gap and this is a problem for high school students in particular.

A quality education is custom design that addresses the unique abilities of each student and has a positive emotional experience. Custom education evaluates natural talent and how the students learn. This is why home schooled students all perform classroom students. Parents learn what works and does not work. With this method, students develop a love to learn and learning because a lifelong process.

Various Definitions on Education

After throwing light on the true meaning of education it is clear that Education is a process of growth and development. However, to make this concept more clearly the following definition is being below.

John Dewey (1859-1952) the American educator, observed... All social institutions have a meaning, a purpose that purpose is to set free and to develop the capacities of human individuals without respect to race, sex, chess or economic status. And this is all one with saying that the test of their value is the extent to which they educate every individual into the full stature of his possibility".

Froebel, **(1782- 1852)** "Education is the process by which the child makes the internal external".

Vivekananda (1863 - 1902) "Education is manifestation of perfection already reached in man".

Meaning of Commerce

Commerce is the strongest and most influential social institution in all societies these days. It is a social institution which provides goods and services. Commerce is operated for a profit that is individuals using the system find it advantageous to pay a money price to have other individuals make goods and renders services of them. Commerce is owned privately by individuals or group of individuals or by Government or partly by Government and partly by individuals; it completes with other commercial units to make goods and render services of the highest quality at the lowest prices and in the shortest possible time; and it is regulated by the Government.

Besides the commercial units which operate for a profit thousands and thousands of institution in India Carry on business activities on a non - profit business. These institution are Government union, state and local, educational institutions, hospital and co - operative enterprises. These institutions have many of the same employment needs for trained business workers as the commercial units which operate for a profit.

The term "Commerce" includes all vocational life. If this is true preparation for the professions and trades must be considered as a function of commerce education. But since commerce educator, as commonly understood, does not perform this function, either commerce teachers are not fulfilling their tasks or the definition is incorrect. Commerce education does not encompass for example the training of physicians and yet the physician helps to satisfy human wants. At the present time, commerce education does not even have a minor place in medical college. If it is presumed that the definition is correct, then commerce education will embrace not only what is generally included in commerce Curriculum but also what is included in agricultural education, in trade and industrial education and in education, in trade and industrial education and in education for the professions and for domestic life. But this is entirely too broad field. Commerce education can make some contribution to the training of all workers but it cannot provide all the training of all workers but it cannot provide all the training. In a comprehensive interpretation of the world, the entire economic structure may be regarded as a complicated form of business enterprises; yet for practical educational purpose, the term must be given a more limited and practical. Thus meaning of commerce in this chapter will be defined as the phase of the economic system which is devoted to the management and distribution of the products of industry and the professions; as such it is the essential integrating element in the whole economic structure.

Definition of Commerce

Evelyn Thomas defines commercial activities as "activities dealing with the buying and selling of goods and the distribution of finished products from the producers to the customers".

Stephenson defines commerce as "the sum total those processes with are engaged in the removal of hindrances of person, place and time in the exchange of commodities by "commerce" the investigator means a subject by the students at higher secondary level.

Meaning of Commerce and Accountancy Education

In 1992 levert S. Lyon defined commerce education as "Education which a businessman has and which makes him a better business man, is for him a business education no matters whether it was obtained in this walls of a school or not". Accounting is defined as, "the art of recording, classifying and summarizing in terms of money transactions and events of a Financial character and interpreting results there of".

History of Commerce Education

During the last quarter of the last century, with rapid advances in technology more and attention was paid towards the scientific management side of the business. A number of laws were passed by Government and so a need was felt for professionals in the field. This created demand for professionalized commercial education. It is said, "Education of commerce was started by private commercial institutions. To short with only book, Keeping was taught we find minims used to train junior minims under their apprenticeship. Later on private commercial institutes started teaching of book keeping and Accountancy".

For such as education, Madras became a pioneer state where it started in 1886. The Government of madras laid the foundation of commerce education by setting up commercial institute in Madras. Two others institutions were established during the next ten years (by 1896). One was set-up at calcite and the other in the state of Kerala.

In the beginning of this century Calcutta Presidency College also introduced the teaching of commerce (1903). By about that time it was also introduced in Delhi. One more commercial institution was started in Bombay in 1912. At the graduate level the commerce education was introduced in 1913 in Sydenham College of commerce and economic in Bombay.

In 1920's (1921-22) the first Fiscal commission was set up and this commission made certain important recommendations. In this light of these recommendations some major improvements were visible in various industrial fields especially in the field of iron and steel industry, sugar industry, tea industry, cotton industry and jute industry. A very rapid growth of commercial educational institution was observed during 1920-40. The India Institute of Bankers was established in 1926, the institute of charted Accounts of India was established in 1934.

Concept of Commerce Education

The view expressed in various journals, and the views of some educationists about the nature of commerce education are given here to acquaint the students about the study of commerce education.

Levert. S. Lyon defined commerce education as 'any education which a business man has and which makes him a better businessman, is for him business education, no matter whether it was obtained in the walls of a school or not.".

According to Herbert A. Tonne. "For school teaching purpose the above definition is not satisfactory in as much as it would label any useful thing learned by a business man as a form of commerce education what Lyon was attempting to do in this definition was to indicate that the school can never do the entire job of training for business. In training for business, teachers must consider not only the specific training place in and out of school, when viewed in this light, Lyon's definition is preeminently sound.

Commerce Education General Education

Tonne, popham and Freeman (1965) illustrate the scope of commerce Education as under.

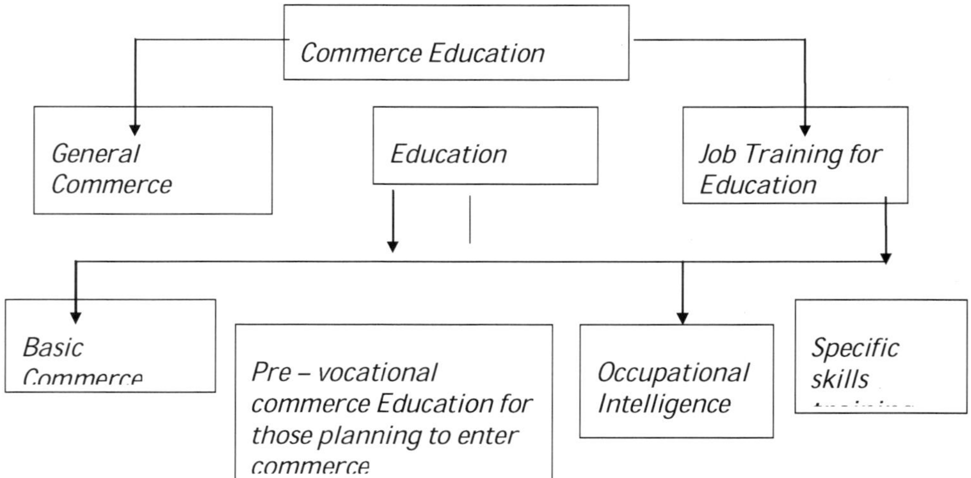

Branches of Commerce

All those activates which are connected with transferring of goods and services from Producers to come under of obstacles have to be crossed. The goal of commerce is to ensure a proper flow of goods and there may be difficulties with regard to trade, transport, distributions, finance, insurance publicity etc.

TRADE

Trade removes hindrance of person through wholesalers, retailers and mercantile agents, goods are owned and possessed by those who produce them unless these goods go in to the hands of the consumers they will have no meaning for the society. Ownership

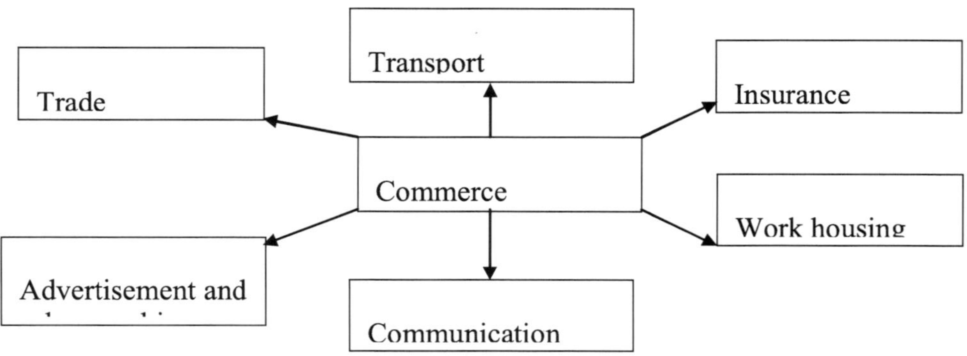

and possession of goods must pass on from the producers to the ultimate consumers. Then only consumers can enjoy these goods.

Transport

Transport removes place hindrance. Goods may be produced at places where they are in less demand. These goods are to be taken to the place of consumption with the help of transport facilities we can create. "Place utility in goods". The various modes of transport i.e. road, rail, sea, air have helped the growth the commerce and industry.

Ware Housing

Ware housing removes hindrance of time, many goods, such as cotton, jute, food grains, sugar etc, are produced during particular seasons of the year. But they are needed throughout the year. To make these goods available throughout the year arrangement must be made for their proper storage. Similarly certain goods are needed in particular seasons. E.g. woolen cloth is required during winter. Rain - coats, umbrellas are essential during rainy season. These goods must be in stock in sufficient quantity before the commencement of the season. This is done with the help of ware housing.

Banking

There is also difficulty of finance. There is always a time gap between the time of production and consumption. During this period of time - gap, traders need funds to carry on their trade. These funds are made available by commercial banks and other financial institutions.

Advertisement Sales Manship

The consumers may not be aware of the availability of various goods in the market. The absence of information about goods is a great hindrance for buying than the producers will also like to have more consumers. Advertisement and sales man ship help in informing the consumers about the availability and use fullness of various products in the market with the advent of T.V, FM Radio, Internet etc., and consumer awareness on various goods in increasing.

Insurance

There is a risk involved in transporting goods from one place to another. This can be a risk of fire or theft. The fee of loss of goods due to any cause is an abstract in the development of trade. The insurance companies provide the coverage for all types of losses of goods the insurance coverage has given a fillip not only to the national trade but also to the international trade.

Communication

The buyers and sellers need the services of various agencies for communicating their message among themselves. The producers inform their customers about the production of goods, the intending send orders to producers for the supply of goods, the services of post offices, private courier services, tax, telephone, cell phone etc, are utilized for communication purpose.

Recent Development in Commerce

(i) Web marketing / Internet marketing and e - commerce.

(ii) Tele-shopping

i. Web marketing / Internet marketing and e - commerce

The growth of trade and commerce has increased the demand for internet and electronic commerce at present geographical coverage of market for products and services in world wide. It enforces the business to carry out its commercial activities like marketing. Selling, delivering, servicing and paying for products and services thought electronic commerce.

Internet

The internet is an international network of computers of carrying unbelievable amount of information. It is a global collection of big powered computers that they connected to each other with network cables, telephone lines, Microwave dishes, satellites etc.

E - Commerce

With the explosive growth in Electronic commerce, referred in general as e -commerce, there was a part in the growth of commerce. The world over e -commerce follows the same basic principles that traditional commerce follows that is buyers and sellers exchange and transport goods from one place to another. But in e – commerce the exchange is facilitated by network computers. Buyers order goods and services online. They track the status of their order in electronic mail and in some cases; they receive the goods they purchase directly over the internet. Computer software, digital music and video online information and other products and services can all be distributed in electronic formats. In such cases, products ordered online are delivered using traditional shipping methods. At the close of the 21st century, retail transactions made up the largest part of e – commerce. Consumers purchased computers, airline tickets, automobiles, clothing, electronics, books, tickets, food, furniture and countless other commodities over the internet.

ii. Tele - Shopping

Tele-Shopping functions according to the principal of the impulse buying in such a way specified. Beyond that is tried to reach with interactive elements customer connection.

With the assortment selection the comparability lacking of market prices plays a role by the spectators. Thus articles of the daily need are sold rarely, for which the spectators could have an approximate price conception. More frequently against it genu ne or alleged innovations are offered, for which there is no well – known market price. A further typical product group is decoration for which for laymen a value evaluation is impossible. To reach at the group of the Cosmetic product frequently self – marks with genuine or alleged however position characteristics sold around this goal.

With sales successes of the transmitters also (sometimes consciously by the moderators more promoted) a self reward effect, as well as the different other methods of the customer influence play like it Markets chreiernand fair propagandists were historically already developed a role.

Recent Development Banking System Internet Banking

Internet Banking or online banking has revolutionized an integral activity of our lives – banking. Internet banking is conducted through a PC, PDA, a hand held communication gadget or any mobile device offering internet connectivity. Broadband internet access uses friendly access and reliable security features of the bank's websites have made online banking the most popular form of e –commerce. Internet banking also facilities an easy, seamless and paperless way to shop, pay bills, buy action items and perform money transfer operations.

The ability to conduct banking services and transactions anytime from home or workplace is the major benefit of online banking, doing away with the need to go traditional bank branch.

MICR - CHEQUE (MAGNETIC INK CHARACTER RECOGNITION)

Magnetic Ink character Recognition, or MICR, colloquially pronounced / mk/ or sometimes / mak / a character recognition technology adopted mainly by the banking industry to facilitate the processing of checks. The process was demonstrated to the American bankers Association in July 1956, and it was almost universally employed by 1963.

Magnetic Ink character Recognition (M.I.C.R) is a character recognition system that uses special ink and character. When a document that contains this ink is to be read it is passed through a machine with a magnetic field that recognizes the characters. It is mostly used by banks to facilitate processing of cheques. The main purpose is to enhance security and avoid losses caused by fraudulent cheques or colored photocopied cheques, because when a colored. Photocopied cheques is scanned the magnetic field will not be able to read the ink.

Electronic Fund Trans (Eft) in India

i. In 1995 the RBI has introduced electronic clearing system for the transfer of funds in Mumbai, Delhi, Calcutta and Chennai.

ii. Floppy input clearing system was introduced in the banking industry in which the data are consolidated for settlement.

iii. In 1997 RBI has introduced Electronic chasing service for payment of electricity bills in Mumbai.

Automatic Teller Machine (Atm)

ATM is Automated Teller Machine. It is to add money into a bank account. It is to open an account in bank. Then you will have to take out that money with the help of cheques or whatever modus operandi. But another simple and easy method is to get that money by help of ATMs. They are very generous in many ways. You just have to get your pin code.

This pin code will be your secret. Don't let anybody know that. This will be purely yours. This will help you out to get money at the time of need. You must have to go for money during off time of bank. At that time you will feel uncomfortable if you are unable to get a cash of the sequel. But ATM will be an awesome help at this time. You will just need to go to ATM machine to get the money you are asking for. You will enter your pin code and amounts of money required. This will make you able to get the money you are seeking for.

Credit Card

A credit card is a small plastic card issued to users as a system of payment. It allows its holder to buy goods and services based on the holder's promise to pay these goods and services. The issuer of the card creates a revolving account and grants a line of credit to the consumer (or the user) from which the user can borrow money for payment to a merchant or as a cash advance to the user.

A credit card is different from a charge card: a charge card required the balance to be paid in full each month. In contrast, credit cards allow the consumers a continuing balance of debt, subject to interest being charged. A credit card also differs from a cash card, which can be used like currency by the owner of the card. Most credit cards are issued by banks or credit unions, and are the shape and size specified by the ISO/IEC 7810 standard as ID - 1.

Scope of Commerce Education

Scope of commerce Education has changed radically during the past six decades. In this contest it would be of interest to note what abbot - wood (1937) report said about commerce education. "This branch (Education for commerce) of vocational education differs so greatly from education for industry, that it demands separate consideration. It must be so framed as to meet the needs of both the two main groups into which we have divided workers in commercial occupations, that is, (a) of the group of which the members have the responsibility for transacting business on an important scale or for performing the professional functions of banking, Accountancy and the like, and (b) of the very large group engaged in recording the transactions of the member of the first group.

Computer in Commerce

Like books, films, blackboards, and laboratory equipments and maps, computer - also can serve the teacher to communicate to the student. But is a very sophisticated monster aid and requires careful preparation for use and higher prerequisite for understanding. Apart from this the computers does some of the teacher's work.

Computer - assisted instruction has two major levels of impact on the teacher. First, the teachers ability to work in an efficient way is increased, because the strenuous works of correcting work books, comparing exercise, maps etc., can be given to the computer. Second, the computer makes the teacher to be more critical and active, because the work is synthesized and regulated by the computer.

Computer is very helpful in preparing balance sheets, maintenance of several types of account books needed in commerce.

To the student it gives immense opportunities for learning more and to rationalize thinking. The learning will become sharp and not speculative. The pervious student involved with facts, ideas and logics, win find fast sequences in learning. The most important factor is that the computer is a 'flexible' teacher not like 'rigid' human teacher. With a level of flexibility, the computer will give alternatives to the learners so that depending upon learning capacity and imaginative power, different options are available to the students.

Importance of Commerce Education

Commerce education is the backbone of business. The success in business depends upon the quality of manpower etc, utilized; commerce education should keep pace with changing trends.

Commerce Education has a crucial role to play in our society including various political parties, religious organizations, where expertise in commercial knowledge is required. The commerce degrees are impended for acquiring a conceptual knowledge and managerial skills in the wide spectrum of business and industry. Today's highly developed industrial, commercial and business world requires highly qualified and smart commerce graduates. Hence it is essential to shape and mould the commerce students to suit the global changes.

Education is a medium through which knowledge and intelligence required by individuals or society can be obtained or properly formulated. Commerce beings with functional aspects and then leads to liberal or ideological aspects. The individual and the society get goods and services at the door steps. The commerce system deals with every part of human life and thus commerce education becomes an - education for better living. The close relationship between the functions of syllabus and social - Economic development and cultural values has led to the increasing realization of the importance of syllabus formation. So we must introduce vocationalization concept in commerce as recommended in 1882 by Hunter's commission. The commission suggested two types of curriculum, namely subjects for higher studies and vocational and practical subjects. It was Gandhiji's Nai Talim (1936), which conceived education as an independent stream with training to prepare students for identified occupations. "There is", as the great philosopher whitened (1861 - 1947) put it, "only one subject matter of education, and that is life in all its manifestation." Trade, commerce and industry constitute as vital part of our life's activities. These aspects of our life's experience are extremely important and if we despise these, all our educational effort will be fruitless toils.

High philosophies apart, the full education for an individual must be both for making a living and for making a life. Thus viewed, the full education of an individual involves both, vocations education' and 'cultural education'. The individual must be able to earn a living for learning a civilized life. In such a perspective, commerce or business education, not inferior or superior to any other phase or branch.

Role of Commerce in The Present Scenario

The present world is characterized by fast changing conditions or demand and technology. There will be much uncertainty than in the past. Our research and development organizations will have to acquire, and adapt latest technologies in improving the quality to stay in the competitive world.

The world is changing very fast. The speed of LPG (Liberalization, privatization and Globalization) has tremendously influenced the various dimensions of commerce education. Most of the scholars are recommending re - orientations of the commerce course. The present syllabi of all universities are not able to meet the different types of challenges posed by industry and business. There are no practical orientations to develop skills and qualities among youngsters, thus there is a need for reorienting and restricting commerce education by introducing uniform syllabi at the national level. Most of the colleges and even a few universities have not recognized the importance of IT and it related skills. Therefore, students are not getting an opportunity to acquaint themselves with tools of information technology. The professional bodies, trade associations, and chambers of commerce have shown very little interest to associate with universities redesign the commerce courses.

"India is rich in resources; culture and education too." It is right time to improve the basic curriculum and the infrastructure facilities. By this way, we can minimize the number of Indian students migrating to foreign countries for quality education. There is a need for globalization of education too, to face the competition from foreign universities and ensuring quality education with placement.

In commerce, transportation of goods from one place to another is unavoidable. In the past, transporting commodities was expensive, time consuming and risky. Therefore commerce was restricted mainly to local markets. With the advancement of technology in transportation, commerce expanded considerably. Today commerce takes place between neighboring households, neighboring cities, and neighboring countries by international shipping, mail services advancement in information technology and Internet enables commerce among people from any location in the world.

Industrial growth effected commerce in a variety of ways and a revolution has taken place in land transportation. There were trade barriers, and depression in some parts of the world, due to the fury of nature war between countries, internal political strife and economic setbacks. These have retarded commerce growth. A series of international conferences and discussions between member countries slowly but steadily dismantled many of the restrictions though not completely. The execution of the General Agreement on Tariffs and Trade (GATT) and the formation of customers unions like European Union, have brought about a significant reduction in tariff reductions.

Later on in 1944, Institute of works and cost Accountants of India was established. In 1955, the Federation of Insurance institutes were established.

AIMS OF TEACHING COMMERCE

1. This knowledge should help the pupil in his daily life.
2. It should be related to the materials with which the pupil is familiar and should not be based an absolute devices and ideas.

3. It should make pupil fit for society.
4. It must provide him some practical experiences which form a part of his learning process.
5. It should inculcate a commercial temper in the student.

Status of Commerce Education The Secondary Schools in India

In India commerce education first started at the secondary level but its real growth and development took place at the college level, up to the middle of twentieth century. In India commerce was not considered as a separate discipline and it was reduced to an insignificant item of the twin department's economics and commerce, in which Economics had an upper hand. It hindered any real progress in the field of commerce for a pretty long time. Only after the report of Mud liar commission an expansion took place in commerce education. The multipurpose higher secondary schools were opened and practical subjects were introduced in many fields including commerce.

To start with in commerce education were introduced such subjects as letter writing, business methods shorthand and Type-writing. Later on many more subjects such as Book-keeping economics, Accountancy, commercial Law, and Taxation etc were introduced. Adopting the recommendation of Dr.V.K.R.V. Rao committee national Diploma in commercial practice was started with a view to prepare qualified and skilled persons needed by the growing economy in the country.

With the rapid growth in the field of trade, commerce and industry, the need for proper education and right type of commerce teachers was felt and to meet the needs of teachers of practical subjects a necessity was must to have Some teachers of practical subjects a necessity was must to have some special type of institutes to provide. For this type of institution N.C.E.R.T. and Regional college of Education did a commendable Job, Till about 1963 no facilities existed for providing training facilities in the field of commerce but now such training is available through regular training in service courses, summer-cum-correspondence course etc. but even now the practical aspect of commerce education programmed is not quite Satisfactory. An effort is needed to accelerate the teaching or short hand and type - writing etc. in views of an enormously increasing demand in these fields.

There is a talk of vocationalisation and work experience in Education. It is thus hoped that in recent Future the commerce education will be much more oriented in favors of practical subjects. It could help to achieve the main objective of commerce education i-e development if employable skills.

Need For the Commerce Education

There has been a history growth in the fields of commerce, industry and science in the recent past. This growth demands a specialized education in various fields concerned with science, commerce and industry. The dependence of commerce on science has been exam pilfer by pointing out the fact that" the management side of commerce is wholly dependent upon computers. In India to the computer is fully accepted by business. Computer education has been introduced in the schools in India and with this it is expected that the School will become the machines of commerce education. However, at present commerce education in schools has not become so advanced that computers are used at school stage in book - keeping or Accountancy"

In Most of the advanced countries the commerce education is totally computerized.

Need and Significance of the Study

In modern world we are enjoying a very happy life and good Standard of living, because of the development of commerce - commerce provided all the things we require to need a happy life. Commerce refers to all those activities which are necessary to bring goods and services from the place of origin to the consumption. Commerce includes trade and aids to trade consist of services such as transport, banking, insurance, ware housing, advertising and communication. Commerce relates of all economic activities resetting in production exchange, distribution and consumption of commodities and services.

Student's performance in different school subject may not be uniform. For example a student studying well in commerce may not do well in subject like chemistry and physics. Learning different school subject requires different skills from the students. For better learning of commerce one should have the knowledge of banking, trade, export, business, marketing etc. If the student fails to acquire knowledge of these dimensions his/her performance in commerce may not be up to the desired level. At the same time the students must acquire the mental ability to increase the reasoning ability for day -to -day life, as each concept in commerce depends on reasoning ability. So in commerce, concepts and reasoning ability are the two sides of the coin.

High Lighting the Learing Problems of Commerce

The main objective at this investigation is to study the learning problems of the commerce students studying in the higher secondary level of the Salem district. The different aspect of the learning problems of commerce students in the higher secondary schools are determined with the consultation of the commerce students in the higher Secondary schools are determined with the consultation of the commerce students in various higher secondary Schools, preference to all these sources led the investigator to approach the study in six different areas Vis.

1. Learning problems in psychological aspects
2. Learning Problems in curriculum aspects
3. Learning Problems in learning aspects
4. Learning Problems in occupation aspects
5. Learning Problems in Health aspects
6. Learning Problems in Economic aspects

Specific aim of the Study

1. To study the problems of learning commerce students under the different variables

* Male and Female commerce students
* Rural and Urban commerce students
* Tamil and English Medium commerce Students
* Hostel and day scholar commerce Students

2. To Study the problems of learning commerce students under the type of schools.

* Government Schools
* Aided Schools
* Matriculation Schools

Scope of the Study

The Scope of this study to enumerate all types of problems by the commerce students in learning commerce. But the issues, selected may represent the most common earning problems by commerce students, Hence the present investigatior deals with the most common and basic problems that are being encountered by the commerce students in the day-to-day learning work. The present study will talk into consideration, the learning problems by the commerce students in the following areas. Learning problems relating to the higher secondary curriculum. Psychological, curriculum, learning, occupation, Health and Economic factors.

Statement of the Problem

The problem of the present study is entitled "problems in learning commerce student's higher secondary school at Salem district".

Commerce : By "Commerce" the investigator means a subject studied by the students at higher secondary level.

Learning : The knowledge we acquire, the language we speak, the habits, attitudes and skills developed in wars are all due to learning. Psychologists define learning as "a relatively permanent change in behavior which occurs as a result of activity, training, practice or experience". Learning is basic to human behavior learning plays a central role in the language we speak. Our customs attitudes and beliefs, our goals, our personality, traits (both adaptive and maladaptive) and even in our perceptions.

Higher secondary school students : By this, the investigator means the students studying in standards XI and XII of higher secondary Schools following state board syllabus. Students studying in first Higher Secondary course of different subject group.

Problems: Something difficult as a problem obstacle, objection or hindrance. The society is tending towards assuring unified challenges for both male and female students. There is therefore the need to give equal opportunities to both male and female students to enable them to develop necessary skills to face the challenges. In the Classroom situation the male and female students are equally exposed to the Methods, Strategies, Teaching to develop problem solving skills. The present study aimed at knowing the differential performance in problem - solving. Tests when the male and female students are exposed to the different methods or strategies of teaching commerce problems. It also aimed to know the relative effectiveness of the methods of teaching.

Delimitation of the Study

The study is limited to only higher secondary commerce student of the Salem District only. The sample was selected as stratified random sampling method to come to the various states as given below.

1. Both the sex.
2. Higher secondary schools in Salem District only.
3. Higher secondary schools in Salem District only.
4. Rural and Urban schools.
5. These study lover's only commerce students studying higher secondary classes.

Organization of the Study

The report of the thesis will be presented according to the following sequences.

The first chapter gives introduction, definitions of terms, statement of problem and limitations of the study.

Second chapter deals with the review of related literature which are done in India and abroad related to this study. Third chapter gives a detailed account of research procedures and methodo-logy used in this study. Fourth chapter deals with the tabulation of analysis and the interpretations of the data in detail. Fifth chapter describes the findings, conclusion and certain recommendations about the study. This is followed by the bibliography which consists of the study and the related matters.

II

Review of Related Literature

Introduction

"A good thesis is one that me how to replicate or extend the previous work with improvement to reduce bias, eliminate flows, consider pertinent variables, settle unsolved issued to check contradictory or uncertain in finding".

The aim of this chapter is to record briefly a survey of literature related to the problems under study. It is necessary to enter on any research project. This will help in understanding the various aspects of the problem.

The research worker must be acquainted with up-to-date information about what has been thought and done in the specific area from which he intends to take up a problem of research.

A review of related literature gives the scholar an understanding of the previous work that has been done in the area, it enables him to know the means of getting to the frontier in the field of his problems, methods and limitations and it enables him to locate compensative data useful in the interpretation of results.

Purpose of Review Literature

The following are the same of the purpose of the review of literature.

1. It provides ideas, theories, explanations or hypotheses valuable in formulation the problem.
2. To avoid the risk of duplicating some of the studies already undertaken.
3. To suggest methods or research methodologies appropriate to the problem.
4. It widens the horizon of the researcher.
5. It suggest valuable basis for hypothesis.
6. It helps delimit the problem.
7. It helps the investigator not to allow the mistake (or) 100 phone (or) pitfall which occurred in the previous findings.
8. To locate compensative data useful in the interpretation of results.
9. It contributed to the investigator for the general scholarship.

According to Best (1977)," familiarity with the literature in any problem area helps the student to discover what is already known, what others have attempted to find out 1 what methods of attacks have been promising or disappointing and what problem remain to be solved."

Mouly (1984) says, "Survey of related literature avoids the risk of duplications, provide theories, ideas, explanations or hypothesis valuable in formulating the problem and contributes to the general scholarship of the investigator.

The review of literature is a necessity for any research for the following reasons. It enables the investigator to study the work done earlier (previously) in the area of research.

Related Studies In India and Abroad on Students

Learning Problems

Desai, B.V.(1981) conducted "A study of the outstanding problem of teachers of standards V to VII of the Marathi language side of municipal primary schools of Bombay".

The main problem of the municipal primary school teachers were the educational apathy of the homes of the children attending the municipal primary schools. Personal, domestic, family and social problems of the municipal primary teachers were relatively fewer. The problem of looking after onisocon children at home was ranked fifth by the teachers.

Sharma, S. (1982) "A study of intellectual factors and academic achievement in arts, science and commerce course at higher secondary stage, PhD education".

The objectives of the investigation to study the productive value of intelligence (verbal and non - verbal) and creativity for success in arts, science and commerce course at the higher secondary stage with anxiety, study habits and social economic status as control variables. BARER . M, Differential out whether the existed a differential pattern of factors required for successful performance in the science, arts and commerce offered at the higher secondary stage.

Sharma, R.C. (1984), conducted "A study of the opinions of parents of out of school children, sired, Rajasthan".

In rural areas the child was an economic unit of the family, a helper in agricultural and animal husbandry, and an important contributor to family income. About 88 percent were ready to sent their children to school if their problems were solved. The reason for the low enrolment girls were, girls needed for household work and early marriage and the feeling that it was not worthwhile to educate girls as they were not an integral part of the family.

Soman, N.B.(1990) conducted "A study of the problems of secondary School students staying in hostels and the problems of administration of these hostels in the state of Maharashtra".

A hostel was better than a home for those students who could continue their education in hostels only. Due to the poor group influence students acquired regularity in studies, but also acquired habits of chewing tobacco, smoking, etc, All the students cpposed friendships based on caste and religion.

Agrawal Sarawsati, (1990) conducted "A study of an investigation into the awareness among primary and secondary school teachers population problem and their attitude towards population education".

Most teachers were aware of and had positive attitudes towards the population problem. Caste seemed to be a significant variable in awareness of attitude towards the population problems and population education.

Mohapatra,T.(1991) conducted "A study of problems of secondary school teachers, a comparative study of government and private schools teachers".

Teachers both male and female came from all classes of society, but the majority of them were from the lower and lower middle - class income groups. As compared to the male teachers, most of the female teachers came from families belonging to the higher secondary educational system. The private school teachers were found more qualified than the government school teachers.

Ramasamy, V. (1992) conducted "A study of problems of adolescents and their achievement in mathematics".

Adolescent boys and girls in the urban areas different with respect to their physical problems. Adolescent boys and girls in the urban areas had problems in social relationship. Acolescent boys and girls in the rural areas faced similar problems regarding physical, school and social areas. Both urban and rural adolescents faced problems in their vocational choice.

Dr.Rajammal, (1996) "Problems faced by the student's teachers in teaching biology of high schools and higher seconcary schools".

From the analysis the students who have opted Tamil & biology face more difficulties that the other two groups.

Santosh gupta (2003) Reported in the criticle "Emerging trends in commerce and management education"(University news weekly journal of high education Vol.401.03.2003)

"Experience - oriented and experimental learning so as to enhance individual's current and future managerial effectiveness. Commerce and management educators and training instruments can play a critical role in executing this task of developing the right perspective and needed skills money the students by redesigning the education programmed and modifying the teaching methods."

Dr.Babu ,R.(2004) "Higher secondary student's attitude towards the study of commerce and their adjustment." journal of educational research & extension Vol.41-2

From the interpretations it is concluded that (1) there is a significant relationship between the higher secondary student's attitude towards the study of commerce and their adjustment. (2) There is significant difference between boys and girls in respect of their attitude towards the study of commerce. (3) There is no significant difference between (i) Rural and Urban students (ii) Government school students and private school students and (iii) Tamil medium and English medium students in respect of their attitude towards the study of commerce.

(4) There is significant difference between the rural students and urban students in respect of their adjustment. (5) There is no significant difference between (i) Boys and Girls,(ii) Government school student's private school students and (iii) Tamil medium and English medium students in respect of their adjustment. (6) The higher secondary school students selected for this study showed a very poor status in respect of their adjustment (emotional, social and educational).

Vinayagamoorthy, A. (2006) "Move with the world changer imminent in commerce education & curriculum" Edu tracks, Vol.6 No.1 page No.17-19.

Stating that commerce Education in the backbone of business and that it should keep pace with the changing trends, the author assists that if we have to compete our educational institutions should impart the most modern skills cost - effectively through innovative teaching and best infrastructure. The two - year master's degree viz, post graduate degree, should focus on the advanced level of the subjects as required nationally and internationally. This exposure should facilitate the students to proceed further to do research on the subject of this choice. There should be courses designed to bridge the gap between designed to bridge the gap between the captains of the industry and the professionals. A short duration course on business laws, drafting and conveyance will be a right choice. The students should be exposed to basic computer knowledge and it should form part of the curriculum viz. Basic packages like TALL 7.2 and Spas). More opportunities should be provided for the students to exhibit their skills, by organizing frequent one-day student's programmers, competitions and quiz programs both within the college and outside. There should be a quarter journal, wherein the students should be encouraged to make their presentations in the form of articles, write – ups etc.

Dr. Harjeet kaur bhata.(2006) "Teaching of commerce at higher secondary stage" Education tracks Vol.5 page No.23.

E – Commerce, business and technological, issues one lightly intertwined. Although this course recognizes the importance of both sets of issues, it does not require prior knowledge of the underlying technologies. The course will give an over – view of E – technologies, best practices and strategies, trends. Furthermore, during the course the impact of -technologies will be analyzed.

The students will understand the issues under p nning today's best practice in commerce and e-business. The students will be awareness of innovative strategies in the field as well as future trends, including the advent of mobile – e – commerce. The students will understand the increased of e-business solutions in e- The Government.

Dr. Chandra sekhar, C. (july 2006) "Problem solving ability of primary school in elementary mathematics" Vol.3 page No. 12-19.

In this case private school teachers more number is in low category the in high category. There is no evidence to prove that the level of problem solving abilities is independent of the type of management. Rural teachers dominated the urban in high and moderate categories, where as in low category, urban number is more than the rural. The level of problem solving abilities is independent of the locality of working. The level of problem solving abilities is independent of the gender.

Dr. Ishwara,P.& Dr. Laxmana,P.(2007) "Participant's attitude to referesher courses in commerce and management in kuvempu university". (experiments in education).

Out of 128 participants 96 suggested that, in order to appreciate the field Conditions and insights into practical experiences, non-academic professionals like executive must also be invited as resource persons besides academicians.

A majority for the participants have suggested that this type of refresher course in necessary once in a year even for experienced teachers. Almost all participants have suggested there should be more seminars / group discussions amount the necessary once in a year even for experienced teachers. Almost all participants have suggested there should be more seminars / group discussions amount the participants, industrial visits / or field trips during the refresher course. Many of them suggested that hostel and library facilities should be provided adequately. A few participants suggested that such refresher course should not be made compulsory for all teachers and it must be made so only for poor performers, the need for refresher course should be ascertained through scientific performance evaluation. More than 87.5 % of the respondent teachers are favorable disposed towards the refresher course. There is no significant difference between the various pairs of sub sample groups which were tested statistically for such difference. It is a micro study conducted on very limited population; there is a strong need to conduct studies of this type on different Population in a more generalized fashion.

Latha, G. & Pancharatham, N.(2007) "Job strees related problems and coping strategies" journal of community guidance and research Vol.24 no. 235-242.

73.5% of software professional has medium job stress. The workload acts as a major stressor for software professionals. Long work hours are associated with increased work family conflict and at least indirectly, with psychological distress. To work long hours creates such tension and stress that individuals are enable to accommodate all their responsibilities at home regardless of the member of hours they work. This implies that the work must be properly planned and executed. A comparison of the actual work with the planned one will be helpful to take corrective action.

Ayodhya (2007) "Emotional problems in secondary school children and its relation to life events and scholastic life events and scholastic achievement". J.C.G. and R. Vol.24 page No. 347-355.

Secondary school students had significantly high rate of emotional problems. Emotionally disturbed students had high life events scores and work number of events. Boys had high life event scores more number of events. The emotional problems found were of minor native depression was the commonest emotional problem. Emotional problems did not have influence on scholastic achievement in the present study.

Awi, Asnaini (2008) "The relationship between teacher's knowledge of the commerce learning experience and evaluation and the teacher's management of the implementation of the commerce in secondary schools", Kualalumpur, master's thesis, University putra Malaysia

The results of data analysis on the problems and challenges faced by commerce teachers in managing the commerce instruction implementation showed that most respondents have problems with the uncoordinated learning experience specifications and as well as limited time to finish up the syllabus. Most respondents suggested that the learning experience specifications should be simplified and extra teaching time should be given. In conclusion, even though there is no significant relationship between the teacher's knowledge of the commerce learning experience and evaluation and the teacher's implementation management of the commerce instruction and also the no significant relationship between the teacher's knowledge of the commerce and demographic factor, all of the problems faced by the teachers and their suggestions need to be taken into considerations by responsible parties in order to find solutions to the real factors that have caused the decline of the students performance in the commerce subject among secondary students in Kuala Lumpur.

Arumugarajan, R.(2008) "Abstract reasoning of commerce students studying in school" (Edu tracts Vol. 8-No.4 page No.34-39.

In this study aimed at finding out the level of reasoning ability of commerce students, the investigators conclude that the abstract remaining ability of the students is moderate while their achievement is average. The level of abstract reasoning ability of higher secondary commerce students in moderate. The level of achievement of higher secondary commerce students is average. There is significant difference between XI and XII standard commerce group students with reference to abstract reasoning. There is significant correlation between the achievement and abstract reasoning ability of higher secondary commerce students with reference to background variables - female students. XI standard students, XII standard students.

III

Methodology

Introduction

The main objective of the study was to find out the problems in learning commerce students among higher secondary School. The need for the study, objectives and the scope of the study were split out in chapter – 1. An extensive review of related literature covering the problems in learning commerce students and higher secondary school and some other related fields were presented in chapter – II. This chapter deals with the design and procedure adopted for the present study. In the simplest way research design is a plan structure and strategy of investigation in order to obtain answer to the research question. "Design is the blue print of the procedures that reaching valid conclusion about relationships between independent and dependent variables" says Best (1978). Hence to be right towards the goal, it is necessary to have a design for the research being carried out at the very beginning. But it is also true that "selection of a particular design," as Best (1978) suggests, "is based on the purpose of the experiment the types of variables to be manipulated and the conditions or limiting factors under which it may be conducted." So it is apparent that the design differs, as the problems differ.

The selection of methods for research work depends upon the nature of problem selected. Mainly methodology consists of tools, techniques and procedures. The success of investigation depends on the priority of the method and the tools and techniques the researcher uses.

Statement of the Problem

The present study is entitled "Problems in learning commerce students among higher secondary school at Salem District".

Objectives of the Study

1. To find out the problems in learning commerce students among higher secondary school between total Male and Female students.
2. To find out the problems in learning commerce students among higher secondary school between total Rural and Urban students.
3. To find out the problems in learning commerce students among higher secondary school between total Government and Aided students.
4. To find out the problems in learning commerce students among higher secondary school between total Aided and Matriculation students.
5. To find out the problems in learning commerce students among higher secondary school between total Matriculation and Government students.
6. To find out the problems in learning commerce students among higher secondary school between total Tamil and English Medium students.
7. To find out the problems in learning commerce students among higher secondary school between total Hosteller and Day scholar students.

8. To find out the problems in learning commerce students between Male and Female with respect to their psychology, curriculum, learning, occupation, health and economic factors.
9. To find out the problems in learning commerce students between Rural and Urban with respect to their psychology, curriculum, learning, occupation, health and economic factors.
10. To find out the problems in learning commerce students between Government and Aided with respect to their psychology, curriculum, learning, occupation, health and economic factors.
11. To find out the problems in learning commerce students between Aided and Matriculation with respect to their psychology, curriculum, learning, occupation, health and economic factors.
12. To find out the problems in learning commerce students between Matriculation and Government with respect to their psychology, curriculum, learning, occupation, health and economic factors.
13. To find out the problems in learning commerce students between Tamil and English medium with respect to their psychology, curriculum, learning, occupation, health and economic factors.
14. To find out the problems in learning commerce students between Hosteller and Day scholar with respect to their psychology, curriculum, learning, occupation, health and economic factors.

Hypothesis of the Study

1. There is no significant different on the problems in learning commerce among higher secondary school between Male and Female students.

2. There is no significant different on the problems in learning commerce among higher secondary school between Rural and Urban students.
3. There is no significant different on the problems in learning commerce among higher secondary school between Government and Aided students.
4. There is no significant different on the problems in learning commerce among higher secondary school between Aided and Matriculation students.
5. There is no significant different on the problems in learning commerce students among higher secondary school between Matriculation and Government students.
6. There is no significant different on the problems in learning commerce among higher secondary school between Tamil and English medium students.
7. There is no significant different on the problems in learning commerce among higher secondary school between Hosteller and Day Scholar students.
8. There is no significant difference on the problems in learning commerce students among higher secondary school between Male and Female with respect to their psychological, curriculum, learning, occupation, health and economic factors.
9. There is no significant difference on the problems in learning commerce students among higher secondary school between Rural and Urban with respect to their psychological, curriculum, learning, occupation, Health and economic factors. There is no significant difference on the problems in learning commerce students among higher secondary school between Government and Aided with respect to their psychological, curriculum, learning, occupation, health and economic factors.
10. There is no significant difference on the problems in learning

commerce students among higher secondary school between Aided and Matriculation with respect to their psychological, curriculum, learning, occupation, health and economic factors.

11. There is no significant difference on the problems in learning commerce students among higher secondary school between Matriculation and Government with respect to their psychological, curriculum, learning, occupation, health and economic factors.

12. There is no significant difference on the problems in learning commerce students among higher secondary school between Tamil and English Medium with respect to their psychological, curriculum, learning, occupation, health and economic factors.

13. There is no significant difference on the problems in learning commerce students among higher secondary school between Hosteller and Day scholar with respect to their psychological, curriculum, learning, occupation, health and economic factors.

Design of the Research

Research design is a plan, a structure and a strategy of investigation conceived to obtain answers to various issues in research. The object to research design is to test the research hypothesis. The research design, therefore, is built in the principle of maximization of variance. A research design however, is not a Highly specific plan to be followed without direction. Rather, it is a series of guide post to keep right direct. Thus, research design is the process of planning a research, choosing methods and procedures that can be expected to yield meaningful and most interpretable results.

The present study belongs to normative survey research. The factors used in the study such as psychological, curriculum, learning, occupation, health and Economics factors problems in learning commerce students among higher secondary among the students.

The tool used in the study are problems in learning rating scale developed by the investigator to access the factors problems in learning commerce students among higher secondary school at Salem District Separately, along with a personal data sheet to know the background of the students. Stratified random samplings a technique was followed in this study. Data were collected from 150 students of six different schools of Salem District. The statistical Technique were used Mean, Standard deviation and't' test.

Table 3.1

Schematic representation of the research design

S. No	Type	Sources
1.	Nature of the research	Normative survey method
2.	Factors	1.Psychology factor 2.Curriculum 3.Learning factor 4.Occupationfactor 5.Health factor 6.Economic factor
3.	Tool developed	Problems in learning commerce students among higher secondary school
4.	Demographic Variables	1.Gender 2.Locality 3.Type of schools 4.Medium of instruction 5.Residency
5.	Sampling Technique	Stratified random sampling
6.	Size of the sample	150 samples, male(77),female(73)
7.	Statistical Technique	Mean, Standard Deviation, 't' test

Methodology of the Study

In this present study was used in normative survey method. Normative survey method is connected with collection of data and describing the present's status. Normally the data is collected either by interview or by questionnaire. It deals with describing, recording, analyzing and interpreting the conditions that exist.

Sample of the Study

For the present study the stratified random sampling method

was used. This method of sampling is used when the population is composed of diverse segments or natural subdivisions of units. The method consists a classifying the population units into a certain number of groups called strata (plural) and then selecting random samples independently from each group or stratum (singular).

Size of the Sample

The sample was selected stratified randomly representing 150 students from different school of Salem District. A total number of 150 students comprising 77 male and 73 Female were drawn from the following school as shown in table.

Table - 3.2

School wise distribution of the sample

S. No	Name of the school	Sample		Total
		Male	Female	
1.	Government Higher Secondary School, Muthunaickenpatty.	17	6	23
2.	Municipal Higher Secondary School, Salem.	10	-	10
3.	Government Girls Higher Secondary School, Salem.	-	36	36
4.	Sengunthar Mahajana Higher Secondary School, Tharamangalam.	22	-	22
5.	Neelambal Subramaniyam Higher Secondary School, Suramangalam.	10	16	26
6.	Sri Gayathri Higher Secondary School, Sithanoor.	18	15	33

Schematic Representation of the Sample

In this study a total number of 150 commerce students at higher secondary level in Salem District were taken as samples. The samples are categorized in the following table.

Tools used for the Study

In the present study was used in Rating Scale method. To access the factors problem in learning commerce students among higher secondary school with the type of Four point Rating scale was developed under the similar six dimensions. They are psychological Factor, Curriculum factor, learning factor, occupation factor, Health factor and Economic Factor. In the tools with the options such as strongly Agree, Agree, Disagree and strongly disagree were utilized. For favorable statement scoring order is 4,3,2,1 and unfavorable statement scoring order is 1,2,3,4. The total score is 160. Then the score is converted to 100 and analyses are done.

Table - 3.3

Distribution of the sample details

Variables	Sub - Categories	Size	Percentage	Total
	Male	77	51.3	150
Gender	Female	73	48.7	
Locality	Rural	58	38.7	150
	Urban	92	61.3	
	Government	69	46.0	150
Type of schools	Aided	48	32.0	
	Matriculation	33	22.0	
	Hosteller	56	37.3	
Residence	Day scholar	94	62.7	150
Medium of	Tamil	83	55.3	
instruction	English	67	44.7	150

Pilot Study

The investigator being a Teacher Educator was going on to write appropriate statements related to the objectives of the study. Moreover she was consulted the higher secondary students. The steps on the different issues based on the experienced teachers, twenty commerce students and others aspects the investigator refine the written statements in all the opionnairres.

For the present study initial hundred statements were constructed for the pilot study. After careful examination of the critical ratio for each item, it was decided to have 40 statements for the final study.

Administration of the Tool

The tool used for the present study is a Rating scale. Psychological aspects consist of 10 statements with deal with the problem in psychological aspects for the commerce students. Curriculum aspects consist of 10 statements about the learning problems in higher secondary commerce curriculum for the commerce students. Learning aspects consists of 5 statements about the problems in earning situation for the commerce students. Occupation aspects consist of 5 statements about the learning problems in occupation aspects for the commerce students. Health aspects consist of 5 statements about the learning problems in Health aspects for the commerce students. Economics aspects consist of 5 statements about the learning problems in Economic aspects for the commerce stucents.

Table - 3.4

Number of statements under each category of problems in learning commerce students among higher secondary school

S. No	Factors	Students		Total
		Positive items	Negative items	
1.	Psychological factors	1,3,4,5,7,8,9,10	2,6	10
2.	Curriculum Factors	11,12,13,14,15,16,18	17,19	10
3.	Learning Factors	22,24,	21,23,25	5
4.	Occupation Factors	26,27,28,30	29	5
5.	Health Factors	31,33,34,35	32	5
6.	Economic Factors	36,38,39,40	37	5
	Total	30	10	40

The above table 3.4 shows the student's opionnairres to access the factors for the problems in learning commerce students among higher secondary school at Salem District. This tool so problems in learning commerce students consists of 4 point scale with 30 positive and 10 negative statements on all the six dimensions such as psychological, curriculum, learning, occupation, health and economic factors.

Collection of Data

The investigator obtained adequate number of copies of the rating scale for the actual collection of data. Selected higher secondary schools were visited and their heads and teachers were contacted for getting permission and co-operation for the collection of data.

The rating scale was then distributed among the students. Adequate instructions were given for marking the responses. Strict uniform procedures were adopted in the administration of the rating scale to commerce students of different schools.

Scoring and Consolidation of Data

The data collected were consolidated, codified and used for suitable analysis. Scoring of the response sheets was done as per the scoring scheme described earlier. The scores were summed up separately and the total score of each individual was taken. The forty statements in the rating scale offer the following comprehensive view. 40 x 4 = 160, 40 x 3 = 120, 40 x 2 = 80, 40 x 1 = 40 thus all the scores would fell maximum 160 and minimum 40 scores. Each response is given numerical scores assigned to all the separate items giving the total score, which is interpreted as positive and negative answer.

S.No	Categories of response	Scores	
		Positive Key	Negative Key
1	Strongly agree	4	1
2	Agree	3	2
3	Disagree	2	3
4	Strongly disagree	1	4

Personal Data Sheet

The personal data sheet serves to collect personal information. Students were asked to write their Name, Gender, Locality, Type of schools, Medium of instruction and Residence that they studied in higher secondary schools.

Reliability of the Tool

According to Garret and Henry (1972), "Reliability means the degree to which a test or tool measure. Something consistently". A reliable test would definitely yield consistent result if it is administrated to the different groups of equal level. On the result of the pilot study the investigator found that the tool was very well understood by the students.

The investigator used Karl Pearson's correlation coefficient product moment correlation, to find out the relationship variables between the variables. The following formula was employed.

$$r = \frac{N\sum xy - (\sum x.\sum y)}{\sqrt{N\sum x^2 - (\sum x)^2 . N\sum Y^2 - (\sum y)^2}}$$

Where,

X = Sum of the X scores
Y = Sum of the Y Scores
X^2 = Sum of the Squared X scores
Y^2 = Sum of the Squared Y scores
XY = Sum of the products of paired X and Y scores
N = Number of paired scores.

Split Half Method

The investigator used split half method to find out the reliability. In this method the test is first divided into two equivalent half's. the first half of the tests represents odd number items 1,3,5,7...etc and second half of the test represent the even number items 2,4,6,8 ...etc. The reliability coefficient of the whole test was calculated and it was found to be 0.9886. Reliability co-efficient of its various factors varies from 0.811 to 0.98.

Reliability coefficient of the whole test.

$$r = \frac{2r}{r+1}$$

$$r = \frac{2(0.97755)}{1.97755}$$

= 0.9886

r = the reliability coefficient of the half test

r_n = the reliability coefficient of the whole test.

Table - 3.5

Split half method reliability of the problems in learning factors.

S. No	Problems in learning factors	No. of items	Reliability co-efficient
1	Psychology factors	10	0.9827
2	Curriculum factors	10	0.8650
3	Learning factors	5	0.9755
4	Occupation factors	5	0.9313
5	Health factors	5	0.882
6	Economic factors	5	0.8117

Validity of the Tool

Henry E Garret defines validity as "The fidelity with which it measures what it purpose to measure". A test is valid when it measures truly and accurately the ability or equality one wants to appraise. Thus the tool was stabilized by finding the content validity. The statement was constructed properly for the final study by the investigator.

Statistical Measurement used in the Study

The following statistical techniques were used by the investigator.

Mean

Mean is used to measure the entire data by one value. Its value is obtained by adding to gather all the items and by dividing the total by the number of items.

$$x = A + (\frac{\sum fd}{N}) \times c$$

Where ,

C = Class interval

Σfd = Total of the products of each class frequency with the steps deviation of the respective class.

N = No. of samples.
X = Arithmetic mean.

Standard Deviation

The standard deviation concept was introduced by Karl Pearson in 1823. It is used to measure dispersion standard deviation is also known as root of the mean of the square deviation from the arithmetic mean.

$$S.D = \sqrt{\frac{\sum fd^2}{N} - (\frac{\sum fd^2}{N})} \times c$$

N = No. of Samples
C = Class interval
D = $\frac{X-A}{c}$
X = Mid point of the class interval
A = Assumed mean
$\sum fd$ = Total of the products of each class frequency with the steps deviation of the respective class.
$\sum fd^2$ = Total of the products of each days frequency with the square deviation of the respective class.

't' Test.

The test of significance of the difference between the two means is known as't' test. 't' is calculated by using the formula.

$$t = \frac{M_1 - M_2}{\sqrt{\frac{SD^2}{N_1} + \frac{SD^2}{N_2}}}$$

M_1 = and are means of the two variables.
N_1 = Number of cases in First sample.
N_1 = Number of cases in second sample.
$SD_1{}^2$ = Standard deviation of first sample.
$SD^2{}_1$ = Standard deviation of second sample.

Delimitations of the Study

1. This study is limited to a sample of 150 commerce students studying in higher secondary school. As Salem is sprawling city, having a good no. of higher secondary schools of all types; the investigation could visit only a small number of schools.
2. The investigation is confined to 69 Government school students, 48 Aided school students and 33 matriculation school students in the present study.

Conclusion

This chapter deals with methodology of the present investigation as enumerated. Thus it gives brief details about selection of sample, pilot study, and administration of tool in the study, data collection and statistical technique used in tool. Having described the detailed methodology of the study in the chapter, analysis and interpretation of the data for the present study is next chapter.

IV

Analysis and Interpretation of the Data

Introduction

The analysis and interpretation of the collected data are the essential part of any dissertation. A detailed statistical analysis and accurate interpretation is attempted in this chapter is to present the result of the study.

Meaning of Analysis

Analysis of data means studying the tabulated data in order to determine the internet factor or meanings. It involves breaking down existing compiled factors into simpler parts and putting parts together in new arrangements for purpose of interpretation. According to wolf "The discovery of order in the phenomena of values, not withstanding their complexity and apparent confusion is rendered possible by the process of analysis and synthesis which are the foundation store of all scientific methods.

Analysis of the Data

Testing of hypothesis

Hypothesis - 1

There is no significant difference between total male and female students on the problems in learning commerce among higher secondary school.

Table - 4.1

Table showing the't' value of male and female higher secondary school students regarding the problems in learning commerce

Variables	N	Mean	Standard deviation	't' Value	Significant at 0. 05 Level
Male	77	68.1948	6.00	1. 6186	1. 98
Female	73	66. 2876	8. 2006		

The arithmetic mean of male and female higher secondary school students are 68.1948 and 66.2876. The calculated't' value is 1.6186. It is less than the tabulated value of 0.05 level of 1.98for df =148. Hence the hypothesis is accepted.

This indicates that there is no significant difference between male and female students on the problems in learning commerce among higher secondary school. From the mean value it is concluded that male have more problems in learning commerce than female.

Hypothesis - 2

There is no significant difference between rural and urban students on the problems in learning commerce among higher secondary school.

The arithmetic mean of rural and urban higher secondary school students are 68.4310 and 67.0176. The calculated 't' value is 0. 1112. It is less than the tabulated value of 0. 05 level of 1.98 for df = 148. Hence the hypothesis is accepted.

Table - 4.2

Table showing the't' value of rural and urban higher secondary school students regarding the problems in learning commerce

Variables	N	Mean	Standard deviation	t' Value	Significant at 0.05 Level
Rural	58	68.4310	7.35	1.1112	1.98
Urban	92	67.0760	7.15		

This indicates that there is no significant difference between rural and urban students on the problems in learning commerce among higher secondary school. From the mean value it is concluded that rural have more problems in learning commerce than urban.

Hypothesis-3

There is no significant difference between Government and Aided students on the problems in learning commerce among higher secondary school.

Table - 4.3

Table showing the't' value of government and aided higher secondary school students regarding the problems in learning commerce students.

Variables	N	Mean	Standard deviation	't' value	Significant at 0.05 Level
Government	69	64.6666	7.8421	3.1630	1.98
Aided	48	68.5208	5.3385		

The arithmetic means of Government and Aided higher secondary school students are 64.6666 and 68.5208. The calculated't' value is 3.1630. It is greater than the tabulated value of 0. 05 level of 1.98 for df =115. Hence the hypothesis is rejected.

This indicates that there is a significant difference between Government and Aided students on the problems in learning commerce among higher secondary school. From the mean value it is concluded that Aided have more problems in learning commerce than Government.

Hypothesis - 4

There is no significant difference between Aided and Matriculation students on the problems in learning commerce among higher secondary school.

Table - 4.4

Table showing the't' value of aided and matriculation higher secondary school students regarding the problems in learning commerce

Variables	N	Mean	Standard deviation	't' Value	Significant at 0. 05 Level
Aided	48	68.5208	5.3385	2. 9255	1.99
Matriculation	33	72.9393	5.0497		

The arithmetic means of Aided and Matriculation higher secondary school students are 68.5208 and 72.9393. The calculated't' value is 2.9255. It is greater than the tabulated value of 0. 05 level of 1.99 for df = 79. Hence the hypothesis is rejected.

This indicates that there is a significant difference between Aided and Matriculation students on the problems in learning commerce among higher secondary school. From the mean value it is concluded that Matriculation has more problems in learning commerce than Aided.

Hypothesis - 5

There is no significant difference between Matriculation and Government on the problems in learning commerce among higher secondary school.

The arithmetic means of Matriculation and Government higher secondary school students are 72.9393 and 64.6666. The calculated't' value is 5.6381. It is greater than table value of 0.05 level of 1.98 for df =100. Hence the hypothesis is rejected.

There is a significant difference between matriculation and Government students on the problems in learning commerce among higher secondary school. From the mean value it is concluded that Matriculation has more problems in learning commerce than Government.

Table - 4.5

Table showing the't' value of Matriculation and Government higher secondary school students regarding the problems in learning commerce

Variables	N	Mean	Standard deviation	't' Value	Significant at 0. 05 Level
Matriculation	533	72.9393	5.0497		
Government	69	64.6666	7.8421	5. 6381	1.98

Hypothesis - 6

There is no significant difference between Tamil and English medium students on the problems in learning commerce among higher secondary school.

Table - 4.6

Table showing the't' value of Tamil and English medium higher secondary school students regarding the problems in learning commerce

Variables	N	Mean	Standard deviation	't' Value	Significant at 0.05 Level
Tamil medium	89	68.1807	6. 20		
English medium	67	66.8805	8. 35	1.0603	1. 98

The Arithmetic means of Tamil and English medium higher secondary school students are 68.1807 and 66.8805. The calculated't' value is 1.0603. It is less than the tabulated value of 0.05 level of 1.98 for df = 148. Hence the hypothesis is accepted.

This indicates that there is no significant difference Tamil and English medium students on the problems in learning commerce among higher secondary school. From the mean value it is concluded that Tamil medium have more problems in learning commerce than English medium.

Hypothesis -7

There is no significant difference between Hosteller and day scholar students on the problems in learning commerce among higher secondary school.

Table - 4.7

Table showing the't' value of hosteller and day scholar higher secondary school students regarding their problems in learning commerce

Variables	N	Mean	Standard deviation	't' Value	Significant at 0.05 Level
Hosteller	56	69.1071	5.0877		
Day scholar	94	65.9255	8.4554	2.8774	1.98

The Arithmetic means of Hosteller and Day scholar higher secondary school students are 69.1071 and 65.9255. The calculated't' value is 2.8774. It is greater than the tabulated value at 0.05 level of 1.98 for df = 148. Hence the Hypothesis is rejected.

There is a significant difference between hosteller and day scholar students on the problems in learning commerce among higher secondary school. From the mean value it is concluded that Hosteller more than problems in learning commerce than Day scholar.

Hypothesis-8

There is no significant difference on the problems in learning commerce students among higher secondary school between male and female with respect their psychology, curriculum, learning, occupation, health and economic factors.

From the above table 4.10 it is understood that the calculated't' values 2.2115 and 2. 2900 are significant at 0.05 levels. It is greater than the tabulated value of 1.98 for df = 148. Hence the null hypothesis of psychology and learning factors are rejected. Whereas the values 0. 2167, 1.7002, 0.3723 and 1.0450 are not significant at 0.05 level. It is less than the tabulated value of 1.98 for df= 148. Hence the null hypothesis of curriculum, occupation, health and economic factors are accepted.

Table - 4.8

't' values of mean scores in total sample with regard to all the factors problems in learning commerce students between male and female higher secondary school

Category	Sample	N	Mean	SD	't' value	Significant at 0.05 level
Psychology factor	Male	77	63.9415	10.4527		
	Female	73	59.9520	11.5749	2.2115*	1.98
Curriculum factor	Male	77	69.7857	12.8354		
	Female	73	70.2260	12.0469	0.2167**	1.98
Learning factor	Male	77	66.3831	13.7000		
	Female	73	71.0068	10.9380	2.2900*	1.98
Occupation factor	Male	77	70.9545	12.8471		
	Female	73	74.6369	13.9957	1.7002**	1.98
Health factor	Male	77	71.6428	12.4687		
	Female	73	72.4452	13.8444	0.3723**	1.98
Economic factor	Male	77	67.4870	12.4903		
	Female	73	65.1849	14.3656	1.0450**	1.98

*Significant at 0.05 level ** Not significant at 0.05 level

From the above table indicates that there exists a significant difference between six factors had problems in learning commerce students among higher secondary school. It is concluded that the factors followed by psychology and learning factors are more learning problems than curriculum, occupation, health and economic factors.

Hypothesis-9

There is no significant difference between Rural and Urban students on the problems in learning commerce among higher secondary school with respect their psychology, curriculum, learning, occupation, health and economic factors.

From the above table 4.11 it is understood that the calculated't' values 1.6788, 1.8533, 0.4715, 0.3722, 0.7014 and 1.1781 are not significant at 0.05 level. It is less than the tabulated value of 1.98 for df = 148. Hence the null hypothesis of psychology, curriculum, learning, occupation, health and economic factors are accepted.

Table - 4.9

't' values of the mean scores in total samples with regard to all the factors of problems in learning commerce students between rural and urban higher secondary school

Category	Sample	N	Mean	SD	't' Value	Significant at 0.05 level
Psychological factor	Rural	58	64. 8448	12. 5900	1.6788**	1. 98
Urban	92		61. 4565	11. 1058		
Curriculum factor	Rural	58	72. 5034	12. 5199	1.8533**	1. 98
	Urban	92	68. 7391	11. 4429		
Learning factor	Rural	58	67. 6034	12. 7585	0.4715**	1. 98
	Urban	92	67. 4347	12. 5574		
Occupation factor	Rural	58	75. 5344	12. 8234	0.3722**	1. 98
	Urban	92	74. 7173	13. 5118		
Health factor	Rural	58	72. 9482	11. 8617	0.7014**	1. 98
	Urban	92	71. 4565	13. 8892		
Economic factor	Rural	58	67. 9482	12. 3947	1.1781**	1. 98
	Urban	92	65. 3695	14. 0379		

* Significant ** not significant

This indicates that there is no significant difference between rural and urban students had problems in learning commerce among higher secondary school with respect to their psychological, curriculum, learning, occupation, health and economic factors, less than that of the tabular value.

Hypothesis-10

There is no significant difference between Government and Aided higher secondary school students on the problems in learning commerce with respect their psychology, curriculum, learning, occupation, health and economic factors.

From the above table 4.12 it is understood that the calculated't' values 2.8839 and 2.2069 are significant at 0.05 level. It is greater than the tabulated value of 1.98 for df = 148. Hence the null hypothesis of psychological and Economic factors are rejected

.Whereas the values 1 8832, 1.3054, 0.0980 and 0.1822 are not significant at 0.05 level. It is less than the tabulated value of 1.98 for df=148. Hence the null hypothesis of curricu um, learning, occupation, and health factors are accepted.

Table-4.10

't' values of the mean scores in total samples with regard to all the factor of problems in learning commerce students between government and aided higher secondary school

Category	Sample	N	Mean	SD	't' Value	Significant at 0.05 level
Psychology factor	Government.	69	58. 2681	11. 6864	2. 8839*	1. 98
	Aided	48	64. 5000	11. 3651		
Curriculum factor	Government.	69	67. 6884	11. 9774	1. 8832**	1. 98
	Aided	48	71. 7916	11. 3172		
Learning factor	Government	69	65. 6594	13. 2465	1. 3054**	1. 98
	Aided	48	68. 6666	11. 5169		
Occupation factor	Government	69	73. 9202	13. 2465	0. 0980**	1. 98
	Aided	48	73. 6666	14. 1173		
Health factor	Government	69	71. 7463	14. 2324	0.1822**	1. 98
	Aided	48	72. 2083	12. 9487		
Economic factor	Government	69	64. 5000	13. 8311	2. 2069*	1. 98
	Aided	48	70. 125	13. 3704		

* Significant ** not significant

From the above table indicates that there exists a significant difference between six factors had problems in learning commerce students among higher secondary school, it is calculated that the factors followed by curriculum and economic factors are more learning problems than psychology, learning, occupation and Health factors.

Hypothesis -11

There is no significant difference between Aided Matriculation higher secondary school students on the problems in learning commerce with respect their psychology, curriculum, learning, occupation, health and economic factors.

From the above table 4.13 it is understood that the calculated t' values 2.0906 and 2.7926 are significant at 0.05 level. It is greater than the tabulated value of 1.98 for df = 78. Hence the null hypotheses of psychology and occupation factors are rejected. Whereas the values 1.8786, 0. 8331, 0.0638 and 1.8990 are not significant at 0.05 level. It is less than the tabulated value of 1.99 for df = 78. Hence the null hypothesis of curriculum, learning, health and economic factors are accepted.

Table 4.11

't' values of mean scores in total samples with regard to all the factor of problems in learning commerce students between aided and matriculation higher secondary school students

Category	Sample	N	Mean	SD	't' Value	Significant at 0. 05 level
Psychology factor	Aided	48	64. 5000	11. 3651	2. 0906*	1. 99
	Matriculation	33	69. 0454	8. 1981		
Curriculum factor	Aided	48	71. 7916	11. 3172	1. 8786**	1. 99
	Matriculation	33	76. 3181	10. 2849		
Learning factor	Aided	48	68. 6666	11. 5169	0. 8331**	1. 99
	Matriculation	33	70. 8636	11. 7596		
Occupation factor	Aided	48	73. 6666	14. 1173	2. 7926*	1. 99
	Matriculation	33	81. 6666	10. 0503		
Health factor	Aided	48	72. 2083	12. 9487	0. 0638**	1. 99
	Matriculation	33	72. 3787	10. 9430		
Economics factor	Aided	48	70. 1250	13. 3704	1. 8990**	1. 99
	Matriculation	33	64. 8030	11. 6734		

* Significant ** not significant

From the above table indicates that there exists a significant difference between six factors had problems in learning commerce students among higher secondary school. It is concluded that the factors followed by psychology and occupation factors are more learning problems than curriculum, learning, health and Economic factors.

Hypothesis -12

There is no significant difference between Matriculation and Government higher secondary school students on the problems in learning commerce with respect their psychology, curriculum, learning, occupation, health and economic factors.

Table - 4.12

't' values of mean scores in total samples with regard to all the factors of problems in learning commerce students between matriculation and government higher secondary school

Category	Sample	N	Mean	SD	't' Value	Significant at 0.05 level
Psychology factor	Matriculation	69	58. 2681	11. 6846	5. 3784*	1. 98
	Government	33	69. 0454	8. 1981		
Curriculum factor	Matriculation	69	67. 6884	11. 9774	3. 7540*	1. 98
	Government	33	76. 3181	10. 2849		
Learning factor	Matriculation	69	65. 6594	13. 2465	2. 0055*	1. 98
	Government	33	70. 2636	11. 7596		
Occupation factor	Matriculation	69	73. 9202	14. 1301	2. 9697*	1. 98
	Government	33	81. 1666	10. 0503		
Health factor	Matriculation	69	71. 7463	14. 2324	0. 2468**	1. 98
	Government	33	72. 3787	10. 9430		
Economics factor	Matriculation	69	64. 5000	13. 8311	0. 1153**	1. 98
	Government	33	64. 8030	11. 6734		

* Significant ** not significant

From the above table 4.14 it is understood that the calculated't' values 5.3784, 3.7540, 2.0055 and 2.9697 are significant at 0.05 level. It is greater than the tabulated value of 1.98 for df = 100. Hence the null hypotheses of psychology, curriculum. learning and occupation factors are rejected. Whereas the values 0.2468 and 0.1153 are not significant at 0.05 level. It is less than the tabulated values of 1.98 for df = 100. Hence the null hypothesis of health and economic factors are accepted.

From the above table indicates that there exists significant difference between six factors had problems in learn ng commerce students among higher secondary school, it is concluded that the factors followed by psychology, curriculum, learning and occupation factors are more learning problems than health and economic factors.

Hypothesis - 13

There is no significant difference between Tamil and English Medium higher secondary school students on the problems in learning commerce with respect their psychology, curriculum, learning, occupation, health and economic factors.

Table - 4.13

't' values of the mean scores in total samples with regard to all the factors of problems in learning commerce students between Tamil and English medium higher secondary school

Category	Sample	N	Mean	SD	't' Value	Significant at 0.05 level
Psychology factor	Tamil	83	64. 7409	10. 5256	2. 0318*	1. 98
	English	67	60. 7686	12. 9100		
Curriculum factor	Tamil	83	70. 8855	12. 0818	0. 0927**	1. 98
	English	67	71. 0671	11. 7881		
Learning factor	Tamil	83	67. 3915	13. 4911	0. 1115**	1. 98
	English	67	67. 6343	13. 0678		
Occupation factor	Tamil	83	75. 2228	13. 2431	0. 2082**	1. 98
	English	67	75. 6940	14. 1971		
Health factor	Tamil	83	70. 2831	12. 0361	1. 3797**	1. 98
	English	67	73. 3059	14. 3071		
Economics factor	Tamil	83	69. 9216	12. 3503	3. 6754*	1. 98
	English	67	62. 1119	13. 3929		

* Significant ** not significant

From the above table 4.15 it is understood that the calculated't' values 2.03186 and 3.754 are significant at 0.05 level. It is greater than the tabulated value of 1.98 for df =148. Hence the null hypothesis of psychology and economic factors are rejected. Whereas the values 0.0927, 0.1115,0. 2082 and 1.3797 are not significant at 0.05 level. It is less than the tabulated values of 1.98 for df= 148. Hence the null hypothesis of curriculum, learning, occupation and health factors are accepted.

From the above table indicates that there exists significant difference between six factors had problems in learning commerce students among higher secondary school, it is concluded that the factors followed by psychology and economic factors are more learning problems than curriculum, learning , occupation and health factors.

Hypothesis - 14

There is no significant difference between Hosteller and Day scholar higher secondary school students on the problems in learning commerce with respect their psychology, curriculum, learning, occupation, health and economic factors.

Table - 4.14

't' values of the mean scores in total samples with regard to all the factors it problems in learning commerce students between hosteller and day scholar higher secondary school

Category	Sample	N	Mean	SD	't' Value	Significant at 0.05 level
Psychology factor	Hostel	56	67. 5357	9. 2428	4. 2896*	1. 98
	Day scholar	94	59. 9255	12. 3482		
Curriculum factor	Hostel	56	75. 0357	9. 3386	3. 8104*	1. 98
	Day scholar	94	68. 1170	12. 7871		
Learning factor	Hostel	56	67. 1785	12. 3186	0. 7702**	1. 98
	Day scholar	94	65. 5638	12. 5872		
Occupation factor	Hostel	56	77. 1785	13. 8217	0. 8837**	1. 98
	Day scholar	94	75. 1382	13. 4327		
Health factor	Hostel	56	73. 4285	13. 0491	0. 8917**	1. 98
	Day scholar	94	71. 4148	13. 9122		
Economic factor	Hostel	56	66. 4642	12. 4527	0. 1190**	1. 98
	Day scholar	94	66. 2021	13. 9635		

* Significant ** not significant

From the above table 4.16 it is understood that the calculated't' values 4.2896 and 3.8104 are significant at 0.05 level. It is greater than the tabulated value of 1.98 for df =148. Hence the null hypotheses of psychology and curriculum factors are rejected. Whereas the values 0.7702, 0.8837, 0. 8917 and C.1190 are not significant at 0.05 levels. It is less than the tabulated value of 1.98 for df = 148. Hence the null hypothesis of learning, occupation, Health and Economic factors are accepted.

From the above table indicates that there exists a significant difference between six factors had problems in leaning commerce students among higher secondary school, it is concluded that the factors followed by psychology and curriculum factors are more learning problems than learning, occupation, Health and Economic factors.

V

Findings and Concusion

Introduction

This section is indented to provide the reader a quick review of what has been done to get the results. This portion of report is probably the most utilized part of the report. This chapter commences with the statement problem and brief description of the procedures followed by the findings and conclusion. The recommendations of the study are also presented and also, suggestions for new studies are given.

Statement of the Problem

The present study is entitled "Problems in learning commerce students among higher secondary school at Salem District"

Objectives of the Study

1. To find out the problems in learning commerce students among higher secondary school between total male and female students.

2. To find out the problems in learning commerce students among higher secondary school between total Rural and urban students.
3. To find out the problems in learning commerce students among higher secondary school between total Government and Aided students.
4. To find out the problems in learning commerce students among higher secondary school between total Aided and Matriculation students.
5. To find out the problems in learning commerce students among higher secondary school between total Matriculation and Government students.
6. To find out the problems in learning commerce students among higher secondary school between total Tamil and English Medium students.
7. To find out the problems in learning commerce students among higher secondary school between total Hosteller and Day scholar students.
8. To find out the problems in learning commerce students between male and Female with respect to their Psychology, curriculum, learning, occupation, Health and Economic Factors.
9. To find out the problems in learning commerce students between Rural and urban with respect to their Psychology, curriculum, learning, occupation, Health and Economic Factors.
10. To find out the problems in learning commerce students between Government and Aided with respect to their Psychology, curriculum, learning, occupation, Health and Economic Factors.
11. To find out the problems in learning commerce students between Aided and Matriculation with respect to their Psychology, curriculum, learning, occupation, Health and Economic Factors.

12. To find out the problems in learning commerce students between Matriculation and Government with respect to their Psychology, curriculum, learning, occupation, Health and Economic Factors.

13. To find out the problems in learning commerce students between Tamil and English medium with respect to their Psychology, curriculum, learning, occupation, Health and Economic Factors.

14. To find out the problems in learning commerce students between Hosteller and day's scholar with respect to their Psychology, curriculum, learning, occupation, Health and Economic Factors.

Hypothesis of the Study

1. There is no significant different on the problems in learning commerce among higher secondary school between Male and Female students.
2. There is no significant different on the problems in learning commerce among higher secondary school between Rural and Urban students.
3. There is no significant different on the problems in learning commerce among higher secondary school between Government and Aided students.
4. There is no significant different on the problems in learning commerce among higher secondary school between Aided and Matriculation students.
5. There is no significant different on the problems in learning commerce among higher secondary school between Matriculation and Government student.
6. There is no significant different on the problems in learning commerce among higher secondary school between Tamil and English medium students.

7. There is no significant different on the problems in learning commerce among higher secondary school between Hosteller and Day Scholar students.
8. There is no significant difference on the problems in learning commerce students among higher secondary school between male and Female with respect to their psychological, curriculum, learning, occupation, and Health and Economic factors.
9. There is no significant difference on the problems in learning commerce students among higher secondary school between Rural and Urban with respect to their psychological, curriculum, learning, occupation, Health and Economic factors.
10. There is no significant difference on the problems in learning commerce students among higher secondary school between Government and Aided with respect to their psychological, curriculum, learning, occupation, Health and Economic factors.
11. There is no significant difference on the problems in learning commerce students among higher secondary school between Aided and Matriculation with respect to their psychological, curriculum, learning, occupation, Health and Economic factors.
12. There is no significant difference on the problems in learning commerce students among higher secondary school between Matriculation and Government with respect to their psychological, curriculum, learning, occupation, Health and Economic factors.
13. There is no significant difference on the problems in learning commerce students among higher secondary school between Tamil and English Medium with respect to their psychological, curriculum, learning, occupation, Health and Economic factors.
14. There is no significant difference on the problems in learning commerce students among higher secondary school between Hosteller and Day scholar with respect to their psychological,

curriculum, learning, occupation, Health and Economic factors.

Findings of the Study

1. There is no significant difference between male and female students on the problems in learning commerce among higher secondary school.
2. There is no significant difference between Rural and Urban students on the problems in learning commerce among higher secondary school.
3. There is a significant difference between Government and Aided students on the problems in learning commerce among higher secondary school.
4. There is a significant difference between Aided and Matriculation students on the problems in learning commerce among higher secondary school.
5. There is a significant difference between Matriculation and Government students on the problems in learning commerce among higher secondary school.
6. There is no significant difference between Tamil and English medium students on the problems in learning commerce among higher secondary school.
7. There is a significant difference between Hosteller and Day scholar students on the problems in learning commerce among higher secondary school.
8. From the table – 4.8 indicates that there exists a significant difference between male female students on problems in learning commerce among higher secondary school, it is concluded that the factors followed by psychology and learning factors are more learning problems than curriculum, occupation, health and economic factors.
9. There is no significant difference between Rural and Urban students on the problems in learning commerce among higher secondary school with respect to their psychological,

curriculum, learning, occupation, health and with respect to their psychological, curriculum, learning, occupation, health.

10. From the table – 4.10 indicates that there exists a significant difference between Government and Aided cn problems in learning commerce among higher secondary school, it is calculated that the factors followed by curriculum and economic factors are more learning problems than psychology, learning, occupation and Health factors.
11. From the table – 4.11 indicates that there exists a significant difference between Aided and Matriculation on problems in learning commerce among higher secondary school, it is concluded that the factors followed by psychology and occupation factors are more learning problems than curriculum, learning, health and Economic factors.
12. From the table – 4.12 indicates that there ex sts significant difference between Government and Matriculation of problems in learning commerce among higher secondary school, it is concluded that the factors followed by psychology, curriculum, learning and occupation factors are more than health and economic factors.
13. From the table – 4.13 indicates that there exists significant difference between Tamil and English medium of problems in learning commerce among higher secondary school, it is concluded that the factors followed by psychology and economic factors are more than curriculum, learning, occupation and health factors.
14. From the table – 4.14 indicates that there exists a significant difference between Hosteller and Day scholar of problems in leaning commerce among psychological higher secondary school, it is concluded that the factors followed by psychology and curriculum factors are more than learning, occupation, Health and Economic factors.

Result and Discussions of the Study

1. The Hypothesis No:1 The calculated 't' value s 1.6186 less

than the tabulated value of 0.05 level there is no significant difference between male and female students on the problems in learning commerce among higher secondary school. So, I conclude that male have more problems in learning commerce than female.

2. The Hypothesis No:2 The calculated 't' value is 0.1112 less than the tabulated value of 0. 05 levels there is no significant difference between rural and urban students on the problems in learning commerce among higher secondary school. So, I conclude that rural have more problems in learning commerce than urban.

3. The Hypothesis No:3 The calculated 't' value is 3.1630 greater than the tabulated value of 0. 05 level there is a significant difference between Government and Aided students on the problems in learning commerce among higher secondary school. So, I conclude that Aided have more problems in learning commerce than Government.

4. The Hypothesis No:4 The calculated 't' value is 2.9255 greater than the tabulated value of 0. 05 level there is a significant difference between Aided and Matriculation students on the problems in learning commerce among higher secondary school. So, I conclude that Matriculation have more problems in learning commerce than Aided.

5. The Hypothesis No:5 The calculated 't' value is 5.6381 greater than table value of 0.05 level there is a significant difference between matriculation and Government students on the problems in learning commerce among higher secondary school. So, I conclude that Matriculation have more problems in learning commerce than Government.

6. The Hypothesis No:6 The calculated 't' value is 1.0603 less than the tabulated value of 0.05 level there is no significant difference Tamil and English medium students on the problems in learning commerce among higher secondary school. So I conclude that Tamil medium have more problems in learning commerce than English medium.

7. The Hypothesis No:7 The calculated 't' value is 2.8774 greater than the tabulated value at 0.05 level there s a significant difference between hosteller and Day scholar students on the problems in learning commerce among higher secondary school. So I conclude that Hosteller more than problems in learning commerce than Day scholar.
8. The Hypothesis No:8 The calculated 't' values 2.2115 and 2. 2900 are significant at 0.05 levels. Whereas the values 0. 2167, 1.7002, 0.3723 and 1.0450 are not significant at 0.05 level. So I conclude that there exists a significant difference between six factors had problems in learning commerce students among higher secondary school. It is followed by psychology and learning factors are more learning problems than curriculum, occupation, health and economic factors.
9. The Hypothesis No:9 The calculated 't' values 1.6788, 1.8533, 0.4715, 0.3722, 0.7014 and 1.1781 less than the tabulated value are not significant at 0.05 level. So I conclude there is no significant difference between Rural and Urban students had problems in learning commerce among higher secondary school with respect to their psychological, curriculum, learning, occupation, health and economic factors, less than that of the tabular value.
10. The Hypothesis No:10 The calculated 't' values 2.8839 and 2.2069 are significant at 0.05 level. Whereas the values 1 8832, 1.3054, 0.0980 and 0.1822 are not significant at 0.05 level. So I conclude that there exists a significant difference between six factors had problems in learning commerce students among higher secondary school, it is followed by curriculum and economic factors are more learning problems than psychology, learning, occupation and health factor.
11. The Hypothesis No:11 The calculated t' values 2.0906 and 2.7926 are significant at 0.05 level. Whereas the values 1.8786, 0. 8331, 0.0638 and 1.8990 are not significant at 0.05 level. So I conclude that there exists a significant difference between six factors had problems in learning

commerce students among higher secondary school. It is followed by psychology and occupation factors are more learning problems than curriculum, learning, health and Economic factors.

12. The Hypothesis No: 12 the calculated't' values 5.3784, 3.7540, 2.0055 and 2.9697 are significant at 0.05 level. Whereas the values 0.2468 and 0.1153 are not significant at 0.05 level. So I conclude that there exists significant difference between six factors had problems in learning commerce students among higher secondary school, it is followed by psychology, curriculum, learning and occupation factors are more learning problems than health and economic factors.

13. The Hypothesis No:13 The calculated 't' values 2.03186 and 3.754 are significant at 0.05 level. Whereas the values 0.0927, 0.1115,0. 2082 and 1.3797 are not significant at 0.05 levels. So I conclude that there exists significant difference between six factors had problems in learning commerce students among higher secondary school, it is followed by psychology and economic factors are more learning problems than curriculum, learning, occupation and health factors.

14. The Hypothesis No: 14 the calculated't' values 4.2896 and 3.8104 are significant at 0.05 level. Whereas the values 0.7702, 0.8837, 0. 8917 and 0.1190 are not significant at 0.05 levels. So I conclude that there exists a significant difference between six factors had problems in leaning commerce students among higher secondary school, it is followed by psychology and curriculum factors are more learning problems than learning, occupation, health and economic factors.

Both male and female had impact in the adolescent stage and there some problem in learning process. The males are mostly involved in sports and other entertainment activities while the females are involved in house hold activities so they had some learning problems. In the rural areas, the problems arising in learning process is due to illiterate parents, improper guidance and the environmental situations. Where as in towns and cities the students are in the hands of computerized modern communication like chat, game, songs and pictures they made a problem in learning process.

Government, government aided, matriculation schools are the way to built capacity to construction of school works, environmental surroundings, teachers, teaching process and timing are the basic needs of students discipline such factors there exists a different problems in learning process among higher secondary students. Tamil medium students are arriving from villages, those students does not get the basic needs which leads to problems in learning commerce.

Hostlers or students in hostel face many problems like lack of affection and kindness, improper diet, rules and regulation of hostels. This affects some problems in learning commerce so the students had the whole syllabus as theory and practical, they face more problems in learning. Job opportunities for commerce students are very few in both government and private institutions which also affects the learning interest of commerce.

Also due to long distance and few Hr. Sec. Schools have commerce subject group. So the student most of the time is devoted to accountancy and did not getting proper nutrition diet which also affects the learning problems in commerce. Most of the students are economically affected, those who could not pay the exam fees, could not buy the basic things for education at the proper time which also affects the learning problems in commerce.

Implications Of The Study

It should be obvious that unit teaching is not only concerned with units of subject matter, but is equally concerned with a process of teaching which takes into account modern psychological principles of learning dealing with individual differences, goals sharing, pupil teacher planning and pupil self – evaluation.

1. Commerce teacher can help the students in the selection of good books in the library.

2. Vocational guidance should be made available to the individual commerce students.
3. The commerce teacher should adopt student - centered method in the teaching learning process.
4. The commerce teacher could make use of audio – visual aids in commerce teaching in the classroom.
5. The Government has to modify the commerce syllabus according to the needs and psychological level of students.
6. Almost all commerce students had suggested there should be more seminars, group discussions, among the students, industrial visits or field trips during the commerce students.
7. Commerce teachers may be trained to teach their lesson linked with recent commerce news.

Suggestions for Further Study

The investigator would like to suggest the following for further researches.

1. A study on difficulties of low experiences teacher in teaching commerce.
2. Study on difficulties faced by student regarding new commerce syllabus.
3. A study of problem faced by post graduate commerce teachers in teaching commerce.
4. Comparative study of difficulties faced by college and school students in learning commerce.
5. A study on difficulties faced by the students in learning commerce.
6. A study of difficulties on teacher trainees in teaching commerce.

Conclusion

The present study made many problems in learning commerce

students among higher secondary school. The findings of the present study reveals that 67.24% of the higher secondary school students had high problems among gender, locality, type of schools, residency, medium of instruction with respect to the Psychological, Curriculum, Learning, Occupation, Health and Economic Factors.

In 21st century, if the school of Education considered about commerce subject and creates job opportunities from Secondary and high school level means the commerce students will make more interest to study and will not face much problems and difficulties in commerce subjects.

Bibliography Books

1. Aggarwal, J.C.(1996). "Education Research". New Delhi: Arya Book Depot.
2. Aggarwal, Y.p.(1986). "Statistical methods". Sterling puplishers private limited.
3. BABU, R. (2002) "commerce Education in Higher Secondary Schools in Tamil Nadu". Chidambaram: Sathya Publications.
4. Basavaraj Vastrad, (2002). "Methodology of Research in Physical Education & Sports Sciences". New Delhi: Vivek Thani Khel Sahitya Kendra.
5. Best John, w.(1983). "Research in Education". Fourth ed., New Delhi: prentice hall.
6. Best. John, W.(1979) "Research in education". New Delhi: prentice Hall of India.
7. Bharti Sharma, b. (2004). "Methodology of Educational Research". New Delhi: Vohra Publishers & Distributors.
8. Khan, M.S. (1982). "Commerce Education". New Delhi: Sterling Publishers Private. Ltd.
9. Kothari, C. K. (1990). "Research Methodology". New Delhi: Wishwa Prakasham Publishers.

10. Dr.Radha mohan, (2003). "Research methods in education". Hyderabad: Neelkamal puplications private limited.

11. Seema Rao,(1995)."Teaching of commerce". New Delhi: Anmol publications Pvt. Ltd.

12. Sharma, K.R.(2004). " Research methodology". New Delhi: National publishers house.

13. Travers, M.W. (1958). "An introduction in to Educational Research".

14. Yogesh Kumar Singh, (2005). "Research Methodology". New Delhi: APh Publishing Corporation.

Part 3

Relationship Between Parental Educational and Student Achievement

I

Relationship between Parental Educational and Student Achievement

Overview

The present study deals with the conceptual framework of the study. It starts with the various definitions of Mathematics, influence, achievement, parents' education, higher secondary students. It also deals Influence of parents' level of education, the relationship between parents' educational attainment and student achievement. This chapter ends with cauterization.

Introduction

Adolescence is an intriguing stage of development followed with many physical, cognitive, social, and emotional changes. At the same time, the increase in academic demands and the complexity of the school structure make the task of academic success for adolescence even more difficult. Because parent involvement parent education have been shown to be very important postured force in a child's life, one would expect that during such a critical and demanding phase the two more important in child development. Home and school would increase the collaboration. Parent education often deals with values classification and the resolution of values and conflicts. For example, a parent who is resistant to offering a child certain freedoms may be acting from out dated belief system. Some group discussion and experimental activities might help parents to become aware of the source of the belief and to rich and understanding that certain belief needs to be updated. To simply of a such parents better communication skills, to teach them how to say limits would ignore deny their own serious problems.

Various Definitions for the Terms

Influence

A power to affect persons or events especially power based on prestige etc.

Parent Education

The term "parent education" was defined as "instruction on how to parent". Parent education, as we will be using the term, refers to a systematic and conceptually based program, intended to impart information, awareness, or skill to the participants on aspects of parenting.

Achievement

Achievement testing plays a significant role in the teaching learning program in school. A class teacher constructs tests to work out the student's performance in a subject but majority of people in India are not in favor of present system of examination. Reason begin, these tests lack objectivity reliability and validity. Objective type test is an improvement upon present system of examination but standardized achievement tests are a step further to this improvement. In India a few steps of standardizing tests in different subjects are made.

According to Super, "An Achievement or proficiency test is used to aeration what and how much has been learnt or how well a task has been performed".

According to Freeman, "A test of educational achievement as a test designed to measure knowledge, understanding, and skills in a specified subject or group of subject".

According to Best, "Achievement test attempts to measure what an individual's has learned-his or her present level of performance".

W.James Papham has defined in the book "Modern educational measurement", "test in the cognitive and psychomotor realm are often focused on an examines attainments at a given time; these tests are usually referred to as achievement tests".

W.Wiersma & S.Gjurs define in their book' "educational measurement and testing", Achievement tests as "a measure of knowledge and skills in a content area".

N.M.Gronlund & R.L.Linn in their book' "Measurement and teaching" discussing about standardized achievement test has observed "These typically have been norm-referenced tests that measure the pupils' level of achievement in various content and skills areas by comparing the test performance with the performance of other pupils in some general reference group". In recent years numbers of criterion-referred achievement tests have also been published.

Mathematics

According to New English Dictionary' "Mathemat cs- in a strict sense is the abstract science which investigates deductively the conclusions implicit in the elementary conception of spatial and numerical relations".

The National Policy on Education (1986) defined Mathematics is should be visualized as an instrument to train a child to think, reason, analyze and to articulate, logically. Apart from being specific subject it should be treated as a concomitant to any subject involving analysis and reasoning".

Marshal H.Stone defined Mathematics is the study of abstract system built of abstract elements. These elements are not described in concrete fashion.

According to Bertand Russel, "Mathematics may be defined as the subject in which are never known we are talking about or whether what we are saying true".

According to Voss, "Our entire civilization depending on the intellectual perpetration and utilization of nature has its real foundation in the mathematical sciences".

According to Benjamin Peirce, "Mathematics is the science that draws necessary conclusion".

According to Galieo, "Mathematics is the language in which God has written the universe".

According to Locke, "Mathematics is a way to settle in the mind of children a habit of reasoning".

Xi Standard Pupils

Pupils who are in the age group 15+ and 16+ and studying XI standard in recognized schools of Rasipuram Taluk following Tamilnadu State Board syllabus.

Need And Significance of the Study

Adolescence is first of all a period of physical and physiological change. This growth furnishes the basis for emotional, social, intellectual and economic maturity.

Parents should understand the child's problem "It is much more important for parents to learn how to promote normal development than to master techniques for correcting distortions in the growth process". Edward C.Lindeman says "My vision of parent education takes the form of a gigantic folk movement in which all participants are consciously preparing themselves for life in a fairer world".

Fundamentally, we are all parents. Teaching is a profession like many others. Even teachers are parents. The first and foremost duty of parents is to look after their children in the best possible way, to take interest in their welfare and to see their progress. For that purpose, parents take effort at the maximum and select and put their children in the best school.

As the investigator is a mathematics teacher she got interested to find out the possible reasons among the XI standard pupils, if there exists any gender differences in influences of parents' education level achievement in mathematics.

The research is restricted the secondary level, XI standard pupils, because it is crazier stage: After completion of this class, they will ready to write the public examination, there by paving the way to their future career. At this stage, the gender differences in Mathematics achievement and Influence of parents' education are to be analyzed. Hence the apt title "Influence of Parents' Education on Achievement in Mathematics" is chosen for investigation.

Influence of Parent's Level of Education

Traditionally, family status variables such as parents' level of Education have been regarded as predictors of children's academic achievement. Increasingly, research has suggested that, rather than having a direct association with children's academic achievement, parents' level of education is part of a larger constellation of psychological and sociological variables influencing children's school outcomes.

Level of Education influences parents' knowledge, benefits, values, and goals about childrearing, so that a variety of parental behaviors are indirectly related to children's school performance. For example, higher level of education may enhance parents' facility at becoming involved in their children's education, and also enable parents to acquire school success. Thus, students, whose parents have higher level of education may have an enhanced regard for learning, more positive ability beliefs, a stronger work orientation, and they may use more effective learning strategies than children of parents with lower of education.

Parents' with higher level of education are also more likely to believe strongly in their abilities to help their children learn. A recent study exploring the relationships between level of parent's education, parent self-efficiency, children's academic abilities, and participation in a Head Start program found that level of parent education and program participation was significantly related to parental self-efficiency. In turn, parental self-efficiency beliefs significantly predicted children's academic abilities.

The relationship between parental educational attainment and student achievement

Parents' play an important role in their children's learning. Aside from being actively involved in their children's education, parents also provide a home environment that can affect learning. Parents serve as a model for learning, determine the educational resources available in the home and hold particular attitudes and values towards education. Although it is difficult to examine the home environment of each student, the educational attainment and occupation of parents serve as an indicator of the values and resources with which parents create this environment.

For Canada as a whole, the average math scores of students whose parents had high school or less were significantly lower than the average scores of students whose parents had college or university. For example, the gap in average performance between students who had at least one parent with a university degree compared to those whose parents had no more than a high school education was about two-thirds of a proficiency level.

However, while there is a positive relationship between the educational level of the parents and student performance in mathematics, there also is considerable overlap in the performance of students from different educational backgrounds. In fact, many students whose parents had a high school education or less scored higher than students whose parents had a university degree. For example, one-quarter of the students who scored in the top 15% of students had parents who had at most a high school education. Similarly, one-quarter of those in the bottom 15% of students had at least one parent with a university degree.

Given the wide range of student performance within each group, it is clear that the success of many students appears to be dependent on factors other than their parents' level of education.

Educated Parents, Educated Children: TowardS a Multiple Life Cycles Education Policy

Given the important intergenerational effects of parents' education level on the achievement of their children, education policies should shift from a focus on one life cycle to a focus on "multiple life cycles". Such a policy would explicitly recognize that adults transfer their educational achievements to the achievement of their children. It would also recognize that adult education should be valued as much as early childhood education, and that nations should provide adult education systems on a par with children's education systems. Poorly educated children are the source of adult functional illiteracy, and functionally illiterate adults are the source of poorly educated children. Perhaps through education based on a Multiple Life Cycles policy, in which children are guaranteed a right to educated parents, the vicious intergenerational cycles of functional illiteracy can be stopped at both sources.

Educated parents make educated children

Educated parents have better educated children irrespective of genetically transmitted personal abilities; a policy promoting education will have long lasting effects in the form of better education for the next generation and an improvement of outcomes in later life such as health, productivity and wealth.

Parent Involvement

"Parent involvement" and "Parent participation" are nebulous terms because there is an array of parent behaviors that these could include. As Carol Ascher (1986) has stated, "Of all education issues, parent involvement is one of the vaguest and most shifting in its meanings. Parent involvement may easily mean quite different things to different people". To define parent involvement more operationally,

Hoover-Dempsey, Bassler, and Brissie (1987) theorized a two-way breakdown into home-based activities (e.g., parent home tutoring) and school based parent involvement activities (e.g., parent volunteering, attendance at parent-teacher conferences).

The Importance of Parent Involvement

1. Lack of parent involvement is one of the biggest problems facing the public school system today.
2. Parent involvement has helped students increase test scores and graduation rates.
3. Parent involvement has increased the number of children attending schools and decreased the number of absences.
4. Parent involvement increases motivation and improves self esteem.
5. Parent involvement has decreased the use of drugs, alcohol, and violent behavior.

Types of Parent Involvement

Gordon's six types of parent involvement are

i. The traditional type of parent involvement type (the parent as audience or bystander-observer);
ii. Parents as decision makers (as in School Advisory Committees or Parent Teacher Associations [PTAs] in which parents participate in school decision making activities);
iii. Parents begin as classroom volunteers;
iv. Parent as a paid paraprofessional or teacher's aide;
v. Parents as learners (e.g., participate in child development or parenting classes)
vi. Parents as teachers of their own children at home.

Epstein (1988), in a slightly different approach, described five types of parent involvement

i. "Basic Obligation of Parents" includes parents providing for the health and safety of their children as well as preparing their children for school.

ii. "Basic Obligation of the Schools" includes the school communicating with parents about school programs and the progress of children.

iii. "Parent Involvement at School," the volunteering of parents in the classroom and attendance at school performances or sports events.

iv. "Parent Involvement in Learning Activities in the Home" parents initiating activities with their child or a child initiating the help through questions.

v. "Parent Involvement in Governance and Advocacy" the parents assuming decision making roles.

Greenwood & Miller, in a slightly different approach, described seven types of parent involvement

a) Parent as communicator

b) Parent as supporter of activities

c) Parent as learner

d) Parent as advocate

e) Parent as decision maker

f) Parent as volunteer / professional

g) Parent as home activities teacher.

Implimentation For Parent Involvement

1. Parents need to be educated as to the importance of their role in education. Many parents need to be disabused of the idea that the school is the domain of the teachers and that school is the place for education. Learning is an experience which happens both at school and at home.

2. The training of teachers in general and specific techniques to invite parents in their children's education is necessary. This needs to be accomplished at both the pre-service level as well as during in-service training sessions.

3. The development of parent involvement programs will need to be funded by the educational community. As society changes, the needs of our students will change and the educational system needs to not only keep up with these changes, but to be on the cutting edge. In order to prepare students for their future.

4. The role of the administration is vital in terms of the support of teacher and parent collaboration. Graduate programs in educational administration need to include information concerning the relevance of parent involvement programs.

The Education Level of Parents' Impacts Involvement in their Child's Education

While the level of education should not be a basis for a child's success in his studies, there is always a difference in the performance of children with educated parents from the children with parents who haven't gone to school. Studies show that the children of educated parents are smarter and more intelligent than children of those who have not gone to school or those who went to school but finished only the elementary grades. The higher the education of the parents, the better is the performance of their children. This is because people who are well-educated have different perceptions as well as visions in life than those who are less-educated.

Children who have follow-up studies at home have better performance in school than children who have no follow-up at home. Generally speaking, parents who are educated could follow-up the studies of their children at home because they know how to teach their lessons. Those who can afford could hire private tutors to do the follow-up. The level of education of parents has a great effect on how the child relates to his studies. Of course, if the parents are educated then they understand what education is all about and they involve themselves in their child's education. This includes having the rights gadgets and materials that the child needs for school.

Kind of environment

The kind of environment where the child lives greatly affects his education. Of course a child whose parents are both lawyers will react differently than a child who comes from parents who are laborers. In a very practical sense the child whose parents who are both lawyers has a far different exposure than the son of the laborers. So they also react differently and perform differently in school. The parent's involvement in the studies of the children makes a very big difference in the child's education. Most career men and women participate in the activities of their children in school and they try their best to coach their child.

Examples from parents

No matter how people look at the situation, parents who have a higher level of education have better examples that their children could imitate. Career parents are able to impart better educational values to their children than parents who have not finished high school.

The level of education of parents is a great factor in determining the actuations and performances of the children. This is because the educated parents are concentrated and concerned with their children's education because they want their child to be like them while the parents who are not educated think that ecucation is not very important in a person's life.

Involving Parents in the Education of their Children

When parents are involved in their children's education, both children and parents are likely to benefit. Researchers report that parent participation in their children's schooling frequently:

a. Enhances children's self-esteem

b. Improves children's academic achievement

c. Improves parent-child relationships

d. Helps parents develop positive attitudes towards school

e. And a better understanding of the schooling process.

Despite these advantages, it is not always easy for parents to find time and energy to become involved or to coordinate with schedules for school events. For some parents, a visit to school is perceived as an uncomfortable experience, perhaps a holdover from their own school days. Others may have their hands full with a job and other children. The availability and cost of babysitters are other factors. Recently, teachers and other school staff have made special efforts to increase communication with parents and encourage involvement in children's learning experiences.

Ways to involve Parents

One kind of parental involvement is school-based and includes participating in parent-teacher conferences and functions, and receiving and responding to written communications from the teacher. Parents' can also serve as school volunteers for the library or lunchroom, or as classroom aides. In one survey, almost all teachers reported talking with children's parents— either in person, by phone, or on open school nights—and sending notices home (Becker & Epstein, 1982). These methods, along with requests for parents to review and sign homework, were most frequently used to involve parents.

Parents' can participate in their children's schools by joining Parent Teacher Associations (PTAs) or Parent Teacher Organizations (PTOs) and getting involved in decision-making about the educational services their children receive. Almost all schools have a PTA or PTO, but often only a small number of parents are active in these groups.

Another kind of involvement is home-based and focuses on activities that parents can do with their children at home or on the teacher's visits to the child's home. However, few teachers involve parents through home-based activities, partly because of the amount of time involved in developing activities or visiting and partly because of the difficulty of coordinating parents' and teachers' schedules.

Ways to Reach Parents

Some programs aim to reach parents who do not usually participate in their children's education. Such programs provide flexible scheduling for school events and parent-teacher conferences, inform parents about what their children are learning, and help parents create a supportive environment for children's learning at home.

Many schools have responded to the needs of working parents by scheduling conferences in the evening as well as during the day, and by scheduling school events at different times of the day throughout the year.

It is important for teachers to keep the lines of communication open. This involves not only sending regular newsletters and notes, but also obtaining information from parents. Phone calls are a greatly under-used technique for keeping in touch. A teacher usually calls a parent to report a child's inappropriate behavior or academic failure. But teachers can use phone calls to let parents know about positive behavior and to get input. Parents justifiably become defensive if they think that every phone call will bring a bad report. If teachers accustom parents to receiving regular calls just for keeping in touch, it is easier to discuss problems when they occur.

Teachers need to consider families' lifestyles and cultural backgrounds when planning home activities. However, some activities can be adapted to almost any home situation. These are activities that parents or children engage in on a day-to-day basis. Teachers can encourage parents and children to do these activities together, and can focus on the opportunities that the activities provide for learning. For example, although television viewing is a pastime for most children and adults, they do not often watch shows together. Teachers can suggest appropriate programs and send home questions for families to discuss. This discussion can be carried over into class.

Busy parents can include children in such everyday activities as preparing a meal or grocery shopping. Teachers can also suggest that parents set aside a time each day to talk with their children about school. Parents may find this difficult if they have little idea of what occurs in school. Notes on what the children have been working on are helpful. Parents and children can discuss current events using teacher-provided questions. Teachers often suggest the activity of reading aloud to children. Reading to children is an important factor in increasing their interest and ability in reading. Teachers can also encourage children to read to parents. In areas where children may not have many books, schools can lend books, and teachers can provide questions for parents and children to discuss.

Home activities allow parents flexibility in scheduling, provide opportunities for parents' and children to spend time together, and offer a relaxed setting. To be most beneficial, home activities should be interesting and meaningful—not trivial tasks that parents and children have to "get through." When teachers plan home activities, they often think in terms of worksheets or homework that will reinforce skills learned in school. But parents often grow tired of the endless stream of papers to be checked and the time spent on "busywork." Another danger of promoting home activities is the possibility that there may arise an unclear distinction of roles, with teachers expecting parents to "teach" at home. Teachers and parents need to understand that their roles are different, and that their act

Difficulties in involving Parents with child education

All teachers experience the frustration of trying to involve parents and getting little response. Teachers complain that parents do not come to conferences or school open houses, check homework, or answer notes. This leads some teachers to conclude that parents do not care about their children's education. While it is true that the emotional problems of a few parents may be so great as to prevent them from becoming involved with their children's education, most parents do care a great deal. This caring is not, however, always evidenced by parent attendance at school events. There are a number of reasons why these parents may not become involved, and teachers need to consider these before dismissing parents as uninterested.

For many parents, a major impediment to becoming involved is lack of time. Working parents are often unable to attend school events during the day. In addition, evenings are the only time these parents have to spend with their children, and they may choose to spend time with their family rather than attend meetings at school.

For many apparently uninvolved parents school was not a positive experience and they feel inadequate in a school setting. Parents may also feel uneasy if their cultural style or socioeconomic level differs from those of teachers (Greenberg, 1989). Some parents who are uninvolved in school may not understand the importance of parent involvement or may think they do not have the skills to be able to help. Even parents who are confident and willing to help may hesitate to become involved for fear of overstepping their bounds. It is the responsibility of teachers and administrators to encourage such parents to become involved.

Parents involvement in Children's Homework

1. Interact with the student's school or teacher about homework.

a. Communicate with the teacher about student performance, progress, homework.

b. Meet school requests and suggestions related to homework (e.g., sign completed tasks, offer requested help, participate in homework intervention program).

2. Establish physical and psychological structures for the child's homework performance.

a. Specify regular times for homework, establish structures for time use.

b. Articulate and enforce expectations, rules, and standards for homework behavior

c. Help student structure time, space, and materials for homework.

d. Structure homework within the flow of family life; ensure parental "availability on demand".

3. Provide general oversight of the homework process.

a. Monitor, supervise, and oversee the homework process.

b. Attend to signs of student success or difficulty related to task or motivation.

4. Respond to the student's homework performance.

a. Reinforce and reward student's homework efforts, completion, and correctness.

b. Recognize and offer emotional support for student performance, ability, effort.

c. Review, check, correct homework.

5. Engage in homework processes and tasks with the student.

a. Assist, help, tutor, "work with" student or "do" homework with student.

b. Teach student in direct, structured, convergent ways (e.g., learn facts, derive answers, drill, practice, memorize).

c. Teach student using indirect, more informal methods (e.g., respond to questions, follow student lead).

6. Engage in meta-strategies designed to create a fit between the task and student knowledge, skills, and abilities.

a. Break learning tasks into discrete, manageable parts.

b. Observe, understand, "teach to" student's developmental level.

7. Engage in interactive processes supporting student's understanding of homework.

a. Model or demonstrate appropriate learning processes and strategies.

b. Discuss problem-solving strategies.

c. Help student understand concepts, check for understanding.

8. Engage in meta-strategies helping the student learn processes conducive to achievement.

a. Support student's self-regulation skills, strategies, personal responsibility for homework processes and outcomes.

b. Help student organize personal thinking about assignments.

c. Encourage student to self-monitor, focus attention.

Teach and encourage the student to regulate emotional responses to homework.

Strategies for Supporting Student Motivation and Performance in Homework

The investigators focus in this section on basic strategies for supporting student motivation and performance in homework. Because teachers often take the lead in communicating learning goals, we focus on strategies teachers can use to encourage parental involvement. We also discuss strategies teachers may use in interacting with parent leaders and after school staff for further support of parental involvement in homework.

Influences of Educational attainment

Educational attainment is influenced by:

i. The highest and lowest educated parent, and the same-sex and different sex parent.

ii. These roles have not changed.

iii. There is no difference between men and women in the effect of parental education.

iv. The effect of parental education has decreased, but this decrease has slowed down.

Achievement Test

As a teacher one is involved directly in the evaluation of the learner. The theory that you have learnt will have to be applied by you as a teacher in the classroom situation. The present block Learner's Evaluation' in general and this unit in particular is concerned wid1 this very important activity of teachers.

Teachers teach and help the learners to learn. The learning that takes place is assessed or evaluated not only for the learner's benefit but also for the teacher to evaluate his/her own work. At the end of a lesson or a group of lessons, the teacher needs to get feedback on wile the learner has achieved, as a result of the teacher's efforts and also, indirectly to assess his her own, Achievement as a teacher. This feedback comes with the help of a tool, generally an achievement test. An achievement test is designed to evaluate a unit during the teaching-learning process. The unit of teaching-learning may be, as has already been mentioned, one lesson or a group of lessons transacted in a particular time period. You have already read about achievement tests in the previous unit. In this unit we will discuss the same in detail.

Objectives of Achievement Tests

a. Discuss the purpose of achievement tests.

b. Describe the steps involved in construct the achievement test.

c. Explain/illustrate how the design and blueprint of an achievement Lest are prepared.

d. A write a variety of questions - objective, short answer and essay.

e. A prepare a sample achievement test with a marking scheme.

f. Describe how an achievement test should be administered.

g. Mark/score an achievement test and interpret test scores.

h. Discuss the different types of grading and their purpose.

Purpose of Achievement Tests

Achievement tests are universally used in classroom mainly for the following purposes:

1. To measure whether students possess the pre-requisite skills needed to succeed in any unit or whether the students have achieved the objective of the planned instruction.
2. To monitor students' learning and to provide ongoing feedback to both students and teachers during the teaching-leaning process.
3. To identify the students' learning difficulties- whether persistent or recurring.
4. To assign grades.

Construction of Achievement Tests

There are several steps involved in the construction of Achievement Tests. We will now discuss these in detail one by one.

Instructional Objectives

The first and the most important step in planning a test are to identify the instructional objectives. Each subject has a different set of instructional objectives. In the subjects of Science, Social Sciences, and Mathematics the major objectives are categorized as knowledge, understanding, application and skill, while in languages the major objectives are categorized as knowledge, comprehension and expression. Knowledge objective is considered to be the lowest level of learning whereas, understanding, application of knowledge in sciences or behavioral sciences is considered higher levels of learning.

Design

The second step in planning a test is to make the "Design". The Design specifies weight ages to different (a) instructional objectives, (b) types (or forms) of questions, (c) units and sub-units of the course content, (d) levels of difficulty. It also indicates as to whether there are any options in the question paper, and if so, what their nature is.

The design, in fact, is termed as an instrument which reflects major policy decisions of the examining agency, whether it is a Board or an individual. A sample format for presenting design of a test is given on the next page.

Blueprint

The third step is to prepare the "Blueprint". The policy decisions, as reflected in the design of the question paper, are translated into action through the Blueprint. It is at this stage that the paper setter decides as to how many questions are to be set for different objectives. Further him/her & decides under which unit/topic a particular question is to be set. Furthermore, he/she packs up various forms of questions. Thereafter, the paper setter decides how all the questionnaire to be distributed over different objectives and content areas so as to obtain the weight ages decided in the Design. The three dimensions of the blueprint consist of content areas in horizontal rows and objectives and forms of questions in vertical columns. Once the blue prints prepared, the paper setter can write/ select the items and prepare the question paper.

Mproving Mathematics Performance

In an effective mathematics program, students learn to reason and communicate mathematically, value mathematics, and become confident in their own mathematical abilities to solve problems in situations that may not be familiar to them. Students need to be equipped as confident, competent, engaged, and persistent problem solvers. The key to mathematical competence is learning with understanding so that students are able to reason, solve problems, and apply their learning to new situations. Students need to be computationally fluent to carry out mathematical procedures flexibly, accurately, efficiently, and appropriately. Students need to be able to understand and use mathematics in everyday life. This understanding must be continually strengthened and expanded throughout their educational experiences. Strong mathematics programs also address the needs of all students, including struggling and highly able students. Early opportunities should be provided for one-on-one or small group assistance. To the extent possible, such supports should not interfere with the student's participation in regular classroom activities and learning. It is important that all students have access to rigorous mathematics, opportunities to engage in rich discourse about mathematics and expectations to think about their mathematical thinking. It is also important to use formative assessment practices to identify when students struggle and to intervene early.

Mathematical proficiency is something that all students can and need to achieve, just as all students need to become proficient readers. "Mathematical proficiency is not something students accomplish when they reach eighth grade or twelfth grade; they can be proficient regardless of their grade. Moreover, mathematical proficiency can no longer be restricted to a select few". Five areas of mathematical proficiency can be viewed as strands of an intertwined rope: Conceptual Understanding, Procedural Fluency, Strategic Competence, Adaptive Reasoning, and Productive Disposition.

In practice, educators need to consider making sure that student:

1. Understand important mathematical concepts, operations, and relations.
2. Develop procedural fluency to carry out procedures flexibly, accurately, efficiently, and appropriately.
3. Are strategic in their thinking and problem solving, able to formulate, represent, and solve mathematical problems.
4. Are able to reason and have the capacity for logical thought, reflection, explanation, and justification.
5. Have positive attitudes about math and confidence in their mathematical abilities and have developed an ability to persist.

6. See math as something that makes sense, is useful and worthwhile, and is applicable to real-life.

Improving Student Achievement in Mathematics

1. The extent of the students' opportunity to learn mathematics content bears directly and decisively on student mathematics achievement.
2. Focusing instruction on the meaningful development of important mathematical ideas increases the level of student learning
3. Students can learn both concepts and skills by solving problems.
4. Giving students both an opportunity to discover and invent new knowledge and an opportunity to practice what they have learned improves student achievement
5. Teaching that incorporates students' intuitive solution methods can increase student learning, especially when combined with opportunities for student interaction and discussion.
6. Using small groups of students to work on activities, problems and increase student mathematics achievement.
7. Whole-class discussion following individual and group work improves student achievement.
8. Teaching mathematics with a focus on number sense encourages students to become problem solvers in a wide variety of situations and to view mathematics as a discipline in which thinking is important.
9. Long-term use of concrete materials is positively related to increases in student mathematics achievement and improved attitudes towards mathematics.
10. Using calculators in the learning of mathematics can result in increased achievement and improved student attitudes.

Statement of the Problem

The statement of the problem is "RELATIONSHIP BETWEEN PARENTAL EDUCATIONAL AND STUDENT ACHIEVEMENT".

Objectives

The following are the objectives of the present study:

1. To find out the level of influence of parental education of higher secondary students in Rasipuram Taluk.
2. To find out the significance difference between Influence of parents' education and achievement in Mathematics of higher secondary students.

Hypotheses

1. There is no significant difference between male and female higher secondary students with respect to Influence of parents' education.
2. There is no significant difference between rural and urban higher secondary students with respect to Influence of parents' education.
3. There is no significant difference among government, aided, private higher secondary students with respect to Influence of parents' education.
4. There is no significant difference between literate and illiterate fathers of higher secondary students with respect to Influence of parents' education.
5. There is no significant difference between literate and illiterate mothers of higher secondary students with respect to Influence of parents' education.

Limitation of the Study

Broadly speaking any study is impossible without limitation. Research studies in general will have limitation due to many factors.

This study too has some limitations. It is the responsibility of the researcher to see that the study is conducted with minimum care in order to be reliable. However, the following limitations were unavoidable in the present study.

1. This study adopted survey method using questionnaires to collect data from respondents.
2. In this study, sample was confined to higher secondary students of various schools in Rasipuram Taluk.
3. The sample respondents belong to age group between 15+ and 16+.

The generalizations of the study are to be viewed in the light of the above limitations that are Inherent in academic research.

Organization of the Thesis

The report of the thesis will be presented according to the following sequences.

The first chapter gives introduction of terms, statement of the problem, objectives, hypothesis and limitations of the study.

Second chapter deals with the review of related literature which are done in India and abroad referred to this study.

Third chapter gives a detailed account of research procedures and methodology used in this study.

Fourth chapter deals with the tabulation of analysis and the interpretations of the data in detail.

Fifth chapter describes the findings, conclusion and certain recommendations about the study.

This is followed by the bibliography and appendices which consist of the tools used for the study and the related matters

II

Review of the Literature

Overview

The present chapter deals about the need of the existence of the review of related literature, classification of the studies identified that were conducted in India and abroad. The analogy of the whole study is presented at the end of the present chapter.

Introduction

Any worldwide research study in any field of knowledge requires an adequate familiarity with the work which has already been done in the same area. A summary of the writings of recogn zed authorities and of previous research provides evidence that the research is familiar with what is already known and what is stil unknown and untested.

Since effective research is based upon past knowledge, this steps helps to eliminate the duplication of what has be done, and provides useful hypotheses and helpful suggestions for significant investigation.

According to Jonathan Anderson, "the review of related literature in a field of work is general to the specific to work from territory and secondary source of information to primary source".

According to Berg.W.R, "the literature in any field forms the foundation upon which all future work will be built. If we fade to build the foundation of knowledge provided by the review of literature our work is likely to be shallow and naïve will often duplicate work that has already been done some better by someone else".

Reviewing the literature has tells phases. In the first phases include identifying all the relevant published material in the problem area and reading that part of its with which we are not thoroughly familiar. The second phases of review of literature involve writing this foundation of ideas into a section of the research and readers. For the researchers it establishes the background in the field for the readers provides a summary of the thinking and research necessary for them to understand the study.

Need For Review of Related Literature

The review of related literature is essential due to the following reasons. One of the early steps in planning a research work is to review research done previously in the particular areas of interest and relevant area quantitative and qualitative analysis of this research usually gives the worker and indication of direction.

1. It is very essential for every investigator to be up-to-date in his information about the literature, related to his own problem already done by others.
2. It provides as sources of problem of study, an analogy may be drawn for identifying and selecting his own problem of research.
3. The review of literature indicates the clear picture of the problem to be solved.

Classification of the Studies

The investigator has gone through the researches related to the present problem. Hence an attempt was made by the investigator to put forth the reviews related to the present investigation. The investigator identified forty eight studies conducted in India and abroad. Out of this, sixteen studies conducted in India and the remaining thirty two studies were done in abroad. The investigator suitably located the related studies and the details of the above studies are presented below:

Studies Conducted in India

The investigator identified sixteen studies conducted in India on influence of parent education, parent involvement, achievement in Mathematics and are presented below in the chronological order:

Srivastava (1976) conducted a study of personality factors on predictors of academic achievement of high school students. He found that learning outcomes, in terms of objective in mathematics and some of personality factors as predictors of academic achievement of high school students.

Jayaratne (1987) found that parents exerted a strong influence on the development of their children's attitudes toward achievement. Children's beliefs about achievement appeared to be related to their parents' expectations about their children's achievement but not to the parents' attitudes in regard to their children's abilities and experiences.

Rangappa (1992) investigated the relationship among self-concept, reading ability and achievement in mathematics. He found no significant difference in the achievement of students having different level of self-concept, but significant difference was observed in the mathematics achievement of students having different levels of reading ability.

Singh and Varma (1992) studied the attitude towards mathematics as a function of some individual characteristics such as sex and intelligence. They found that students of lower age group (i.e. 13 years) and intelligence with average and high intelligence showed more favorable attitude towards mathematics as compared to students of higher age group (i.e. 14+ & 15+) and lower intelligence.

Maya (2001) found that parental level of education did not have significant effects on adolescent's achievement motivation. Parents' education and income level are not important determinants of student's achievement motivation in comparison to parental support and encouragement.

Davis-Kean (2005) found that achievement motivation in other areas are not significantly influenced by parents' education probably because motivation in dramatics, general interest and sports of the child is influenced by other factors such as their interest in dramatics and sports, their aptitude and opportunities for extracurricular activities in the school that parents' education.

Vamadevappa (2005) conducted a study on impact of parental involvement on academic achievement. The objective of the study were,

1. To find out the extent of relationship parental involvement and academic achievement among higher primary student.
2. To find out the difference between high achievers and low achievers with respect to parental involvement
3. To find out difference between boys and girls on high and low parental involvement.

Nirmala.P (2006) conducted a study on optimization of academic achievement in mathematics a linear programming approach. The objective of the study were,

1. To study the contributing factors of academic achievement in mathematics.
2. To study the optimizing the variables of the academic achievement in mathematics using linear programming approach.

Rita Chopra & Surabala Sahoo (2006) conducted a study on self-esteem of secondary school students in relation to parent involvement. The objectives of the study were,

1. To find out the relationship between self-esteem students and parent involvement.

2. To find out the difference between the self-esteem students belonging to high parent involvement group and low parent involvement group.

Shoni Thomas (2006) conducted a study on "the influence of mathematical aptitude on achievement in accountancy of higher secondary students". He has been conducted on a sample of 246 higher secondary students selected from six higher secondary schools in Kottayam revenue district, Kerala. This study revea s that 15.44%, 17% and 12.6% of students have high, moderate and low level of achievement in accountancy respectively. The correlation coefficient of the relationship between mathematical aptitude ar d achievement in accountancy was 0.811 and so it reveals that there is a significant relationship in accountancy and mathematical aptitude.

Kalaiyarasan.G (2007) conducted a study on effect of incentives in enhancing the academic achievement of students in learning mathematics at the higher secondary level. The main objective of the study was to find out influence of incentives in learning mathematics at the higher secondary level.

B.William Dharma Raja & R.Grace (2008) did a study, "Do college wards get parental involvement?". They concluded that teachers should study the level of parental involvement on studies of their wards and if it is found to be not satisfactory, necessary should be taken to be improving it.

Manish Kumar Yadav & Tyagi (2009) conducted a study on accuracy of self assessment of achievement in mathematics in relation to some personality related variables of eight graders. The major finding of the study were,

1. The accuracy of self assessment of achievement in mathematics was found to be independent of gender, intelligence and their interaction, when achievement and dependence were taken as covariates.
2. The accuracy of self assessment of achievement in mathematics was found to be independent of dependence and as well as the interaction between gender and dependence when intelligence and achievement and taken as covariates.

3. The accuracy of self assessment of achievement in mathematics was found to be significantly influence by the achievement level of students when intelligence and dependence were taken as covariates. High achievers were found to self assess themselves more accurately than the low achievers.

4. The accuracy of self assessment of achievement in mathematics was found to be independent of interaction between gender and achievement when intelligence and dependence were takes as covariates.

Noorjehan.N.Ganihar & Wajiga (2009) conducted a study on factors affective academic achievement of IX standard students in mathematics. This study conclude that many factors like mathematical creativity, attitude towards mathematics, achievement motivation and a low level of anxiety in influence the academic achievement in mathematics at secondary stage.

Harish.G.C (2010) conducted a study on, "impact of integrated critical thinking skills on achievement in mathematics of secondary school students". The major findings of the study were,

1. There is a significant difference between the post test achievement of control and experimental group.

2. There is a significant difference between the mean scores of boys and girls in the post test achievement.

3. There is a significant interaction between group and gender on post test achievement.

4. There is a significant difference between the mean scores of group and gender in the post test achievement with respect to total integrated critical thinking skills.

5. There is a significant interaction between group and gender on total integrated on critical thinking skills on achievement after the intervention program.

Lourdusamy (2010) carried out parental influence on academic achievement of higher secondary students. The main objectives of the study are to study the level of parental influence of higher secondary students and parental influence on academic achievement of higher secondary students. The research reveals that 12% of higher secondary students have high level of parental influence and there is a significant relationship between academic achievement and parental influence of higher secondary students.

Studies Conducted in Abroad

Hanrsley & Eligabeth (1982) found that fathers' education had strong influence on academic achievement of girls in early grades, whereas it is effect on boy's academic achievement.

Wigfield (1983) conducted a study on students' perception on parents' beliefs conserving the academic competence. He found that parents' beliefs about their own achievement in regard to mathematics and their background in mathematics were not related to the children's mathematical belief. However, parents' beliefs about the children were related their children's beliefs. A though some parents may have lower expectations for girls in mathematics, they did not appear to directly influence the intentions of either girls or boys to take more mathematics, the children seemed to have less sex differentiated views in regard to mathematics than did their parents.

Song & Hattie (1984) indicated that parents from different socio-economic group create different learning environment that affects child's achievement motivation.

McDevitt & Hoss (1985) found that parents direct control techniques hampered children's cognitive development by influencing their self appraisals. Mothers who maid appeals based on the authority had children who tended to attribute failure to lack of ability and did not attribute success to ability. It could be that not allowing more self exploration, these controlling mothers foster a lack of confidence in their children.

James Comer (1986) reported that many low income parents participating in a parent involvement program become role models for their children by virtue of continuing their own education, taking new jobs, and eventually leaving the welfare rolls.

Yee (1986) found that children's attitudes about mathematics are influenced by: (a) parents' perceptions of their own academic abilities, (b) the value and importance that they place on various academic subjects and (c) the ways in which they structure their children's environment.

Stevenson (1990) found a significant body of research that links parent involvement. A short survey, developed for guidance counselors, revealed the following information about student performance: 77% of the counselors agreed that parent education can improve parent perceptions of their parenting skills; 68% agreed that that parent education, which addresses individual student and parent needs, can improve the school performance of students, and 64% agreed that parent education, that improves student school performance, can also improve teacher perception of the student.

Thind (1990) conducted a study on impact of the socio-economic status of parents on the mathematical problem solving ability of school students. In this investigation, he pointed out that father's and mother's occupation had no effect on both rural and urban children's problem solving ability. Further, education of the father had no effect on the problem solving ability of rural as well as urban children's. However the problem solving ability of urban children was affected by mother's education.

In this study four factors were considered in socio-economic status.

1. Father's educational qualification
2. Mother's educational qualification
3. Father's occupational qualification
4. Mother's occupational qualification

Blevins-Knabe & Musun-Miller (1991) suggested that parental beliefs are related to parental actions and, thus, these beliefs influence the environment that parents provide for their children. For many children, early number skills are intuitive and develop with little direct intervention from parents.

Gotlfried (1991) found that the more involvement of parents increases the children's perception of confidence and enhances their performance in school settings.

Drazen (1992) conducted a study on measuring student achievement and its relationship to socio-economic standing. This study investigates that 75% of the time, level of parents' education was the number one factor related to the performance of their children in the areas of reading and math achievement.

Janine Bempechat (1992) carried out the role of parent involvement in children's academic achievement. This study examined the research on parent involvement in their children's education by exploring socialization patterns that foster high achievement and describing the structure and effectiveness parent involvement programs.

Leder (1992) studied the relationships between home experiences and mathematical skills. It was found that parents from a variety of backgrounds reported a number of different activities and games they provided in the home in order to support their child's mathematical development. Also, the provision of such mathematical activity seemed to be correlated with success in school.

Benjamin (1993) conducted a study on the most important factors that influence a child's achievement in school. This study revealed that more highly educated mothers succeed greater in providing their children with the cognitive skills that promote achievement in school. Factors other than directly helping children with homework were also found to have a strong effect on student achievement. These factors include,

1. Parent involvement and support in school in child's after school activities.
2. Time spent interacting with the child at home.
3. Emotional climate at home.
4. Level of financial stress of parent.
5. Enrichment activities.

Gailey (1993) compiled a bibliography of 159 children's books that are connected to mathematics. In this bibliography, there are many excellent suggestions for mathematically based children's literature to be read at home.

Alexander (1994) found that parents with more education for their children's education which facilitates the greater educational attainment for their children.

Gunn & Duncan (1994) found that both mothers' education and family income were important predictors of the physical environment and learning experiences in the home.

Anderson (1997) conducted a study which was focused on families and mathematics. In this study of parent-child interactions, three interrelated theoretical perspectives were examined: (a) contextualized learning, (b) social constructivism, and (c) mediated learning.

Brooks-Gunn & Klebanov (1997) carried out an investigation of the literature on achievement. This study revealed that parent education is important in predicting children's achievement.

Khalid (1997) focused his research on factors affecting mathematics achievement. The investigator found that confidence, socio-economic status, gender beliefs, peers, location of school, school environment, ethnicity beliefs and previous achievement in mathematics were significant contributors of mathematics achievement in Malaysian school.

Klebanov & Smith (1997) found that association between parents' education and children's academic achievement was mediated by the home environment.

Stevention & Baker (1997) found that well educated parents are involved more in their children's education than less educated parents. Such parental involvement in children's education is fruitful. The more actively involved parents are in their children's education, the higher their children's perceptions of competence and better they perform in school and enhance their achievement motivation.

Hao & Burns (1998) argued that family income, education and occupation is less influential for achievement motivation of adolescents than parental interaction with children, involvement in the children education and expectation for their children.

Teng (1998) recounted many real life mathematics experiences provided by parents about their interaction with their children. Parents reported that they wanted their children to be curious and knowledgeable about numbers. Many believed that the earlier that their children learned mathematics, the more success they would achieve. Several parents shared their experiences:

1. One mother reported that she had seen other young children be successful in learning mathematics, so she decided her child should be introduced to it as early as possible.
2. Another parent wanted her son to be skilled in problem solving.
3. A third parent wanted his son to acquire good study habits and understand the methods involved to prevent frustration when the mathematics became more difficult.

Peressini (1998) found that parents' involvement in mathematics education through the lens of the school mathematics reform literature. He maintained that it was important to study the role of parents in school reform as well as their role in their children's mathematics education. Also, parents should be involved in the mathematics reform movement. Peressine stated that "To effectively involve parents in the reform of school mathematics, the mathematics education community needs both an understanding of the research regarding parental involvement and a commitment to future research on parents in mathematics education".

Zang & Carrasquillo's (1998) found that Chinese parents had an important influence in the academic performance of their children. Parents assigned mathematics homework to their preschoolers and kindergartners; some bought workbooks in Taiwan or Hong Kong; and many developed their own mathematics work sheets for their children. This early formal teaching of mathematics by parents was linked closely to these children's higher than average scores on mathematics assessments in comparison to their Anglo American peers.

Jimerson, Egelande & Teo (1999) conducted a longitudinal study of achievement trajectories factors associated with change. This study suggests that influence the beliefs and behaviors of the parent, leading to positive outcomes children and youth.

Corwyn & bradldy (2002) indicated that maternal education had the direct influence on cognitive and behavioral development of the child.

Pamela E.Davis-Kean (2005) conducted a study on the influence of parent education and family income on child achievement. This study examines the process of how socio-economic status, specifically parents' education and income directly relates to children's academic achievement through parents' beliefs and behaviors.

Alen Bisop & Helen Forgasz (2006) conducted a study on perceived parental influence on Mathematical learning. This study explores perceived parental influence on mathematics learning among over 700 students across three year level in China and Australia. It was found that the PPI of students was less strong as year levels increased in both countries. Students in China had stronger perceived parental encouragement and higher perceived parental educational expectation than students in Australia.

Irene Hleanthous & Julian Williams (2010) carried out a study on perceived parental influence on students' mathematical achievement, inclination to mathematics and dispositions to study further mathematics. The findings of this study is perceived parental aspiration where statistically significantly related to students' inclination to mathematics. Students' who are positively disposed towards mathematics reported higher perception of parental aspiration.

Suresh Kumar & N.Vellymalay (2010) conducted a study on parental involvement in children's education. Does parents' education really matter?. This study investigates the relationship between parent education level and parent involvement in their children education among National Medium Tamil Schools in Malaysia. Parent involvement in this study focuses on the involvement strategies implemented by parents' in their children's education at home and at school. Findings of the study suggest that there are no significant differences between parents' education level and most of the parents' involvement strategies in their children's education.

Analogy

Out of the total forty eight studies identified the investigator found sixteen studies conducted in India and thirty two studies conducted abroad. Majority of the studies belonged to survey studies and few of them are experimental studies.

Most of the studies followed random sampling technique in the collection of data and the size of the selected samples ranges from 40 to 2400 samples. In majority of the studies data was collected from the school students and in few of the studies data was collected from the teachers and parents. In majority of the students the questionnaire, Opionnarrie Rating Scale developed by the investigator was utilized as a tool. Since all the reviewed studies were selected to influence of parent education, parent involvement, achievement in Mathematics among higher secondary students. In majority of the studies data was collected only from the school students. Mean, Standard deviation, t-test were the statistical technique followed in the majority of the students.

The studies like Thind (1990), Klebanov & Smith (1997), Steven-tion & Baker (1997), Hao & Burns (1998) and Corwyn & bradldy (2002) states that well educated parents are involved more in their children's education than less educated parents. This finding is related to the present study.

Conclusion

The study so far conducted concerned mainly on the role of parents' education and its influence among higher secondary students towards Mathematics achievement. It is felt only a few studies were done on influence of parents' education and its influence towards Mathematics achievement. So the investigator wishes to know whether factors like gender, literacy of parents', type of the school of students' etc., have any influence on achievement in Mathematics. The following chapter deals with the methodology of the present study.

III

Methodology

Overview

The methodology followed in the present study is described in this chapter. The present study is a normative survey research which aimed to measure the influence of Parental education cn achievement in Mathematics.

Introduction

Research may be termed as a systematic enquiry for verified knowledge. It is an organized deliberate effort to collect information to analyze it, to put it together and finally evaluate it (Nair 1975) methodology is illuminated as science and art of using appropriate modes and order of procedure. A detailed description of the procedures adopted in conducting the present study is presented in this study. It depicts the design of the study, including samples selected for the study, the tool developed method and cata collection.

Design of the Study

Research design is a plan, a structure and a strategy of investigation conceived to obtain answers to various issues in research. The object of research design is to test the research hypotheses. The research design, therefore, is built in the principle of maximization of the results of study, minimization of variance. A research design however, is not a highly specific plan to be followed without direction. Rather, it is a series of guideposts to keep right direction. Thus, research design is the process of planning a research, choosing methods and procedures that can be expected to yield meaningful and most interpretable results.

TABLE 3.1

Schematic Representation of the Research Design

S. No.	Type	Sources
1.	Nature of the Research	Survey research
2.	Tool Developed	Influence on Parental Education on Achievement in Mathematics
3.	Demographic variables	Students
4.	Variables	Boys, Girls (Gender) Rural, Urban (Locality) Government, Aided, Private (Type of the School) Literate, Illiterate (Father's educational qualification) Literate, Illiterate (Mother's educational qualification)
5.	Sampling Technique	Stratified Random sampling Technique
6.	Size of the sample	Students – 150 (Boys-75, Girls-75)
7.	Statistical Techniques used	Mean, Standard Deviation and 't' test

The present study belongs to survey stay Research. The Demographic variables used are Gender, Locality, Type of the school, Father's educational qualification and Mother's educational qualification. The tool "IPEAM" used in the study is 11th standard students in Rasipuram Taluk for sample selection. Stratified Random sampling technique was followed in this study. Data were collected from 150 students and the statistical techniques mean, SD, 't' test and Average were used.

Selection of the Topic

Thought, in principle, all behaviors can be programs the devices to produce different kinds of stimulation and to record the different responses of the learner may not be available to all programs in a particular situation. Keeping this in mind as the basis for the selection of topic, a particular unit in Mathematics was taken depending upon the task analysis in terms of the stimuli required to be presented and flexibility of the available devices in the rural area where the research was conducted. The units was taken after consultation with exports in Mathematics Subject, educational scholars, programmers and senior teacher of Mathematics rich experience at the secondary level. The topic selected is introduced as Matrix and Vector Analysis.

Preparation of Achievement Test

Discussions with the professors of Mathematics, well experienced teachers of Mathematics were consulted. The researcher wanted to conduct an achievement test on the basis of Mathematics at the end of the research. The content validity of the achievement test was reviewed by a panel of two members, consisting of a professor of Mathematics, a well-experienced teacher of Mathematics.

Blueprint

TABLE 3.2

BLUEPRINT FOR ACHIEVEMENT TEST

Objectives	Knowledge			Under			Application standing			Skill			Total
Forms of questions /Content Unit	E	S.A	O	E	S.A	O	E	S.A	O	E	S.A	O	
Matrices	-	-	9	-	-	6	-	-	5	-	-	5	25
Vector Algebra	-	-	7	-	-	5	-	-	10	-	-	3	25
Sub total			16			11			15			8	50
Total (in %)		32			22						30	16	100

Note :

E – Essay Type
S.A – Short Answer
O – Objective Type

Pilot Study

Before administering the questionnaire to the actual sample, pilot study was conducted. The aim of pilot study is not only to test and refine the tools of research but also to force the nature of analysis and processing that may be needed at a later stage. After a questionnaire was prepared. It was given a trial on small sample. This is necessary to know XI standard students whether they are meaningful and whether there is any ambiguity in thought or in the wording of questions.

Objectives

1. To find out the level of influence of parental education of higher secondary students in Rasipuram Taluk.
2. To find out the significance difference between Influence of parents' education and achievement in Mathematics of higher secondary students.

Hypotheses

1. There is no significant difference between male and female higher secondary students with respect to Influence of parents' education.
2. There is no significant difference between rural and urban higher secondary students with respect to Influence of parents' education.
3. There is no significant difference among government, aided, private higher secondary students with respect to Influence of parents' education.
4. There is no significant difference between literate and illiterate fathers of higher secondary students with respect to Influence of parents' education.
5. There is no significant difference between literate and illiterate mothers of higher secondary students with respect to Influence of parents' education.

Research Methods

The investigator followed Survey method as this study aims of eliciting the opinions of the XI standard students on achievement in Mathematics.

Research Method Used For the Study

Research studies require a systematic collection of data from the sample through the use of appropriate data gathering devices. For the present study a Survey method was selected which gathers data from a relatively larger number of samples and provides the information useful to the solution of local problems.

Tool used for the Study

1. Achievement test with multiple choice questions
2. A questionnaire was prepared to get the information about matrix and vector Analysis in XI std students
3. Test method – Achievement test of 50 marks was conducted

Sample of the Study

A sample is a small proposition of a population selected for observation and analysis. "A good sample of a population with great accuracy" - Corwell (1960). By considering here the research which proposes to ascertain what is the normal or typical condition or practice at the present time". It is the only means through which opinions, attitudes and suggestions for improvement and such other data can be obtained. Survey studies help in contributing to other types of investigations and cover a large number of traits and characteristics of the group.

A sample of 150 students of Higher Secondary level was selected from the following. Five difference higher secondary schools in Rasipuram Taluk of Namakkal district.

TABLE 3.3

DISTRIBUTION OF SAMPLES

S.No.	Variables	Category	No. of Samples
1.	Gender	Male	75
		Female	75
2.	Locality	Rural	79
		Urban	71
3.	Type of the School	Government	51
		Aided	50
		Private	49
4.	Fathers' Educational Qualification	Literate	91
		illiterate	59
5.	Mothers' Educational Qualification	Literate	64
		illiterate	86

TABLE 3.4

LIST OF SCHOOLS TAKEN FOR SAMPLES

S.NO.	NAME OF THE SCHOOL	NO. OF SAMPLES
1.	Sengundhar Mahajana Higher Secondary School, Gurusamypalayam.	30
2.	Government Boys Higher Secondary School, Vennandhur.	38
3.	Government Girls Higher Secondary School, Vennandhur.	24
4.	Sri Vidhya Mandhir Higher Secondary School, Rasipuram.	35
5.	Sivanandha Govt. Girls Higher Secondary School, Rasipuram.	23

The personal data sheet servers to collect personal information. Students were asked to write their name, gender, locality, age, name the school, type of the school, father's and mother's educational qualification.

Procedure

The questionnaire was prepared which included questions in XI standard Mathematics given to the students during extra periods. The students wrote the truthful answers. Further the classification and analysis of the results was carried out.

Questionnaire

A Questionnaire usually contains a series of well-planned and well-framed questions on the chosen topic. Which the subjects were asked to answer. "In general the word questionnaire refers to a device for securing answer questions by using a form which the responded fills himself".

Barn, David and Johnson define questionnaire "A systematic computation of question that are submitted to a sampling of population from which information is desired"

Scoring Key

The three types of opionnarrie consist of questions. The total maximum scores 1 and minimum scores 0.

Statistical Techniques

For the analysis of data following statistical technique were adopted.

They were,

1. Arithmetic Mean
2. Standard Deviation
3. 't'- test
4. 'f'- test

Arithmetic Mean

$$M = \frac{\sum fx}{N}$$

f = Frequency of each class interval

x = Midpoint of each class

N = Total number of scores.

Standard Deviation

Σfx^2 $(\Sigma fx)^2$

x = Deviation of each score from mean

N = Total number of score.

i = class interval

't' - test

$$t = \frac{M_1 - M_2}{\sqrt{\frac{SD^2}{N_1} + \frac{SD^2}{N_2}}}$$

m_1 = Mean of first sample

m_2 = Mean of second sample

SD_1 = Standard Deviation of first sample

SD_2 = Standard Deviation of second sample.

N_1 = Total Number of first sample

N_2 = Total Number of second sample

't' - test

$$f = \frac{Variancedifference}{Variancewithin}$$

Delimitations of the Study

Broadly speaking, any study is impossible without delimitation. Research studies in general will have delimitation due to many factors. This study too has some delimitation. It is the responsibility of the researcher to see that the study is conducted with maximum care in order to be reliable.

However, the following delimitations were unavoidable in the present study. The present investigation is confined to the students studying in Rasipuram Taluk, Namakkal District in Tamil Nadu. The study is confined only to a sample of 150 students from higher secondary schools located in rural and urban area. In this present study the investigator analyzed about the variables such as gender, locality, type of the school, father's educational qualification and mother's educational qualification.

Conclusion

The design of the study various stages involved the experimentation and the data collection procedures were explained in this chapter in detail. The analysis and interpretation of data related to the hypotheses framed have been presented in the next chapter.

IV

Data Analysis

Overview

The present chapter deals with the analysis of the data. The collected data according to the procedures discussed in this chapter iii was carefully processed and systematically analyzed. The appropriate statistical techniques such as f-test and t-test and correlation coefficient 'r' were properly applied to draw the conclusion rationally. The results are presented in this chapter under their discussion where are given below.

Introduction

The analysis and the interpretation of data represent the application of the inductive and deductive logic to the research process. it is a very important step in the total procedure of research. Analysis of variation of data means studying the tabulated materials. It involves breaking down exiting complex factor in to simple parts and putting the parts together in new arrangements for the purpose of interpretation. Interpretation of calls for a critical examination of results of once analysis in the light of all limitation of this data gathering.

Analysis of data means studying the tabulated material in order to determine the inherent falls or meaning. Data accepted by the investigator got their meaning, when they are channelized into the process of statistical analysis. It will give the investigator an insight in to the problem. It simplifies the masses of number and facts and presents them in an understandable manner. Therefore analysis must lead to interpretation of data.

The purpose of present investigation is to study the influence of parental education on achievement in mathematics. The data for the study were collected from the students by means of a questionnaire. The analysis of data was attempted as per the objectives of the study. In the present study the data was anglicized using mainly the following techniques.

1. Percentage
2. Arithmetic mean
3. Standard deviation
4. 't'- test
5. 'f' – test

Table 4.1

LEVEL OF INFLUENCE IN TOTAL AMONG HIGHER SECONDARY STUDENTS TOWARDS PARENT EDUCATION

N	MEAN	S.D.
150	46.06	13.31

The table 4.1 shows that the total mean value of higher secondary students towards parents' education is 46.06 and standard deviation is 18.31.

Hypothesis: 1

There is no significant difference between male and female higher secondary students with respect to influence of parents' education.

Table 4.2

SIGNIFICANT DIFFERENCE BETWEEN MALE AND FEMALE HIGHER SECONDARY STUDENTS WITH RESPECT TO INFLUENCE OF PARENTS' EDUCATION

Category	N	Mean	S.D.	't' value	Significance at 0.05 level
Male	75	44.83	17.62	4.51	**No**
Female	75	57.5	16.73		**Significant**

Table 4.2 examines the mean, standard deviation, 't' value and level of significance of male and female student's towards parents' education.

The mean scores of male and female shows that there is significant difference in their influence of parents' education. The scores indicate that the two groups have difference.

The 't' value of the group is 4.51 at 0.05 level. The calculated 't' value exceeds the tabulated value (1.98) at 0.05 level.

Hence the null hypothesis is accepted.

Hypothesis: 2

There is no significant difference between rural and urban higher secondary students with respect to influence of parents' education.

Table 4.3

SIGNIFICANT DIFFERENCE BETWEEN RURAL AND URBAN HIGHER SECONDARY STUDENTS WITH RESPECT TO INFLUENCE OF PARENTS' EDUCATION

Category	N	Mean	S.D.	't' value	Significance at 0.05 level
Rural	79	43.72	14.64	5.86	**No**
Urban	71	59.44	17.8		**Significant**

Table 4.3 examines the mean, standard deviation, 't' value and level of significance of rural and urban student's towards parents' education.

The mean scores of male and female shows that there is significant difference in their influence of parents' education. The scores indicate that the two groups have difference.

The 't' value of the group is 5.86 at 0.05 level. The calculated 't' value exceeds the tabulated value (1.98) at 0.05 level. Hence the null hypothesis is accepted.

Hypothesis: 3

There is no significant difference among government, aided, private higher secondary students with respect to influence of parents' education.

Table 4.4

SIGNIFICANCE DIFFERENCE AMONG GOVERNMENT, AIDED, PRIVATE HIGHER SECONDARY STUDENTS WITH RESPECT TO INFLUENCE OF PARENTS' EDUCATION

Category	N	Mean	S.D.	'f' value	Significance at 0.05 level
Government	51	51.97	23.16		
Aided	50	39.7	10.6	1.56	Significant
Private	49	66.31	15.75		

Table 4.4 examines the mean, standard deviation, 'f' value and level of significance of male and female student's towards parents' education.

The mean scores of government, aided and private shows that there is significant difference in their influence of parents' education. The scores indicate that the two groups have difference.

The 'f' value of the group is 1.56 at 0.05 level. The calculated 'f' value not exceeds the tabulated value (3.06) at 0.05 level. Hence the null hypothesis is rejected.

Hypothesis: 4

There is no significant difference between literate and illiterate fathers of higher secondary students with respect to influence of parents' education.

Table 4.5

SIGNIFICANT DIFFERENT BETWEEN LITERATE AND ILLITERATE FATHERS' OF HIGHER SECONDARY STUDENTS WITH RESPECT TO INFLUENCE OF PARENTS' EDUCATION

Category	N	Mean	S..	't' value	Significance at 0.05 level
Literate	91	56.15	18.86		
illiterate	59	43.63	14.55	4.56	No

Table 4.5 examines the mean, standard deviation, 't' value and level of significance of male and female student's towards parents' education.

The mean scores of literate and illiterate fathers' shows that there is significant difference in their influence of parents' education. The scores indicate that the two groups have difference.

The 't' value of the group is 4.56 at 0.05 level. The calculated 't' value exceeds the tabulated value (1.98) at 0.05 level. Hence the null hypothesis is accepted.

Hypothesis: 5

There is no significant difference between literate and illiterate mothers of higher secondary students with respect to influence of parents' education.

Table 4.6

SIGNIFICANT DIFFERENCE BETWEEN LITERATE AND ILLITERATE MOTHERS OF HIGHER SECONDARY STUDENTS WITH RESPECT TO INFLUENCE OF PARENTS' EDUCATION

Category	N	Mean	S.D.	't' value	Significance at 0.05 level
Literate	64	55.6	20.34		**No**
illiterate	86	47.94	15.92	2.49	**Significant**

Table 4.6 examines the mean, standard deviation, 't' value and level of significance of male and female students towards parents' education.

The mean scores of literate and illiterate mothers' shows that there is significant difference in their influence of parents' education. The scores indicate that the two groups have difference.

The 't' value of the group is 2.49 at 0.05 level. The calculated 't' value exceeds the tabulated value (1.98) at 0.05 level. Hence the null hypothesis is accepted.

Conclusion

Thus the analysis of the data generated by the administration of the tool on the sample of 150 students in Rasipuram Taluk has yielded many interesting results, which are summarized in the succeeding chapter v.

V

Findings, Conclusions and Recommendations

Overview

In this chapter an attempt had been made to consolidate all the findings of the present study, the investigator also made some recommendation, which include the relevant area of for this research and lastly the conclusion. The findings are based on the result collected from the attitude scale.

The Study in Retrospect

The aim of the present investigation was to find out level of influence of parents' education on achievement in Mathematics.

Methodology in Brief

For the present study normative study method was adopted. For the sample of the study, 150 students of 5 different higher secondary schools in Rasipuram Taluk were contacted. The tool used for the collection of data is achievement test.

Re-statement of the Problem

The problem under the study is entitled as "*INFLUENCE OF PARENTS' EDUCATION ON ACHIEVEMENT IN MATHEMATICS AMONG HIGHER SECONDARY STUDENTS IN RASIPURAM TALUK*".

Major Findings of the Study

From the present study the investigator came to the following findings

1. There is no significant difference between male and female higher secondary students with respect to Influence of parents' education.
2. There is no significant difference between rural and urban higher secondary students with respect to Influence of parents' education.
3. There is a significant difference among government, aided, private higher secondary students with respect to Influence of parents' education.
4. There is no significant difference between literate and illiterate fathers of higher secondary students with respect to Influence of parents' education.
5. There is no significant difference between literate and illiterate mothers of higher secondary students with respect to Influence of parents' education.

Suggestions

1. Parents should monitor their children to use mass media/ internet for necessary information.
2. Parents should educate their children in all their stages to overcome the teen age problems and help them out by providing their needs.
3. Parents should bear in mind that it is a temporary phase with

most children. Some of the most destructive children have later on grown up to be among the most creatively constructive. Many of them outgrow this in time.

4. We should be very friendly with the child. Parents can instill the best of everything into their child. Try to improve yourselves to be his/her best companions. The child must have complete trust in you. Children usually love to try their hands at new things. Appreciate them and try a test their intelligence quotients (IQ).

Educational Implications

Parents' education plays key role in performance of their children. In the last 50 years, there has been a striking increase in inequality in children's home environments across families where parents have different levels of education. Given that the tendency is rooted in the experience of each family, it is difficult for the welfare system to import change and direct interventions require the invasion of family autonomy and privacy. The authors of CEPR assess an alternative potential policy, which targets future parents while still in their youth by affecting their education before they start forming a family. Their findings suggest that parental education plays a substantial role in transmitting inequality in home environments and child outcomes, which supports the view that educational policy can make a difference in their future.

In summary, all parental influences derived from this study have implications for Mathematics. These influences, which include parents serving as role models of altruism, parental support for career goal achievement, high grade expectations, introductions to the positive aspects of teaching, parents involving children in hands-on learning experiences, and the creation of environments that nurture the discovery of vocational content are all important in creating interest in Mathematics.

Areas of Research for the Future

Research is a chain activity. The purpose of any research in education is to find solutions for problems related to teachers, students, learning etc. But investigation on one problem always leaves many related research questions that can be investigated by other researchers; some of the areas for research in the future may be as follows:

1. The research done by the investigator can be replicated with primary and high school level.
2. This study was confined only to five institutions in one Taluk. Study may be conducted by taking area, at district and regional level or state level. (i.e.) large sampling covering
3. Similar study may be done with other variab es like parents' socio-economic status and parental involvement in student achievement.
4. A comparative study on influence of parents' education and parental involvement in student achievement among different level of school students.
5. The present study is done only to higher secondary level. Similar study can be conducted for the college students especially for professional course students.

Conclusion

Education plays a vital role in enhancing the level of thinking and standard of living. Educated parents transfer the value of education to their children, which intern affects the aspiration level and achievement of the child. Why children success or fail in school is most enduring questions for educational research. The findings of the present study and earlier researches supported the notion that parents' education is one of the most important factors influencing child's achievement motivation. Highly educated parents have greater success in providing their children with the cognitive and language skills that contribute to early success in school. The relationship of parents' education to their children's achievement motivation in academic area is meditated by parents' beliefs and behaviors are likely to be influenced by their educational experiences and how these parental beliefs and behaviors actually influence children's achievement motivation in academic area.

Part 4

Women Empowerment and School Teachers

I

Women Empowerment and School Teachers

Introduction

"If you educate a man, you educate a person but if you educate woman you educate a nation" -Mahatma Gandhi

Education

Education is the heart of all development. It is essential pre-requisite for equality, dignity and lasting peace. Education is the weapon which strength the personality and makes one confident. Education in earlier days had the privilege of boys and men but now education has been spread all over breaking up the sex barrier and everyone is concerned about girl education as ecucation is an investment and not an expense which gives its returns in long urn in a positive way acknowledging the status of women in family which is the first step of progress and development.

Education is the unique investment for the present and future. It is backbone of a progressing nation. In a modern society, education alone can provide the most dependable and effective investment for accelerating growth and development in all phases of human activity.

Education means 'to draw out' facilitates realization of self potential and latent talents of an individual. Education is a fundamental right for all people, women and men throughout the world. Every person, child, youth and adult shall be able to benefit from educational opportunities designed to meet their basic learning needs to be able to survive, to develop their full capacities to live and work in dignity to improve the quality of their capacities to make informal decisions. Basic education should be provided to all children, youth and adults.

Education is a human right and an essential tool for achieving the goal of equality, development and peace. Education unlocks a woman's potential and is accompanied by improvements in health, nutrition and well being of women and their families.

Education is the basis of human development social transformation and national regeneration. India urgently needs a man making and nation building education as pointed out by Swami Vivekananda a hundred years ago. Our education needs the great vision to go ahead to inspire us and spiritual dynamism and unity to strengthen us. We need to "fight against the education which teaches that a country us greater than the ideals of humanity" as emphasized by Gurudeve Rabindranath Tagore.

Education as on the one hand "Opening up the world" material education and on the other hand "Creating openness in the individual". Formal education knowledge and thinking is an essential aspect of empowerment. Education enables a person to think for himself and others.

Education is empowerment. It is the key to establishing and reinforcing democracy, to development which is both sustainable and humane and to peace founded upon mutual respect and social justice. Indeed, in a world in which creativity and knowledge play an ever greater role, the right to education is nothing less than the right participate in the life of the modern world. The priority of priorities must be the education of women and girls there can be no ending success in basic education until the gender gap is closed.

Swami Vivekananda said "Just as a bird could fly with one wing only, a nation would not march forward if the women are left behind"

Mahatma Gandhi was very sensitive towards the problems of women he considered the women among the weakest and most deprived in society. Education can't deliver results overnight but it is only a part of the larger learning process. Nothing can change in a day or two. It cannot change you overnight but it gives something new to think about some new experiences.

Recovery embodies the process of reclaiming hope, humanity, equality, and dignity birthrights that women were stripped by society at large. They were denied the opportunity to express their views and to introspect and analyse their performance. There is need to stem to tide through a tremendous amount of awareness building through education and this should be our immediate objective. If we don't realize this we fail to harness women power.

Women's role in the contributing to the national development is significant women have started making headway as leaders, administrators and decision makers in different fields women also have the ability to think; They have the capacity for hard work and they are trying best to become proficient in several activities and professions.

Women constitute half of the world's population, accomplish about two third of its working hours receive one tenth of the world's income and the rural women in India in agriculture 77% of the female population. They are active workers in agriculture environment conservation and for production. In some families they are the sole bread winners. It has been recognized that if nation has to progress the deprived half-women must be equal partners.

A teacher takes a pivotal role in any system of education as the teacher has a key role to play in this total process. Teachers acts as an importance formative force on the development of society. It is only a competent teacher who can in some measure be worthy of trust that is placed on him by society.

Aims of Education

Instead of the traditional aim of education like "All round development" (physical, intellectual, social and spiritual) this frame work has listed the following

1. Independence of thought and action.
2. Sensitivity to others well being and feelings.
3. Learning to respond to new situations in a flexible and creative manner.
4. The ability to work towards and contribute to economic process and social change.
5. Predisposition towards participation in democratic process.

Educational Policy

The educational policy as contained in our national vision 2020 is as follows

1. Achieve universal basic education and educate each individual to his or her adult maximum potential.
2. Eradicate adult literacy.
3. Increase female enrolments and completion rates at all levels in the educational system.
4. Increase school enrolments and reduce drop-out rates of rural populations at all levels of the educational system.
5. Improve the quality of education and give greater emphasis to science and technology at all levels.
6. Expand and increases access to secondary and tertiary education

EMPOWERMENT: It's about what you do, not what you say

"Empowerment" is a term all too frequently used like paradigm and "thinking outside the box" after a while we get tired of hearing it. Since it is often overused and misused, it begins to lose its true meaning and usefulness, often ignored or rejected. Empowerment means to give someone power or authority.

Empowerment refers to increasing the spiritual, political, social or economic strength of individual and communities. It often involves the empowered developing confidence in their own capacities. Empowerment is then the process of obtaining these people or through the help of non-marginalized others who share their own access to these opportunities. It also includes encouraging and developing the skills for self-sufficiency with a focus on eliminating the future need for charity of welfare in the individuals of the groups.

Empowerment can have four components: cognitive, psychological, economic and political.

1. The cognitive component would include the "women are understanding of their conditions of subordination and the causes of such conditions at not micro and macro levels of society. It involves acquiring new knowledge to create a different understanding of gender relations as well as destroying old beliefs that structure powerful gender ideologies."
2. The psychological component would include the "development of feelings that women can act upon to improve their condition. This means formation of the belief that they can succeed in change efforts."
3. The economic component "requires that women be able to engage in a productive activity that will allow them some degree of autonomy, no matter how small and hard to obtain at the beginning.
4. The political component would encompass the "ability to organize and mobilize for change.

Empowerment refers to accelerate and also to develop the self, spiritual, political, socio economical strength.

Empowerment implies

1. Self development and self identity

2. Access to knowledge and information's
3. Ability to bring changes
4. Capacity building
5. Increasing self confidence and esteem
6. Realizing potentialities and identities

Empowerment Means 'M' Powerment

There are three M's for empowerment – Money power, Mind power and Muscle power

Money Power

This can be translated into financial independence, employment, economic security, which is the most important factor of empowerment. It gives to the individual. Economic independence builds up self confidence. Money power provides social status. It harnesses individuality of a person. Education is the key to achieve money power.

Mind Power

This symbolizes strong psyche, independent decision making freedom of thoughts, conviction and taking responsibility of one's decision. If you have strong self-image, it builds up confidence; clarity of thoughts is necessary for achieving goals in life; emotional management is required to lead the life with conviction. Knowledge and awareness of present situation develop positive personality. Strong mind and personality reduce the risk of vulnerability.

Muscle Power

Here it translates as physical strength. Women are always believed to be weak. This makes them more susceptible to surrender to any violence are atrocities. To fight against these, realization of physical strength is necessary in women. They play secondary role hence do not pay any attention towards themselves. To keep fit, women should have proper balanced diet. For self-defense, mind and body should work in tandem. Participation in sports activities increases physical and mental strength.

Indicators of empowerment

Understanding that empowerment is a complex issue with varying interpretations in different societal, national and cultural contexts, the participation also came out with a tentative listing of indicators.

At the level of the individual women and her household

1. Participation in crucial decision-making process
2. Extend of sharing of domestic work by men
3. Extend to which a women takes control of her reproductive functions and decides on family size
4. Extend to which a woman is able to decide where the income she has earned will be channeled to
5. Feeling and expression of pride and value in her work
6. Self-confidence and self –esteem and
7. Ability to prevent violence

At the community and/or organizational level

1. Existence of women's organizations
2. Allocation of funds to women and women's projects
3. Increased number of women leaders at vil age, district, provincial and national levels
4. Involvement of women in the design, development and application of technology
5. Participation in community programmes, productive enterprises, politics and arts
6. Involvement of women in non-traditional tasks

7. Increased training programmes for women and
8. Exercising her legal rights when necessary.

At the national level

1. Awareness of her social and political rights
2. Integration of women in the general national development plan
3. Existence of women's networks and publications
4. Extent to which women are officially visible and recognized and
5. The degree to which the media take heed of women's issues.

The process of empowerment

The process which enables individuals/groups to fully access personal/collective power, authority and influence, and to employ that strength when engaging with other people, institutions or society. In other words, "Empowerment is not giving people power; people already have plenty of power, in the wealth of their knowledge and motivation, to do their jobs magnificently. We define empowerment as letting this power out (Blanchard.K)." It encourages people to gain the skills and knowledge that will allow them to overcome obstacles in life or work environment and ultimately, help them develop within themselves or in the society.

Empowerment includes the following or similar capabilities

1. The ability to make decisions about personal/collective circumstances
2. The ability to access information and resources for decision-making
3. Ability to consider a range of options from which to choose (not just yes/no, either/or.)
4. Ability to exercise assertiveness in collective decision making

5. Having positive-thinking about the ability to make change
6. Ability to learn and access skills for improving personal/ collective circumstance.
7. Ability to inform other's perceptions though exchange, education and engagement.
8. Involving in the growth process and changes that is never ending and self-initiated
9. Increasing one's positive self-image and overcoming stigma
10. Increasing one's ability in discrete thinking to sort out right and wrong.

Women Empowerment

The empowerment of women also called gender empowerment, has become a significant topic of discussion in regards to development and economics. Entire nations, businesses, communities, and groups can benefit from the implementation of programs and policies that adopt the notion of women empowerment. Empowerment is one of the main procedural concerns when addressing human rights and development. The Human Development and Capabil ties Approach, The Millennium Development Goals, and other credible approaches/ goals point to empowerment and participation as a necessary step if a country is to overcome the obstacles associated with poverty and development.

Women empowerment needs require focus because

1. Women constitute one half of the segment of population in India. We cannot afford to keep them out of him main streams.
2. Women are vital and productive workers in India's national economy.
3. Women make up one third of the labour force.
4. The poorer the family the greater is the dependence on women's economic productivity is an important households below the poverty line.

5. Women's earning has positive correlation with children's health nutrition levels and education.
6. Today woman are no longer regarded as slaves or drudges. Our constitution grants them equality of status and opportunity with men.

Concept of women Empowerment

Women empowerment is a process by which women gain greater control over material and intellectual resources, it is a changing of power in terms of resources distribution and changes in ideology. Today women are emerging as leaders in a large number of fields be it aeronautics, medicine, space engineering, law, politics, education, you name the profession and they are there women currently hold nearly 16% of the top executive positions in the universities of the United States and the same trend is being seen in India too. The nature of empowerment renders it difficult to define. On the one hand, it is often referred to as a goal for many development programmes / projects. On the other hand, it can also be conceived as a process that people undergo, which eventually leads to changes.

Women empowerment has five components

5. Women's sense of self-worth
6. Their right to have and to determine choices
7. Their right to have access to opportunities resources
8. Their right to have the power to control their own lives, both within and outside the home
9. Their ability to influence their direction of social change to create a more just social and economical order, nationality and internationality

Strategies For Empowerment of Women

Empowerment is a multidimensional process which should enable individuals or a group of individuals to realize their full identity and powers in all sphere of life. It consists of greater access to knowledge and resources, greater autonomy in decision making to enable them to have greater ability to plan their lives, or have greater control over the circumstances that influence their lives and free them from shackles imposed on them by custom, belief and practice. Generally, development with justice is expected to generate the forces that lead to empowerment of various sections of population in a country and raise their status.

Pandit Jawaharlal Nehru said "To awaken the people, it is women who must be awakened; once she is on the move, the family moves, the village moves and the nation moves"

The empowerment mechanism is easily enumerated. We all agree that women should have

1. Higher literacy and education
2. Better care of health for herself and her children
3. Higher age at marriage
4. Acceptance of a small family norm
5. Greater work participant in modernized sector
6. Self reliance, self respect and dignity among women
7. Better consciousness of their rights
8. No dependent on males
9. Higher standard of living etc

Let us empower our students first by

1. Removing sex bias in our curriculum and by designing course incorporating women's dimensions
2. Emphasizing on the multiple role of women
3. Developing the ability to think creatively about situations hurdles to face, possibilities of change, the coping mechanism

etc.,

4. Overcoming social taboos and traditional beliefs
5. Encouraging late marriages
6. Sensitizing them to laws related to property, marriage, divorce, minimum wages, maternity leave benefit etc
7. Encouraging them to take careers seriously
8. Encouraging to believe in their own ability and a sense self worth
9. Helping them to develop interest in application of science
10. Making them aware of possibilities of self employment
11. Educating parents on the importance of making women economically self sufficient

Policy for the Empowerment of Women

In order to address the concerns of women in society, the Government of India has established the Department of women and Child development with the Ministry of Human Resources Development. A National Policy for the Empowerment of Women, 2001, provides the framework for addressing women's issues. The objectives of the policy are as follows

1. Creating an environment through positive economic and social policies for full development of women to enable them to realize their full potential
2. The de-jure and de-facto enjoyment of all human rights and fundamental freedom by women on equal basis with men in all spheres -political, economic, social, cultural and civil.
3. Equal access to participation and decision-making of women in social, political and economic life of the nation.
4. Equal access of women to health care, quality education at all levels, career and vocational guidance, employment, equal

remuneration, occupational health and safety, social security and public office etc.

5. Strengthening legal systems aimed at elimination of all forms of discrimination against women.
6. Changing societal attitude and community practices by active participation and involvement of both men and women.
7. Mainstreaming a gender perspective in the development process.
8. Elimination of discrimination and all forms of violence against women and the girl child.
9. Building and strengthening partnerships with civil society, particularly women's organizations.

Policies adopted for implementation on women

1. Five year plan approach
2. Integrated rural development programme (centrally sponsored scheme)
3. Training or rural youth for self employment (TRYSEM)
4. Mahila Samridha Yojana(Aug 95. This scheme aimed at empowering women through a sustained process of awareness generation and their direct access to resources)

Despite tremendous efforts made to make women equal with men in education as well as in socio-economic development in India

Empowering Quotes for Women

If a woman can only succeed by emulating men, I think it is a great loss and not a success. The aim is not only for a woman to succeed, but to keep her womanhood and let her womanhood influence society. - Suzanne Brogger

Women's empowerment is intertwined with respect for human rights. - **Mahnaz Afkhami**

My mother told me to be a lady. And for her, that meant be your own person, be independent. - Ruth Bader Ginsburg

I was raised in Boston by three older brothers and a very strong and empowering single mom. - Eliza Dushku

Woman must not accept; she must challenge. She must not be awed by that which has been built up around her; she must reverence that woman in her which struggles for expression. - Margaret Sanger

The beauty of empowering others is that your own power is not diminished in the process. - Barbara Colorose

What is empowerment and what empowers women?

Empowerment is both a process and a result, that cannot be measured nor can it be taken by some individual or institution/ organization and given to somebody else. A woman can only empower herself; organizations (through logistic support) and, governments (through their gender just policies) can play a role in supporting the journey and providing an enabling environment.

Women are empowered when they become aware of the unfair power relations they face and are able to take the challenge to overcome inequality. Empowerment enables women to take control over their lives and builds self-confidence and self- reliance.

In order to build self-confidence and to evolve a female agenda, besides education, formation of coalitions to have a united strong voice is equally important. Women's movement advocated country wide formation of grassroots and professional women's groups/ coalitions around a common goal. And thus empower women to ask for gender just laws and institutions and if justice is being denied to law in their own hands. Through women's activism, introduction of equality in discriminatory laws relating to marriage, dowry, divorce, inheritance and domestic violence have been introduced and this has empowered women.

The government of India under pressure from the women activity and international aid agencies has followed a policy of positive discrimination in government employment and in changing the legal system to bring about gender equality in access to education and health and participation in local decision making.

It set up a Commission in 1975 to identify the extent of inequality and discrimination and another enquiry to evaluate the effect of gender just policies after quarter of a century in 2002 which reported that, "After 55 years of Independence, gender equality is nowhere in view".

Women are still unequal to men, but the last quarter of a century has seen tremendous improvement in their status through progress in education, in having better health and longevity of life and entry into jobs in the organized sectors. While we have found no direct correlation between increase in education with female work participation rate and representation in legislatures, education does lead to individual development and creates awareness about individual rights and is thus empowering at the individual level.

Ways to Empower Women

One way to deploy the empowerment of women is through land rights. Land rights offer a key way to economically empower women, giving them the confidence they need to tackle gender inequalities. Often, women in developing nations are legally restricted from their land on the sole basis of gender. They encounter tremendous barriers to claim the land that should rightfully be theirs. Having a right to their land also gives women a sort of bargaining power that they wouldn't normally have, in turn; they gain the ability to assert themselves in various aspects of their life, both in and outside of the home.

Another way to provide women empowerment is to allocate responsibilities to them that normally belong to men. When women have economic empowerment, it is a way for others to see them as equal members of society. Through this, they achieve more self-respect and confidence by their contributions to their communities. Simply including women as a part of a community can have sweeping positive effects.

In a study conducted by Bina Agarwal, women were given a place in a forest conservation group. Not only did this drive up the efficiency of the group, but the women gained incredible self-esteem while others, including men, viewed them with more respect. Participation, which can be seen and gained in a variety of ways, has been argued to be the most beneficial form of gender empowerment.

Political participation, be it the ability to vote and voice opinions, or the ability to run for office with a fair chance of being elected, plays a huge role in the empowerment of peoples. However, participation is not limited to the realm of politics. It can include participation in the household, in schools, and the ability to make choices for one. It can be said that these latter participations need to be achieved before one can move onto broader political participation.

When women have the agency to do what she wants, a higher equality between men and women is established. It is argued that Micro credit also offers a way to provide empowerment for women. Governments, organizations, and individuals have caught hold of the lure of microfinance. They hope that lending money and credit allows women to function in business and society, which in turn empowers them to do more in their communities.

One of the primary goals in the foundation of microfinance was women empowerment. Loans with low interest rates are given to women in developing communities in hopes that they can start a small business and provide for her family. It should be said, however, that the success and efficiency of micro credit and micro loans is controversial and constantly debated

Economic Benefits of Women Empowerment

Most women across the globe rely on the informal work sector for an income. If women were empowered to do more and be more, the possibility for economic growth becomes apparent. Eliminating half of a nation's work force on the sole basis of gender can have detrimental effects on the economy of that nation. In addition, female participation in counsels, groups, and businesses is seen to increase efficiency. For a general idea on how an empowered women can impact a situation monetarily.

Economics and empowerment

In economic development, the empowerment approach focuses on mobilizing the self-help efforts of the poor, rather than providing them with social welfare. Economic empowerment is also the empowering of previously disadvantaged sections of the population.

Role of education in empowering Women

1. An educated woman can be of immense help on different ways for the family.
2. Education gives power to a woman to become strong physically by giving her knowledge about sports, exercise health-related aspects, and good physical health; this will definitely benefit her mental health.
3. Education helps in the mental development of women and a mentally satisfied and contented woman is an asset to a family, society and nation and she can use her efficiency and potential in right manner. She can maintain a proper balance between physical health and mental health with good education.
4. Education promotes team work rather than making a woman individualistic. It develops the feeling of us.
5. Education provides financial and economic security to a woman and a secured woman can do anything. Feeling of security always motivates a person to do constructive activities and with that she can prove her worthiness.
6. Every woman has got her own aspiration which may be high or low but education helps to maintain a balanced aspiration knowing her interest, ability and potential which further helps her to choose a correct field of her work so that she can become a contributing factor to the family, society.
7. An educated woman is a guiding light for her children, family members, society and nation. She knows how to have a happy family and balanced and health relations with others. As it is rightly said, "There is a woman behind the success of every-man"

8. Education gives knowledge about values of life; it teaches us about how to accept and face the challenges of life.
9. Educated women can solve many problems of the society. It makes her self-disciplined and gives her version.
10. An educated woman can bring change in the attitude of family members and society by questioning the conservative thoughts of the people and blind faith. It helps in removing mal-traditions like Sati, Partha, Dowry, early marriage, etc
11. Education provides a clear perspective of life to women
12. Education plays an important role in making women self-reliant
13. Education has played an important role in solving the problem of gender bias; it helps women in time management
14. Women empowerment is possible with education as it helps her become socially, economically, politically, culturally and morally strong.

The Profile of Empowered Woman

The empowered woman appreciates the time she spends on domestic work and outside the home. She is aware that over work is harmful to her physical and mental condition and that health is vital. She is able to question her double responsibility and seeks help from others to have enough leisure to spend on learning and participating in the social and political life of the community.

The empowered women understand that she is a human being and can control her own life. Hence, she could and should question the family and social practices which negatively affect her. She seeks to get scientific insights into superstitions, and challenges those which are unjust to women. She has freedom of movement and expression on a par with men. She appreciates her strength and weaknesses and seeks self-improvement. She can lead and serve as a positive role model for other women.

The empowered woman is aware of her rights as a citizen and protects them actively. She is convinced of her equality with men. She knows which laws and legal process treat women unfairly and seeks to use her legal knowledge to product her own and other women's rights.

The empowered woman respects herself dares take credit and responsibility for her contribution and action. She looks for absence and makes informed decisions. She dares to be different and creative. The empowered woman appreciates and supports other women. She is aware that organization means strength and seeks to strengthen her organizational, management and leadership skills.

The empowered woman is aware that her health is related to the number of children she has. She respects the dignity of womanhood and appreciates daughters in the same way she does sons. The empowered woman nurtures herself. She wants everybody to understand that, as a human being, she is entitled to happiness in the same way that others are. She has a zest for life.

Definition of the Terms

Awareness

Paraphrasing Website's Collegiate dictionary, awareness implies vigilance in observing something or experience and alertness in drawing influences from what one observes.

Awareness in a personal development which helps sense is a consciousness of which you are being and the impact that you are having others. Heighten your awareness by imaging a small creature on your think and what you do and whispers what he observe in your ear.

Empowerment

Definitions of empowerment vary but Paz is most succient, it is "the ability to direct and control one's own life" (Paz 1990)

Empowerment defines as a "a process to change the distribution of power both in interpersonal relations and in institutions throughout society"- Nelly Stromquist

Empowerment is a sociopolitical concept that goes beyond "formal political participation" and "consciousness raising". A full definition of empowerment must include cognitive, psychological, political and economic components.

School Teachers

School Teachers is any school recognized by Government of Tamilnadu for giving instructions to students at the terminal stage of school education.

Scope of the Study

The topic is an investigation of the awareness on women empowerment among teachers. Since this is the survey study. The investigator attempt to know the awareness on women empowerment among the teachers.

This study will be grate help for the educationists particularly for the teachers. Since the concept of women empowerment has been changed from time to time.

The awareness may differ person to person. One can learn he had a better awareness towards it. If we compel anybody to do any work in which one does not have good awareness and then it may be the root cause for many problems. It may give a mental fatigue to a person. Thus he can't do it effectively. In this context the investigator attempts to study the Awareness on women empowerment among teachers in various schools in Sivakasi Taluk.

Objectives of the Study

1. To find out the level of significant difference between Male and Female teachers with respect to awareness on women empowerment.
2. To find out the level of significant difference between the locality of male and female teachers with respect to awareness on women empowerment.

3. To find out the level of significant difference between Age group (below-35) of male and female teachers with respect to awareness on women empowerment.
4. To find out the level of significant difference between Age group (above-35) of male and female teachers with respect to awareness on women empowerment.
5. To find out the level of significant difference between educational qualification (UG) of male and female teachers with respect to awareness on women empowerment.
6. To find out the level of significant difference between the educational qualification (PG) of male and female teachers with respect to awareness on women empowe-ment.
7. To find out the level of significant difference between teaching experience (below 10 years) of male and female teachers with respect to awareness on women empowerment.
8. To find out the level of significant difference between teaching experience (above 10 years) of male and female teachers with respect to awareness on women empowerment.
9. To find out the level of significant difference between married male and married female teachers with respect to awareness on women empowerment.
10. To find out the level of significant difference between unmarried male and unmarried female teachers with respect to awareness on women empowerment.

Hypothesis of the study

1. There is no significant difference between Male and Female teachers with respect to awareness on women empowerment.
2. There is no significant difference between the localities of male and female teachers with respect to awareness on women empowerment.
3. There is no significant difference between Age group (below-35) of male and female teachers with respect to awareness on

women empowerment.

4. There is no significant difference between Age group (above-35) of male and female teachers with respect to awareness on women empowerment.
5. There is no significant difference between educational qualification (UG) of male and female teachers with respect to awareness on women empowerment.
6. There is no significant difference between the educational qualification (PG) of male and female teachers with respect to awareness on women empowerment.
7. There is no significant difference between teaching experience (below 10 years) of male and female teachers with respect to awareness on women empowerment.
8. There is no significant difference between teaching experience (above 10 years) of male and female teachers with respect to awareness on women empowerment.
9. There is no significant difference between married male and married female teachers with respect to awareness on women empowerment.
10. There is no significant difference between unmarried male and unmarried female teachers with respect to awareness on women empowerment.

Delimitations of the Study

Broadly speaking, any study is impossible without limitation. Research studies in general will have limitation due to many factors. This study has some limitations. It is the responsibility of the researcher to see that the study is conducted with the maximum care in order to be reliable. However the following limitations were unavoidable in the present study,

1. The study has been limited to Sivakasi Taluk.
2. The investigator was unable to investigate to all the schools,

few schools were selected to investigate on it. The study was concerned to only thirteen schools in Sivakasi Taluk.

3. In this present study the investigator analysed about the awareness of the variable such as gender, locality, age, educational qualification, teaching experience, marital status.

In spite of the above mentioned limitations, sufficient care has been taken in selecting the sample, constructing the tool, gathering reliable data applying appropriate a statistical analysis etc.

Organisation of the Study

The report of the study will be presented according to the following sequences

S.NO	Chapters	Overview
1	Chapter-I	The first chapter deals with introduction, definitions of the terms, Objectives, Hypothesis and Limitations of the study.
2	Chapter-II	Second chapter deals with the review of literature which are done in India and abroad related to this study.
3	Chapter-II	Third chapter gives a detailed account of research procedures and methodology used in this study.
4	Chapter-IV	Fourth chapter deals with the statistical analysis and the interpretations of the data in detail.
5	Chapter-V	Fifth chapter describe the findings, conclusions and certain recommendations for the further study

This followed by the bibliography

The ensuring chapter deals with the Review of Related Literature.

2

Review of Related Literature

Introduction

"A good Dissertation is one that me how to replicate or extend the previous work with improvement to reduce bias, eliminate flaws, consider pertinent variables, settle unsolved issues to check contradictory or uncertain finding". The aim of this chapter is to record briefly a survey of literature related to the problems understudy. It is necessary to enter on any research project. This will help in understanding the various aspects of the problem. The research worker must be acquainted with up to-date information about what has been thought and done in the specific area from which he intends to take up a problem research.

A review or related literature gives the scholar an understanding of the previous work that has been done in area, it enables him to know the means of getting to the frontier in the field of his problems, methods and limitations and it enables him to locate comparative data useful in the interpretation. A review of literature is the mirror of earlier studies, which enriches the researcher and helps to identify the gaps for further research.

Purpose of Review Literature

The following are the some of the purpose of the review of literature.

1. It provides ideas, theories, explanations or hypothesis valuable in formulation of the problem
2. To avoid the risk of duplicating some of the studies already undertaken
3. To suggest methods or research methodology appropriate to the problem
4. It widens the horizon of the researcher
5. It suggests valuable basis for hypothesis
6. It helps delimit the problem
7. It helps the investigator not to allow the mistake (or) loophole (or) pitfall which occurred in the previous findings
8. To locate comparative data useful in the interpretation of results
9. It contributes to the investigator for the general scholarship

Review of Related Literature

A review of previous investigations relevant to the research study taken by the investigator is necessary to gain better perspective of the problem. Such a review being new thought and helps in the development of the research procedures and instrument.

"Practically all human knowledge can be found in book and library. Unlike other living beings that must start new with each generation, man build upon the accumulated and recorded knowledge of the past"- Best.A

Therefore in this chapter an attempt has been made to have survey of various studies conducted by others in the topic of women empowerment. The researcher has taken 11 studies from India and 6 studies from Abroad.

Studies Conducted in India

Title: Women literacy and empowerment an analysis of the Nellore experience in AndraPradesh

Author : Anita Dighe (1993)

She has identified the following categories of empowerment: Empowerment of marginalized groups, process orient nature empowerment, holistic nature of empowerment, empowerment for dealing with strategic rather than practical gender interests, cognitive, psychological and economic components of empowerment. She also states that the empowerment for democratization and empowerment for understanding the native character of literacy influences the specific nature of empowerment.

Title : Empowering rural women

Author(s) : Sakuntala Narasimha(1999)

Sakuntala Narasimha in her study on empowering rural women focused that the rural women's development through self help groups received priority for the first time during the 6th plan period. The emphasis, however, continue to be on the economic front through programme such as Development of women and children in rural area and others. It was conceded that none of these projects has delivered the expected results in the form of overall betterment of women's status in SC/ST communities. The reasons are lack of identification with the spirit of prokects among the official entrusted with the implementation procedural bases and most failure to involve the beneficiary populations as participants.

Title : Capacity building for effective empowerment of women

Author(s) : Gupta.V.S.(June 2002)

Gupta in his research study stresses the importance of empowerment of women. He refers empowerment as a process of exposing the oppressive power of existing gender relations. The study focus on bringing together and learning lessons from efforts to strengthen the capabilities of women from marginalized sections towards their empowerment.

Title: The role of education in the empowerment of women in a district of West Bengal

Author(s) : Haimanti Mukhopadhyay (2002)

This study confirms that "women's status is inferior to men" in Malda district. Women face discrimination within families as well as in society maintains double standards in the case of education, marriage spousal relationships, domestic violence, laws of patriarchal society, property laws, dowry system, sexual morality, sexual harassment as well as discrimination social stigma and also less recognition and respect for women's work.

Title : Programme for empowering rural women

Author(s) : Hemalatha (2002)

Hemalatha conducted a study on programme for empowering rural women. She focused that gender is very important in development, significantly as it gives not only an opportunity for women to take up the development process but also have control over their lives. According to her study, the development of women and children in rural area programme has enabled the women not only to augment their income through self help groups but also to make a decision on spending the same. The development of women and children in rural area programme indirectly influenced the women's development as they have improved their awareness on the various development programme.

Title : Women empowerment and development of women and children in rural area

Author(s): Narasim Huluk and Annapurna.K(2002)

Narasim Huluk and Annapurna made a study on Women empowerment and development of women and children in rural area. In the study, they bring out that to nerve the purpose of women empowerment. The Government of A.P has taken up the theme of women's empowerment as one of the main agenda to tackle rural poverty and socio-economic issues. Women have taken up self help movement through thrift and savings a mass movement to shape their future destiny. The state government is consciously making an effort to asses these self help group's by providing revolving fund under development of women and children in rural area. The study gives the details of development of women and children in rural area groups in Chittor district. The problems of development of women and children in rural area members have been found out and suggestions have been given as the researcher.

Title : Women empowerment through self help groups

Author(S) : Dr.K.A.Rasure (2002)

Rasure in his study on women's empowerment through self help groups endorse that empowerment should be externally induced, so that women can exercise a level of autonomy. There should be self-empowerment so that women can look at their own lives. The findings reveal that the genesis of self help groups could be treated to mutual aid in a form of co-operation. He has stated that the self help and reliance are strategies of survival as well as development of the poor.

Title : Empowerment of Rural Women

Author(s): Sujit kumar Dulta and Dilip Kumar Ghose (2002)

Sujit kumar Dulta and Dilip Kumar Ghose made a study on women empowerment through literacy in Birbhum district of West Bengal. The study mainly concentrates on Integrated Rural Development programme, a major strategy for poverty alleviation in rural India. From the findings of the study it becomes clear hat literacy is indispensable for reaping the benefits of programme, which is meant to meet the need of the poor.

Title : Women's empowerment: experience from watershed project, Social Welfare

Author(s) : Joshi, Meenakshi. (2004).

This paper analyzed the impact of interventions on women in a project being implemented in Uttaranchal. The study covers rural areas of District Pauri, Nainital and Udhamsingh Nagar. It was found that there were 496 SHGs linked with 6700 women. Construction of water harvesting tanks, irrigation channels, biogas and fodder plantation have reduced the drudgery of women to a certain extent. These interventions have resulted in women saving around two to three hours, which is utilized for awareness programmes, group activities, and Income Generating Activities (IGAs), Capacity Building Activities, and so on. Women in the project area now have greater awareness regarding their roles, responsibilities and rights. Women have generated group savings of about Rs.30 lakhs. The average group fund size is approximately Rs.6000/-. SHGs members have been earning between Rs.500- 6000 since taking up various IGAs. Capacity building, support and involvement in economic activity have helped women to gain respect and self-confidence. The study also found increased role of "women as a group" in solving community problems by their 'shramdan'. Participation in Panchayati Raj institutions and their role in decision-making had also increased. Study suggests that the State could capitalize on project interventions in agriculture and horticulture by developing a brand name for Micro enterprise products of SHGs from Uttaranchal. These efforts need to be maintained and strengthened, and should aim at placing women at the center of project activities.

Title : Economic empowerment of women through Information Technology

Author(s) : Dr.P.N.Prasad and Dr.Sreedevi (2007)

As a result of this, gender gap in the digital divide is increasing in many developed countries. It is imperative to ensure that women in developing countries understand the significance of ICT and use them for their economic and social empowerment. In the days to come, lack of proper use of ICT becomes a significant factor in the marginalization of women from the economic, social and political mainstream of their countries. Information technology can offer significant opportunities for virtually all girls and women in developing countries, including poor women in rural areas. They have begun to consider ICT as a tool for attaining knowledge and development by everyone. The strategy to encourage the participation of the poor women in the digital revolution is expected to reduce the gap in digital and gender divide in this state. The economic empowerment of women via ICT enables them to challenge discrimination and overcome gender barriers.

Title : Enhancing women's empowerment through information and communication technology : a report.

Author(s) : Voluntary Association for People Services, Virudhunagar (2008).

The present study was carried out to assess ICT infrastructure in rural areas vis-à-vis that in urban areas for women's empowerment, and to assess the status of ICT in education in terms of policies regarding scholarships, reservations, business development programmes, etc. For self-employment opportunities for women. The study was conducted in all five major corporations in the state of Tamil Nadu, i.e. Chennai, Thiruchirappalli, Madurai, Coimbatore, and Thirunelveli. The total sample size was 500 women/ girls. Out of 500 respondents, the highest number of women/ girls interviewed was in the age group of 32 years, followed by girls below 17 years. Majority of the respondents were college educated (374), followed by school educated (57), technically educated (44), and the rest were just literate or those who had no schooling. It was found that ICT introduction has made life easier for 284 respondents, followed by 169 who somewhat agreed. Only 24 and 19 respondents said that they did not know, or could not say respectively, whereas only 3 respondents said that they did not agreed with the idea. 224 respondents said that ICTs were easily available, 23 respondents disagreed, and 52 said that they did not know. Only 30 respondents said that they used information technology, 12 for booking tickets, 27 to get information about different aspects of life, and 5 persons said they used IT for banking and insurance. Out of the 500 respondents, 111 said they got information from the Internet, which showed that Internet facility was available in their locality. 90 respondents said communication was through print media, and 33 mentioned radio as a source of information. Of the respondents who said there was easy availability of the Internet, the highest number (170) said they preferred cyber cafes. 116 said they used IT in the office, both for official purposes and personal work. Respondents used Internet according to their need, but only 103 said that they used it almost regularly. 118 respondents used Internet once a week, 88 used it when they felt it necessary, 66 used it very rarely and also said that it was not necessary for them to use Internet daily or for unnecessary purposes. 48 said that they never used the Internet. 234 respondents strongly agreed that ICT had enabled women to know what is happening across the globe more easily. 376 respondents said that it was essential in their job. Regarding the facility of working from home, 215 respondents said they were to some extent provided this facility of working from home. Also, 132 strongly agreed that ICT enabled people to work from home. About 204 respondents said it took away women's relaxation time. Majority (258) of the respondents wanted to make use of ICT for the next generation. It was concluded that the use of ICT helps to bridge the gap between people's opportunities for self-employment in the informal economy and the high growth sectors of the world's economy.

Studies CONDUCTED IN abroad

Title : Empowerment of women in South Asia in speaking out women's Economic empowerment in South Asia

Author(s) : Srilatha Batlivala(1996)

She says that those who promote women's empowerment through integral rural development programme describe women's disempowerment to their lack of education, low economic status, lack of access of resources and low decision making power. Those who promote women's empowerment through awareness building and organizing women see women's disempowerment as stemming from a complex interplay factors-historical, culture, social and economic and political.

Title : Women empowerment and Youth Perception in Pakistan

Author(s) : Iram Naz and Sami Ullah (1998)

The study was conceived to find out the attitude of male youth along with their family practice towards women empowerment. They have shown positive attitude and proactive family practice. It shows that because of better level of education and awareness on gender issue, the attitude of male youth has been transform. At the same time they also show positive practice in the areas of voter registration and vote casting which may be is a result of personal gains of family males to support the desired person. They also have shown positive practice in giving ownership of property to their family women because of the respect for Islamic and inheritance right. The results suggest that on these areas the attitude was positive but the practice in the family was limiter. IT shows that the male youth have gathered positive awareness on the issues of women empowerment and they have transformed their attitude according to it. But on the other hand they are not able to transform it in practice because of the present social setup. Youth have positive attitude because of their better educational background but on the other hand the parents have educational background that is more of inferior quality which is a reason of worse practice in the family. But Women empowerment is a social phenomenon so any change in a social phenomenon is gradual and slow in nature. It will take time to bring a change in the situation of women empowerment in the country.

Title: The Determinants of women empowerment in Southern Punjab (Pakistan)

Author(s): Imran Sharif Chaudhry (1999)

He concluded that women empowerment which is declared as Millennium Development Goal by UNDP, could be achieved only when all concerned bodies will work in cooperation and understanding the factors analyzed in this paper. The society as a whole has to understand women's capabilities and their contributions to the developmental process. Empowering women is an important end in itself not only as human right issue but also having the potential to enhance human well being. Empowering women and improving their status are essential ingredients for realizing the full potential of the economic and potential development of the entire society thus ensuring sustainable development.

Title: Women Empowerment in Oman: A study based on Women Empowerment Index

Author(s): Dr.Thresiamma Varghese (2002)

Women's empowerment is a process whereby women become able to organize themselves to increase their own self-reliance, to assert their independent right to make choices and to control resources which will assist in challenging and eliminating their own subordination" (Keller and Mbwewe, 1991).Empowering women is one of the most crucial concerns of the Millennium Development Goals of the United Nations. One of the national priorities and goals of the Human Resource Development Strategic Plan outlined by the Social Sector of the Ministry of Economic Development in Sultanate of Oman includes the vision of the development of women, upgrading the status of women and facilitating their integration into the total social development. The key objective of this research article is to measure the women empowerment in Oman by identifying the household decision making ability of women, to assess the economic decision making capability of women and evaluate the freedom of mobility of women for giving recommendation and suggestions to boost women empowerment in Oman. We have taken a sample of 150 women in Sohar region, Sultanate of Oman, with a structured questionnaire. Statistical package for social science (SPSS) is the main tool for data analysis and we used regression model and frequency tables. For quantitative analysis, we have taken by selecting five main variables as independent variables and total women empowerment as dependent variable. We have done a hypothesis testing by taking five hypotheses out of that four have accepted and one rejected. In qualitative analysis we have framed total women empowerment index that shows that women in Sohar are good decision makers. Another finding is that women in Oman are better in household decision making and economic decision making than social empowerment. We have also taken perception analysis via addressed different issues in legal and political side. The result shows that majority of women in Sohar region are aware about their rights and duties. Finally the study has given certain recommendations to further improve the empowerment of women in Sohar region.

Title: Girls' and Women's Education and their Empowerment among Pastoral Societies Case Study of Eritrea

Author(s): Abrehe Zemichael(2005)

Most of the recent literature on women and development focuses on education as an important instrument in the empowerment of women as it expands their knowledge and skills. Without education it is difficult to achieve women's empowerment. This paper analyzes girls' and women's education in Eritrea in general, and among pastoral societies in particular. The study attempts to point out early marriage, luck of adequate schools in rural areas, and gender stereotypes and gender biased ideologies in Eritrea are the major barriers that hinder girls and women's access to education thus, affecting their ability to achieve empowerment. These barriers are not tackled among the pastoral society and mere imposing formal education as an automatic solution proved to be unsuccessful. Accordingly, for empowering pastoral societies, particularly women, non formal education principles are likely to be more effective than mainstream formal education. Non formal education is more flexible and responsive in sustaining livelihood strategies of pastoralists.

Title: Women's Empowerment in Disaster Reconstruction: Critical Perspectives on Policies and Frameworks

Author(s): Thurairajah. N, Amaratunga. D, Haigh. R, School of the Built Environment, University of Salford (2006)

The post disaster stage, the impact of natural disasters and the consequent partial reconstruction efforts have presented many challenges to women. Hence, there is a need to enhance women's position within post disaster context. Further, many studies have acknowledged that although women are disproportionately affected by these disasters, their role in preventing and mitigating the effects of natural disasters is not well explored. Within this context, the main research investigates into empowerment of women during post disaster reconstruction in Sri Lanka. There are many factors which influence women's empowerment such as their contribution to household, access to resources, participation in household decision making, perception on gender awareness, etc. Among factors that influence women's empowerment, existing policies and frameworks is one of the important factors that can play a major role within post disaster reconstruction. Further, although there are legislations and policies to provide assistance to women, the lack of implementation of these remains a problem. Hence, in order to gain an understanding on the existing framework on women's empowerment, this study firstly examines the way the concept of empowerment has been viewed within development studies and later analyses the national and international policies and frameworks that exist within post disaster context in Sri Lanka. This study has been based on a theoretical as well as practical ideas obtained through a comprehensive literature review and interviews carried out among experts within the practice in Sri Lanka.

Analogy

Out of 17 studies identified, the investigator found 11 studies are conducted in India and 6 studies conducted in Abroad. Majority of the studies belonged to survey studies. Most of the studies followed random sampling technique in the collection of data and the size of the samples range from 100 to 500. In majority of the study the questionnaire opionnarie rating scale developed by the investigator was utilized as a tool. Mean, standard deviation t-test was the statistical technique followed\wed in the majority of the students. Since all the reviewed studies were selected to uses and awareness of women empowerment.

The findings of Anita Dighe(1993), Abrehe Zemichzle(2005), Haimhopadhayay(2007) states about the literacy . This finding is related to the present study.

The result of the few studies by Sakuntala Narasimha(1999), Sujit Kumar dulta and Dilip Kumar Ghose(2002), NArasim Huluk and Annapurna.K(2002), Hemalatha(2002) states the development of women in rural area programme indirectly influenced the women's development as they have improved their awareness on the various development programme. This result is related to the present study.

The findings of Dr. K.A.Rasure(20020,Dr.P.N.prasad and Dr.Sreedevi(2007), Iram Naz and Sami Ullah(1998) and Imran sharif chaudhry(1999) are new result to the present study.

The ensuring chapter deals with the Methodology.

III

Methodology

Introduction

This chapter deals about the plan and procedure of the entire study. Research is an essential and powerful tool in leading man towards progress. Without systematic research there would have been very little progress. John.W.Best (1996) said the secret of our cultural development has been research pushing back the areas of ignorance by discovering new truths, which intern lead to better ways of doing things and better products. Research is endless guest for knowledge or continuous search for truth. Research is considered to be the more formal, systematic and intensive process of carrying on a scientific method of analysis.

Educational research is a new field of research. Educational research involves an application of the main principles of scientific research to the solution of educational problems. According to John.W.Best (1996), Educational research is that activity which is directed towards development of a science of behavior in educational situation.

Statement of the Problem

The problem of the present study is stated as "A STUDY ON AWARENESS ON WOMEN EMPOWERMENT AMONG TEACHERS IN SIVAKASI TALUK".

Research Design

Research design decides the fate of the research proposal and it's out come. As such, it is regarded as the heart of any research; designing provides a picture for the whole study before starting the work. It is in a sample language, a plan of action. It is therefore, desirable to have a methodically designed research plan. Decisions regarding what, where, when, how much by what means concerning an inquiry of a research study constitute a research design. It is the arrangement of conditions for collection and analysis of data.

Objectives of the Study

1. To find out the level of significant difference between Male and Female teachers with respect to awareness on women empowerment.
2. To find out the level of significant difference between the locality of male and female teachers with respect to awareness on women empowerment.
3. To find out the level of significant difference between Age group (below-35) of male and female teachers w th respect to awareness on women empowerment.
4. To find out the level of significant difference between Age group (above-35) of male and female teachers with respect to awareness on women empowerment.
5. To find out the level of significant difference between educational qualification (UG) of male and female teachers with respect to awareness on women empowerment.
6. To find out the level of significant difference between the

educational qualification (PG) of male and female teachers with respect to awareness on women empowerment.

7. To find out the level of significant difference between teaching experience (below 10 years) of male and female teachers with respect to awareness on women empowerment.
8. To find out the level of significant difference between teaching experience (above 10 years) of male and female teachers with respect to awareness on women empowerment.
9. To find out the level of significant difference between married male and married female teachers with respect to awareness on women empowerment.
10. To find out the level of significant difference between un-married male and unmarried female teachers with respect to awareness on women empowerment

HypothesEs of the study

1. There is no significant difference between Male and Female teachers with respect to awareness on women empowerment.
2. There is no significant difference between the localities of male and female teachers with respect to awareness on women empowerment.
3. There is no significant difference between Age group (below-35) of male and female teachers with respect to awareness on women empowerment.
4. There is no significant difference between Age group (above-35) of male and female teachers with respect to awareness on women empowerment
5. There is no significant difference between educational qualifications (UG) of male and female teachers with respect to awareness on women empowerment.
6. There is no significant difference between the educational qualifications (PG) of male and female teachers with respect to awareness on women empowerment.

7. There is no significant difference between teaching experience (below 10 years) of male and female teachers with respect to awareness on women empowerment.
8. There is no significant difference between teaching experience (above 10 years) of male and female teachers with respect to awareness on women empowerment.
9. There is no significant difference between married male and married female teachers with respect to awareness on women empowerment.
10. There is no significant difference between unmarried male and unmarried female teachers with respect to awareness on women empowerment.

Method of the Study

Research methodology is a way to solve the research problem systematically. It is necessary for the researcher to know not only the research methods and the techniques but also the methodology. The methodology varies from problem to problem. ¯he researcher has to specify very clearly what decisions were selected and why he did select them and how they can be evaluated by others. The purpose of study may vary from researcher to researcher. But in any form of researcher, the investigator has to follow certain methods.

George J. Mowly has classified research methods into three basic types, namely.

1. Historic or documentary method
2. Experimental method
3. Normative survey method

In order to realize the objectives, the normative survey method is employed. Normative survey method studies describe and interpret what exists at present. They are concerned with exists at present. They are concerned with women empowerment; such investigations are termed in research literature as descriptive survey or normative survey.

Normative Survey Method

The Word 'survey' has been derived from the words 'sur' or 'ser' and 'vecir' or 'veidor' which means 'over' and 'see' respectively that is the term normally implies the determination of normal or typical conditions.

The normative survey method of education research is very common. It is the method of investigation which attempts to describe and interpret what exists at present in the form of conditions. It is concerned with the phenomena that are typical of the normal conditions.

Characteristics of Survey Method

1. It gathers data from a relatively large number of samples.
2. It involves defined problem and definite objectives.
3. It provides information useful to the solution of local problem.
4. It is not concerned with the characteristics of individuals.
5. It does not seek to develop and organized body of scientific principle.

In the present study the investigator intended to measure the "Awareness on Women Empowerment among Teachers". So here normative survey method is the best method for conducting research study.

Sample of the Study

It is a collection of a population which is select for the express purpose representing of the sample. One can make certain inferences about the characteristics of the population from which it is drawn.

There are certain well accepted methods often adopted for the selection of good samples. They are

1. Random sampling

2. Stratified sampling
3. Cluster sampling
4. Incidental sampling

TABLE 3.1

SCHEMATIC REPRESENTATION OF THE SAMPLE

S.NO	TYPE	SOURCE
1	Nature of the Research	Normative Survey method
2	Variables	(a) Locality (b) Gender (c) Age (d) Qualification (e) Teaching Experience (f) Marital Status
3	Tools used	➢ A scale to measure attitude towards women – B.R.Bhadra and P.R.Girija ➢ Status of women empowerment-B.A.Parikh ➢Attitude towards women scale – Nandhini Deevan From this the investigator consolidated women empowerment scale to 40 questions
4	Sampling Technique	Stratified Random Sampling
5	Size of the sample	150 (Male-75, Female-75)

For the present study the stratified sampling method was used. When employing this technique the researcher divides his population is strata on the basis of some characteristics and from each of this smaller homogenous groups draws at random a predetermined number of units for this study while selection the sample following categories of Women Empowerment shown in table 3.2. The researcher selected 150 (75 Male and 75 Female) samples for the study.

Different Sampling Technique

The process by which a relatively small number of individuals or measures of individuals, objects or events or selected or analyzed in order to find out something about the entire population of the universe from which it was selected (Cornell).

TABLE 3.2

SCHEMATIC TABLE ON VARIABLES AND CATEGORY WISE SAMPLE

Variables	Sub-categories	Size	Total
Gender	Male	75	150
	Female	75	
Locality	Rural	76	150
	Urban	74	
Age	Below 35 yrs	79	150
	Above 35 yrs	71	
Educational qualification	UG		
	PG	73	150
		77	
Experience	Below 10 yrs	87	150
	Above 10 yrs	63	
Marital Status	Married	87	150
	Unmarried	63	

W.G.Coehran has said, "The purpose of sampling theory is to make sampling more efficient . It attempts to develop method of sample selection and of estimation that provide at the lowest possible cost estimate that are precise enough for our purpose".

Random Sampling

The alternate method used for sampling is called random sampling. This technique is based on a rational which is the exact opposite of what is followed in purposive sampling. The random sampling does not have and design behind the selection. All the individuals in the population are treated alike in the selection. In random sampling the sample is formed in such a way that every member of the population has the same chance of being selected. The selection of any individual in this group does not influence the selection of any other member. Hence this method of sample selection is also called equi-probability sampling.

Tools Used

To carry out any type of educational research, data are required because answers to research questions are ought on the basis of empirical data. Data are gathered using readily available tools or those which are modified of developed by the researcher. The investigator must take important decisions concerning the selection of appropriate data collecting tools.

There are many types of tools and each type has its unique characteristics and each should be considered for its appropriateness for collecting certain kinds of data on a selected research problem. It is necessary for the research to become familiar with the different types of research tools so that he/she could select his tools wisely from the available ones or modify one of these construct one by himself.

In this study the investigator used the following tools

(a) Personal Data Sheet

To know the background of the lecturers, the investigator used personal datasheet. It consisted of details regarding their sex, locality, age, educational qualification, teaching experience, marital status. The teachers were asked to fill the particulars given in the personal data sheet.

(b) Women Empowerment Scale

The women empowerment taken from the following tools

- A scale to measure attitude towards women - **B.R.Bhadra and P.R.Girija**
- Status of women empowerment- **B.A.Parikh**
- Attitude towards women scale - **Nandhini Deevan**

From this the investigator consolidated women empowerment scale to 40 questions

Scoring

It is a four point scale based on the lines of Likert four alternatives to each item. Scoring of these five alternatives follows a system of 1,

2, 3&4 from upper to lower end. The item wise scores are to be transferred to the table to obtain different women empowerment scores. The Women Empowerment Questionnaire consists of questions to be answered positively or negatively. Questions 2, 3, 6, 7, 15, 22, 24, 26, 27, 33 and 40 are to be scored negatively. Other questions are positively scored. The answer against each question can be scored as shown below.

	Strongly AgreeAgree		Disagree	Strongly disagree
Positive questions	4	3	2	1
Negative questions	1	2	3	4

Reliability

"The term reliability refers to the extent to which it gives consistent result on testing and retesting" - Frank S. Freeman. A test is said to be reliable to the extend the scores obtained through it are consistent over time and over different samples of the test items. They are not do the errors of measurement crept in by the nature of the test. Reliability refers to the results obtained with an evaluation instrument and not to the instrument itself. An estimate of reliability always relates to a particular type of consistency of scores over different samples of questions. Low reliability can restrict the degree of validity that is obtained, but high reliability provides no assurance for a satisfactory degree of validity. Reliability is primarily statistical in nature in the sense that the scores obtained on two successive occasions are correlated with each other. This coefficient of correlation is known as self-correlation and its value is called the 'reliability coefficient'.

Test - Retest Reliability

Checking the test–retest reliability by giving the test again.

To estimate reliability by means of the test-retest method, the same test is administered twice to the same group of pupils with a given time interval between the two administrations of the test. The resulting test scores are correlated and this correlation coefficient provides a measure of stability, that is, it indicates how stable the test results are over a given period of time. So it is otherwise known as a measure of stability. The estimate of reliability in this case will vary according to the length of time interval allowed between the two administrations.

Split-half Method

Checking test reliability by splitting a test two halves

Since a test consist of many questions, all the questions in a test together try to measure related to a particular aspect. When the test is divided into two halves they would represent two equivalent forms, and each of them would still measure the same aspect. It is a general expectation that the total scores of students on each half should be consistent. Here, the reliability of the test is estimated in terms of the consistency of the scores over the two halves of the test. The usual procedure to split the test into halves that are most equivalent is to score the even-numbered items separately. This provides two scores for each pupil, the correlation between which provides a measure of internal consistency. This gives the reliability of the scores on the fall length test, the following formula is used;

$$\text{Reliability on full test} = \frac{\text{2xreliability on the first 1/2 test}}{\text{1+Reliability on second 1/2 test}}$$

Kuder-richardson Estimates

Kuder and Richardson developed two formula KR-20 and KR-21 which could avoid the question of how to split a test into halves. These formulas provide the means of all possible split-half estimates of reliability of a test. The most popular formula is KR-21 which is given below;

KR-21:

N Epq

R = [1-]

N-1 sx2

Where N = Number of items in the test

P = † Number of persons answering item correctly / Number of persons taking the test

Q = † Number of persons answering item wrongly / Number of persons taking the test

E = summation sign indicting the pq is summated over all items

Sx2 = variance of the total test

R = Reliability of a test

Validity

Boring defines validity as the decree to which the test succeeds in measuring what is sets out to measure. Validity refers to how will a tool tries measure what it intends to measure.

Types of Validity

Broadly, five types of validity are discussed in the literature on testing. They are;

1. Content validity
2. Criterion - related validity
   a) Con-current
   b) Predictive
3. Construct validity
4. Face validity
5. Factorial validity

Statistical Anlysis of Data

The data collected from the sample was analyzed by using appropriate statistical technique. The investigator used descriptive analysis, differential analysis to study the data. The scores obtained by each respondent on each item were calculated. The minimum and maximum score obtained by respondents have been identified.

To know the significance of the all variables such as their locality, age, educational qualification, experience and marital status, mean, S.D, t-test and f- test were calculated.

Statistical Techiques Used

Mean

Mean is the most popular and widely used measure for representing the entire data by one value. It is centre of gravity in a distribution. Mean is more stable an suitable for further statistical treatments.

$$A.M = \frac{\sum fx}{N}$$

f = frequency of each class interval

x = mid point of each class

N = Total Number of scores.

Standard Deviation

It is the most widely measures of dispersion. It measures the scatteredness of the values, homogeneity or heterogeneity of the distribution. A small standard deviation shows high degree of uniformity and homogeneity of the series. The greater amount of dispersion or variability greater is the standard deviation.

$$S.D. = \sqrt{\frac{\sum fd^2}{N} - (\frac{\sum fd}{N})^2} \times c.1$$

N = Number of samples

C.I = Class interval

$$d = \frac{x - A}{C}$$

x = midpoint of the class interval

A = Assumed mean

Σfd = Total of the products of each class frequency with the steps deviation of the respective class.

Σfd^2 = Total of the products of each class frequency with the square deviation of the respective class.

t- TEST

The t- test has a wide number of applications in statistics. It can be used to test the significance of the difference between the means of two independent groups. By using the mean and S.D of the two groups, t-value is calculated. If the calculated value of 't' is 2.59 and above, then the difference between mean is significant at 0.01 level. If the calculated value of 't' is 1.96 and above, then the difference between mean is significant at 0.05 level.

$$t = \frac{M_1 - M_2}{\sqrt{\frac{SD^2_1}{N_1} + \frac{SD^2}{N_2}}}$$

m_1 = mean of first sample

m_2 = mean of second sample

SD_1 = standard deviation of first sample

SD_2 = standard deviation of second sample

N_1 = Total number of First sample

N_2 = Total number of Second sample

The ensuring chapter deals with the Analysis and Interpretation.

IV

Analysis and Interpretation of Data

Introduction

The analysis and interpretation of data represents the application of the inductive and deductive to the research process. It is a very important step in the total procedure of research. Analysis of (variance or data) means studying the tabular material. It involves breaking down existing complex factor into simple parts and putting the parts together in new arrangements for the purpose of interpretation

Analysis of data means studying the tabulated material in order to determine the inherent material falls or meaning. Data accepted by the investigator got heir meaning, when they are channelized into the process of statistical analysis. It will give the investigator an insight into the problem. It simplifies the masses of number and facts and presents them in an understandable manner. Therefore analysis must lead to interpretation of data.

The purpose of present investigation is to study the awareness on women empowerment among teachers. The data for the study were collected from the teachers by means of a questionnaire the present study, the data are analysed using mainly the following statistical techniques.

1. Arithmetic mean
2. Standard Deviation
3. t -value

Objectives of the Study

1. To find out the level of significant difference between Male and Female teachers with respect to awareness on women empowerment.
2. To find out the level of significant difference between the locality of male and female teachers with respect to awareness on women empowerment.
3. To find out the level of significant difference between Age group (below-35) of male and female teachers with respect to awareness on women empowerment.
4. To find out the level of significant difference between Age group (above-35) of male and female teachers with respect to awareness on women empowerment.
5. To find out the level of significant difference between educational qualification (UG) of male and female teachers with respect to awareness on women empowerment.
6. To find out the level of significant difference between the educational qualification (PG) of male and female teachers with respect to awareness on women empowerment.
7. To find out the level of significant difference between teaching experience (below 10 years) of male and female teachers with respect to awareness on women empowerment.
8. To find out the level of significant difference between teaching experience (above 10 years) of male and female teachers with respect to awareness on women empowerment.

9. To find out the level of significant difference between married male and married female teachers of male and female teachers with respect to awareness on women empowerment.

10. To find out the level of significant difference between unmarried male and unmarried female teachers of male and female teachers with respect to awareness on women empowerment.

HypothesEs of the study

1. There is no significant difference between Male and Female teachers with respect to awareness on women empowerment

2. There is no significant difference between the localities of male and female teachers with respect to awareness on women empowerment.

3. There is no significant difference between Age group (below-35) of male and female teachers with respect to awareness on women empowerment.

4. There is no significant difference between Age group (above-35) with respect to awareness on women empowerment.

5. There is no significant difference between educational qualifications (UG) of male and female teachers with respect to awareness on women empowerment.

6. There is no significant difference between educational qualifications (PG) of male and female teachers with respect to awareness on women empowerment.

7. There is no significant difference between teaching experiences (below 10 years) of male and female teachers with respect to awareness on women empowerment.

8. There is no significant difference between teaching experiences (above 10 years) of male and female teachers with respect to awareness on women empowerment.

9. There is no significant difference between married male and

married female teachers with respect to awareness on women empowerment.

10. There is no significant difference between unmarried male and unmarried female teachers with respect to awareness on women empowerment.

Hypothesis -I

There is no significant difference between Male and Female teachers with respect to awareness on women empowerment.

Table 4.1

SIGNIFICANT DIFFERENCE BETWEEN MALE AND FEMALE TEACHERS WITH RESPECT TO AWARENESS ON WOMEN EMPOWERMENT

S.No	Gender	No. of samples	Mean	S.D	t-value	Level of significance
1	Male	75	72.13	5.80	3.48	0.05
2	Female	75	75.47	5.97		

Table 4.1 examines the mean, standard deviation, 't' value and level of significance of male and female teachers in women empowerment score.

The mean scores of male and female shows that there is significant difference in their awareness on women empowerment. The scores indicate that the two groups have difference.

The 't' value of the group is 3.48 at 0.05 level. The calculated 't' value exceeds the tabulated value (1.98) at 0.05 level. Hence we conclude that the null hypothesis, i.e., there is no significant difference between male and female teachers with respect to the awareness on women empowerment among teachers is rejected.

Hypothesis -2

There is no significant difference between Rural Male and Female teachers with respect to awareness on women empowerment.

Table 4.2

SIGNIFICANT DIFFERENCE BETWEEN RURAL MALE AND FEMALE TEACHERS WITH RESPECT TO AWARENESS ON WOMEN EMPOWERMENT

S.No	Category	Gender samples	No. of	Mean	S.D	t-value	Level of significance
1	Rural	Female	38	75.37	6.15	2 08	0.05
2		Male	38	72.61	5.44		

Table 4.2 examines the mean, standard deviaticn,'t' value and level of significance of male and female teachers in women empowerment score.

The mean scores of male and female shows that there is significant difference in their awareness on women empowerment. The scores indicate that the two groups have difference.

The 't' value of the group is 2.08 at 0.05 level. The calculated 't' value exceeds the tabulated value (1.99) at 0.05 level. Hence we conclude that the null hypothesis, i.e., there is no significant difference between rural male and female teachers with respect to the awareness on women empowerment among teachers is rejected.

Hypothesis -3

There is no significant difference between Urban Male and Female teachers with respect to awareness on women empowerment.

Table 4.3

SIGNIFICANT DIFFERENCE BETWEEN URBAN MALE AND FEMALE TEACHERS WITH RESPECT TO AWARENESS ON WOMEN EMPOWERMENT

S.No	Category	Gender	No. of samples	Mean	S.D	t-value	Level of significance
1	Urban	Female	37	75.84	5.07	2.85	0.05
2		Male	37	72.19	5.26		

Table 4.3 examines the mean, standard deviation,'t' value and level of significance of urban male and female teachers in women empowerment score.

The mean scores of male and female shows that there is significant difference in their awareness on women empowerment. The scores indicate that the two groups have difference.

The 't' value of the group is 2.85 at 0.05 level. The calculated 't' value exceeds the tabulated value(1.99) at 0.05 level . Hence we conclude that the null hypothesis, i.e., there is no significant difference between urban male and female teachers with respect to the awareness on women empowerment among teachers is rejected.

Hypothesis -4

There is no significant difference between Age group (Below 35Yrs) Male and Female teachers with respect to awareness on women empowerment.

Table 4.4

SIGNIFICANT DIFFERENCE BETWEEN AGE GROUP (BELOW 35 Yrs) MALE AND FEMALE TEACHERS WITH RESPECT TO AWARENESS ON WOMEN EMPOWERMENT

S.No	Category	Gender	No. of samples	Mean	S.D	t-value	Level of significance
1	Below	Female	39	76.08	5.51		
2	35 yrs	Male	40	72.19	5.40	2.67	0.05

Table 4.4 examines the mean, standard deviation,'t' value and level of significance of below 35 yrs male and female teachers in women empowerment score.

The mean scores of male and female shows that there is significant difference in their awareness on women empowerment. The scores indicate that the two groups have difference.

The 't' value of the group is 2.67 at 0.05 level. The calculated 't' value exceeds the tabulated value (1.99) at 0.05 level. Hence we conclude that the null hypothesis, i.e., there is no significant difference between below 35 yrs male and female teachers with respect to the awareness on women empowerment among teachers is rejected.

Hypothesis –5

There is no significant difference between Above 35 yrs Male and Female teachers with respect to awareness on women empowerment.

Table 4.5

SIGNIFICANT DIFFERENCE BETWEEN ABOVE 35 YRS MALE AND FEMALE TEACHERS WITH RESPECT TO AWARENESS ON WOMEN EMPOWERMENT

S.No	Category	Gender	No. of samples	Mean	S.D	t-value	Level of significance
1	Above	Female	36	75.08	6.40		
2	35 yrs	Male	35	72.43	6.30	1 75	0.05

Table 4.5 examines the mean, standard deviaticn,'t' value and level of significance of Above 35 yrs male and female teachers in women empowerment score.

The mean scores of male and female shows that there is significant difference in their awareness on women empowerment. The scores indicate that the two groups have small difference.

The 't' value of the group is 1.75 at 0.05 level. The calculated 't' value not exceeds the tabulated value (1.99) at 0.05 level. Hence we conclude that the null hypothesis, i.e., there is no significant difference between rural male and female teachers with respect to the awareness on women empowerment among teachers is accepted.

Hypothesis –6

There is no significant difference between Educational qualification (UG) Male and Female teachers with respect to awareness on women empowerment.

Table 4.6 examines the mean, standard deviation, 't' value and level of significance of Educational qualification (UG) of male and female teachers in women empowerment schools.

The mean scores of male and female shows that there is significant difference in their awareness on women empowerment. The scores indicate that the two groups have small difference. The 't' value of the group is 1.42 at 0.05 level. The calculated 't' value not exceeds the tabulated value (1.99) at 0.05 level. Hence we conclude that the null hypothesis, i.e., there is no significant difference between educational qualification (UG) of male and female teachers with respect to the awareness on women empowerment among teachers is accepted.

Table 4.6

SIGNIFICANT DIFFERENCE BETWEEN EDUCATIONAL QUALIFICATION (UG) MALE AND FEMALE TEACHERS WITH RESPECT TO AWARENESS ON WOMEN EMPOWERMENT

S.No	Category	Gender	No. of samples	Mean	S.D	t-value	Level of significance
1	Educational	Female	37	75.03	5.50	1.42	0.05
2	Qualification (UG)	Male	36	72.86	6.60		

Hypothesis -7

There is no significant difference between Educational qualification (PG) of Male and Female teachers with respect to awareness on women empowerment.

Table 4.7

SIGNIFICANT DIFFERENCE BETWEEN EDUCATIONAL QUALIFICATION (PG) OF MALE AND FEMALE TEACHERS WITH RESPECT TO AWARENESS ON WOMEN EMPOWERMENT

S.No	Category	Gender samples	No. of	Mean	S.D	t-value	Level of significance
1	Educational qualification	Female	38	76.29	5.88	4.20	0.05
2	(PG)	Male	39	71.29	4.44		

Table 4.7 examines the mean, standard deviation, 't' value and level of significance of Educational qualification (PG) of male and female teachers in women empowerment score.

The mean scores of male and female shows that there is significant difference in their awareness on women empowerment. The scores indicate that the two groups have difference. The 't' value of the group is 4.20 at 0.05 level. The calculated't' value exceeds the tabulated value (1.99) at 0.05 level.

Hence we conclude that the null hypothesis, i e., there is no significant difference between Educational qualification (PG) of male and female teachers with respect to the awareness on women empowerment among teachers is rejected.

Hypothesis -8

There is no significant difference between teaching experience (Above 10 yrs) of Male and Female teachers with respect to awareness on women empowerment.

Table 4.8

SIGNIFICANT DIFFERENCE BETWEEN TEACHING EXPERIENCE (ABOVE 10 YRS) OF MALE AND FEMALE TEACHERS WITH RESPECT TO AWARENESS ON WOMEN EMPOWERMENT

S.No	Category	Gender	No. of samples	Mean	S.D	t-value	Level of significance
1	Teaching experience (Above 10 yrs)	Female	30	75.33	5.73	1.23	0.05
2		Male	33	73.45	6.43		

Table 4.8 examines the mean, standard deviation, 't' value and level of significance of Teaching experience (Above 10 yrs) of male and female teachers in women empowerment score. The mean scores of male and female shows that there is significant difference in their awareness on women empowerment. The scores indicate that the two groups have small difference. The 't' value of the group is 1.23 at 0.05 level. The calculated 't' value not exceeds the tabulated value (1.99) at 0.05 level. Hence we conclude that the null hypothesis, i.e., there is no significant difference between teaching experience (Above 10 yrs) of male and female teachers with respect to the awareness on women empowerment among teachers is accepted.

Hypothesis -9

There is no significant difference between teaching experience (below 10 yrs) of Male and Female teachers with respect to awareness on women empowerment.

Table 4.9

SIGNIFICANT DIFFERENCE BETWEEN TEACHING EXPERIENCE (BELOW 10 YRS) OF MALE AND FEMALE TEACHERS WITH RESPECT TO AWARENESS ON WOMEN EMPOWERMENT

S.No	Category	Gender samples	No. of	Mean	S.D	t-value	Level of significance
1	Teaching experience	Female	45	75.78	5.92	3.78	0.05
2	(Below 10 yrs)	Male	42	71.33	5.05		

Table 4.8 examines the mean, standard deviation, 't' value and level of significance of Teaching experience (below10 yrs) of male and female teachers in women empowerment schools. The mean scores of male and female shows that there is significant difference in their awareness on women empowerment. The scores indicate that the two groups have difference. The 't' value of the group is 4.20 at 0.05 level. The calculated 't' value exceeds the tabulated value (1.98) at 0.05 level. Hence we conclude that the null hypothesis, i.e., there is no significant difference between teaching experience (Above 10 yrs) of male and female teachers with respect to the awareness on women empowerment among teachers is rejected.

Hypothesis -10

There is no significant difference between marital status (married) Male and Female teachers with respect to awareness on women empowerment.

Table 4.8 examines the mean, standard deviation, 't' value and level of significance of marital status (married) of male and female teachers in women empowerment score.

The mean scores of male and female shows that there is significant difference in their awareness on women empowerment. The scores indicate that the two groups have difference. The 't' value of the group is 2.30 at 0.05 level. The calculated't' value exceeds the tabulated value (1.98) at 0.05 level.

Table 4.10

SIGNIFICANT DIFFERENCE BETWEEN MARITAL STATUS (MARRIED) MALE AND FEMALE TEACHERS WITH RESPECT TO AWARENESS ON WOMEN EMPOWERMENT

S.No	Category	Gender	No. of samples	Mean	S.D	t-value	Level of significance
1	Marital status	Female	45	75.11	6.10	2.30	0.05
2	Married	Male	42	72.05	6.29		

Hence we conclude that the null hypothesis, i.e., there is no significant difference between marital status (married) of male and female teachers with respect to the awareness on women empowerment among teachers is rejected.

Hypothesis -11

There is no significant difference between marital status (unmarried) Male and Female teachers with respect to awareness on women empowerment.

Table 4.11

SIGNIFICANT DIFFERENCE BETWEEN MARITAL STATUS (UNMARRIED) MALE AND FEMALE TEACHERS WITH RESPECT TO AWARENESS ON WOMEN EMPOWERMENT

S.No	Category	Gender	No. of samples	Mean	S.D	t-value	Level of significance
1	Marital status	Female	30	76.50	5.35	3.16	0.05
2	Unmarried	Male	33	72.24	5.09		

Table 4.11 examines the mean, standard deviation, 't' value and level of significance of marital status (unmarried) of male and female teachers in women empowerment score.

The mean scores of male and female shows that there is significant difference in their awareness on women empowerment. The scores indicate that the two groups have difference. The 't' value of the group is 3.16 at 0.05 level. The calculated 't' value exceeds the tabulated value. Hence we conclude that the null hypothesis, i.e., there is no significant difference between marital status (unmarried) of male and female teachers with respect to the awareness on women empowerment among teachers is rejected. The ensuring chapter deals with the findings and conclusion.

V

Summary, Findings and Suggestions

Introduction

This chapter deals with the study in major findings, educational implications and suggestions for further research. The present chapter portrays a brief re-statement of the problem, a description of the procedures used in the study, a detailed discussion of the procedures used in the study, a detailed discussion of the findings and the educational implications of the present study. In addition to this, suggestions for replicating the study in other settings and with different samples and tools are also listed.

Need For The Present Investigation

Education is a complex concept and refers to both a process as well as a product. Education as a product is viewed as the sum total of what is received through learning that is acquisition of knowledge, skills, attitudes, interests, and values, transmission of culture, development of personality and liberation of self-actualization. As a process, education involves the act of developing these products in someone else or in our self. Education is very important, for education determines interests, technology, productivity as well as vertical and horizontal mobility of pupils.

Major Findings of the Study

The following are the findings which show the relation about awareness on women empowerment. The major findings of this study shows that the variables of gender, locality, teaching experience, educational qualification marital status and age factor also play a vital role in this empowerment study. The findings are listed below:

1. The findings of this study show that both male and female teachers shows differential taught on their women empowerment more over the rural and urban teachers shows same significant level in their awareness. This \firms the studies of Anita Dighe(2002), Hamimanti Mukhopadhayay (2007)
2. In this empowerment study the age factor, educational qualification, teaching experience of male and female teachers shows a significant difference with respect to awareness on women empowerment. This finding is new finding to the present study.
3. This empowerment study shows more significant level of difference between married and unmarried male and female teachers because it states that their views taught towards this vary. This finding is also new finding to the present study.

Summary of Conclusions

The present study shows that there is a significant difference between male and female teachers towards women empowerment, because male are dominating women from the beginning of ancient day itself.

Locality plays a vital role towards women empowerment because of their socio-economic dependence. The awareness of women empowerment of female is more than the male, because now-a-days the aware of education spread all the area even interior area.

In earlier days the parents are interested to educate male alone. After the 33% allotment for female about the jobs from the government, the parents are very enthusiastic to educate their female child. Due to globalization in various fields, women emerged difference between below 35 yrs male and female, because male become short temper and they unable to bear the development of women. But there is no difference between above 35 yrs male and female. Because men are able to underestimate them due to economic factors, the family can run smoothly with male and female incomes. Man as a social being changes his mentality often, he concentrate only on his benefit women has positive thoughts and interest in the development of their environment and themselves. The present study shows that there is a significant difference between married, unmarried male and female.

Educational Implications

Even after 61 years of independence, and much advancement in science and technology and drastic social change the genuine place of women could not be as curtained by attracting them towards education and providing them suitable jobs according to their qualifications.

The women have been educated and involved in the progress of nation the progress would have been much more than that of today. A woman needs to be physically healthy in order to take the challenges of life. Education and health continue to be the priority areas for the state government in the matter of social upliftment.

Muhammad yunas (an economist from Dhacca Universuty, Bangladesh) Nonel Laurate for peace in 2006 has appealed earnestly (through his book "Creating a World without Poverty" published in 2008) for women's role as drivers of the coming economic and social revolution in society.

Education as on the one hand "Opening up the world" material education and on the other hand "Creating knowledge and thinking as essential aspect of empowerment. Education enables a person to think for himself and others. Thus the educational process results in empowering women to respond to concrete situations. So that women education is high return investment in socio economic development for society as a whole since, by educating a woman one is educating a entire family.

Suggestions For Further Research

Research is a chain activity. There purpose of any research in education is to find solutions for problems related to teachers, students learning ect. But investigation on one problem always leaves many related research questions that can be investigated by other researcher; Based on the findings of the present study further studies are suggested to be conducted in future are as given below.

1. A similar study on awareness on women empowerment may be conducted among the different types of schools such as government, Aided, Municipal, Public and Matriculation.
2. The present study was confined to the teachers. In further the study may be extended to working women, men, students and others.
3. The similar study may be done with other variables like socio-economic status, caste ect.,
4. This study was confined only to 11 schools on one taluk. Study may be conducted by taking large area at regional level or state level.
5. Only the school level was taken for this study can be extended to other levels like college levels.

Conclusion

The final purpose of educational research is to ascertain principles and develop procedures in the field of education. The purpose of present investigation was to study the awareness on women empowerment among teachers with reference to some selected variables, and the study indicated significant relationship among the variables. This study may enrich the educators in the field of education to teach the students and the findings of this study serve as a data-base for the further research.

Bibliography

Books

1. Digumarti Bjaskara Rao, & Digumarti Pushpalatha Rao, (2003). Women, Education and Empowerment.
2. Haleh Afshar, (1998). Women and Empowerment; Illustrations from the Third World
3. Marta Lundy & Beverly Younger, (1995). Empowering women in the workplace: Perspectives, innovations, and techniques for helping professionals.
4. Setty, E.D. & Krishna Moorthy, P. Women Empowerment through Entrepreneurship Development.

Thesis

1. Abrehe Zemichael, (2005). Girls' and Women are Education and their Empowerment among Pastoral Societies Case Study of Eritrea.
2. Anita Dighe, (1993). Women literacy and empowerment an analysis of the Nellore experience in AndraPradesh.
3. Gupta, V. S. (june 2002). Capacity building for effective empowerment of women.
4. Haimanti Mukhopadhyay, (2007). The role of education in the empowerment of women in a district of West Bengal
5. Hemalatha, (2002). Programme for empowering rural women.
6. Iram Naz, Sami Ullah, (1998). Women empowerment and Youth Perception in Pakistan.
7. Imran Sharif Chaudhry, (1999). The Determinants of women empowerment in Southern Punjab(Pakistan).
8. Joshi, Meenakshi, (2004). Women's empowerment: experience from watershed project. Social Welfare.

9. Narasim Huluk, Annapurna, K. (2002). Women empowerment and development of women and children in rural area.
10. Dr.P.N.Prasad, P.N. Dr.Sreedevi, (2007). Economic empowerment of women through Information Technology.
11. Dr.Rasure, K.A. (2002). Women empowerment through self help groups.Voluntary Association for People Services, Virudhunagar(2008). Enhancing women's empowerment through information and communication technology : a report.
12. Sakuntala Narasimha,(1999). Empowering rural women.
13. Srilatha Batlivala, (1996). Empowerment of women in South Asia in speaking out women's Economic empowerment in South Asia.
14. Sujit kumar Dulta, Dilip Kumar Ghose, (2002). Empowerment of Rural Women.
15. Dr.Thresiamma Varghese, (2002) Women Empowerment in Oman: A study based on Women Empowerment Index.
16. Thurairajah. N. Amaratunga. D. Haigh. R. (2006). Women's Empowerment in Disaster Reconstruction: Critical Perspectives on Policies and Frameworks.

Journals

1. Adam Paul, P. (2008). Awareness of legal rights among women teachers. EDUTRACKS, 7 (9), 38-40.
2. Dr.Archla Bhstia, (2010). Education and Empowerment of Women. Miracle of Teaching, 10 (1), 12-15.
3. Dr.Dhineshkumar, Miss.Pushpa Gautam, (2010). Some Constraints in empowerment of women education. Miracle of Teaching, 10 (2), 20-23.
4. Jaspritkarur Soni, (2007). Women's education investment will never fail. Miracle of Teaching, 7 (2), 91-92.
5. Dr.Kanwalijit Karur, (2008). Education A means of empowering women. Miracle of Teaching, 8 (2), 72-75.

6. Dr. Panna Akhani, Shemb\ekar, I. (2005). 'M' Powerment of women. Miracle of Teaching, 5 (2), 113-115.

7. Dr.Ranjan Bhatia, (2007). Women empowerment in Educational management and Developing Leadership Qualities in Women. EDUTRACKS, 6 (7), 16-18.

8. Dr.ShakunPaharaya, (2009). Women Empowerment. Miracle of Teaching, 9 (1), 31-35.

9. Dr.Vinodkumar, P. (2009). Women education in 21st century. Miracle of Teaching, 7 (1), 25-27.

Part 5

Invariable Fears of Teachers

1

Invariable Fears of Teachers

Introduction

Stress has been acknowledged inherent in the process of teaching. Most teachers, howsoever bright, well read, experienced and well prepared experience some amount of stress while going to lecture in front of the student, but manage to handle it. It is also true that some feel more stressed than others and face occasional difficulty in coping with it. Some teachers find it quite heavy on them and extremely difficult carry on the work, as they are not able to either structure the work environment or exercise control over the factors underlying the stress, or to enhance their capability to cope. It then threatens to adversely impact their physical health reduces their teaching commitment and effectiveness to the extent of their needing professional help. Prolonged periods of intense stress, if not taken care of, can produce feelings of emotional exhaustion, reduce personal accomplishment, induce a sense of professional failure, and even a tendency to act with the clientele in a depersonalized manner, the symptoms which define burnout. Stress and burnout among teachers found directly influence their functioning and survival in the system, and quality of educational and related services offered to all students, and without exception for those with special needs.

Stress And Burnout In Indian Context

As stated in the introduction and other subsequent places in the book, although the definitional complexities in the assessment of stress and burnout are enormous and difficult to be resolved in general. An additional problem has been confronted by researchers in the understanding and assessment of stress and burnout in educational institutions of south Asia because of the specific cultural values of obedience of authority, nurturance of the young, etc. The socio-cultural situations have though, undergone gradual changes in the post independence period, and the difficulty of such unmet unconditional expectations now characterize the numerous interpersonal problems at all levels from administrative heads to students. The emotional strains of interpersonal emotional distances and the non-reciprocal relationships among different sections often operate at the latent level, and camouflage the severity of stress effects.

Like many of the educational institutions in south Asia, teachers in contemporary Indian schools are confronted with the reality of diverse social groups of educators and pupils, large size of class and raised expectations , leaving for them little scope and time for personal interaction with students and colleagues. Over the years, as social power and money have become important personal and social values, and the new professions have emerged, the teaching profession has got devalued. Teachers do not have the desired social respect, nor do they get adequate financial rewards/support for their work. Teachers expected to confer knowledge, and make every child the best achiever in every domain of activity. The task is challenging and demanding, but the teachers represent a mixed lot, with varied levels of skills, capabilities, resources, etc. Teachers who are capability and good, generally respected and appreciated, but instances are uncommon, when parents and students alike so not give a hot to the teachers, and blame them for any shortcomings observed in children/ school. Many parents do not wish their chilc to be a teacher. Many (parents, husbands and in-laws) view teaching as an ideal profession for women, as they can finish their work by the afternoon and take care of their home and children (a part time employee on full salary).

There has been little research in the Indian schools in areas of teacher concerns, stress and burnout. The first and School Surveys of Research in Education (Buch, 1974, 1979) did not include any study on teacher stress and burnout. A later bibliography (Dave and Murry, 1933) included three studies, each emphasizing a different aspect of burnout. As the pressures to perform from various quarters continue to rise, despite the adverse conditions of functioning of teaching institutions, teachers need familial and social support in differentiating across variety of stresses and in handling the day to day stresses, and thus prevent burnout.

Introduction: Setting the Scene

Stress, burnout and coping researches have been confining for years to clinical areas, and the terms have acquired negative connotations, with which the inflicted struggled in a bid to find relief, and in the process depleted and/or exhausted the resources under their control. This indicates an unquestionable acceptance of the underlying assumption of persons going through the stressful experiences, having no control/volition or an alterrative path out, and thus the need of therapy. The common experience as well as the evidence from research does not validate it. There neither is adequate logical ground to argue and suggest that all types of stress are necessarily negative and unhealthy for ones funct oning, nor are the stress and burnout equivalents. A distinction been made in the literature between positive and negative stress, and between stress and burnout. Positive stress called eustress, and negative stress labelled distress. In fact, the positive affect has nct been entirely neglected in the classical models of stress either. It has been discussed in relation to the (a) primary appraisal of stressful situations as challenges, which signal the probabi ity of makings gains and characterized by positive emotions, I ke eagerness, excitement, and confidence. (b) Appraisal of the resolution of a stressful encounter as successful leading to emotions of happiness and pride. (c) Cessation of aversive conditions, when people are likely to experience an offsetting positive emotion, such as relief, and (d) Examining of the other positive outcomes of stressful events, even if the events have not been favorably resolved. The positive outcomes may include perceived benefits of stressful encounters, newly acquired skills and resources that may help in coping, and spiritual/ religious transformation in thinking and attitudes.

Meaning of Stress

Stress is a condition stream on ones emotions, thought processes and physical conditions. When it is excessive, it can pretend once ability to cope with environment. (Hans Selye, 1976) "Stress is the general term applied to the pressures; employs developed various symptoms of stress as, "an adjective demand placed on the organism".

From the above definitions, it may understand that stress pretends the wellbeing of the organism; conditions that tend to because stress called pressure. In this age of anxiety, stress considered as an inevitable aspect of human life, forcing him to cope up with it for successful and happy life. The main factors of creating stress in individual are Biological, Psychological and Socio-Cultural. Biological factors influence all aspects of our behavior including our intellectual capabilities, basic temperament, primary reaction tendencies and stress tolerance. Psychosocial factors of stress also influence the well-being of the individual in contemporary life. Stress due to failure, losses, personal limitations, guilt and loneliness leads to self-deviation. Modern living is a bundle load of pressures acting on individuals. Each individual experience his own unique pattern of pressures such as competing with others, meeting educational, occupational, and marital depends and coping with the complexity and in rapid pace of modern life . There are other socio-cultural factors creating stress on modern man such as problems of war and violence, group prejudice and discrimination, economic and unemployment problems, rapid social change existential anxiety.

Job Stress

In this last decade of twentieth century, many people are unable to cope up with stress generated because of circumstances forcing them to adopt fact-paced life styles. This position is highly significant when people are at work. A rational and logical inference one can make, now basing on the above premises is that working styles are also subjected to change in accordance to the fast changing life styles, mat be a presupposition for work stress or job stress. Therefore, job stress has received an increasing concern to the researchers in the areas of organizational behavior and social psychology, who have been undertaking evidences about the effects of stress on the organization, worker output, and the physical and emotional well-being of the worker.

Teachers Stress

Job stress is the most common psychological phenomena that are prevalent among people who are in different jobs and professions. The stress studies are initially directed toward industrial organization. With the private sector. Researchers have come to believe that stress may be especially prevalent among human service professions, particularly the teaching profession, (Kryacou and Suteliffe 1977-78; Pettigrew and Wolf 1982, Cherniss 1980; and Cooper and Marshall 1980). As teaching is a human service profession, stress within the teaching profession is considerable and may have far-reaching consequences on the entire education system. Teaching is a complex process were in teacher is expected to exhibit many skills. This makes a teacher to experience stress in the profession.

Further Pettergrew and Wolf (1982) opined, "Teacher stress has a Nation-wide concern and relatively new area of empirical research". Concerns regarding stress among schoolteacher have been raised for over 40 years (Tunk, Meeks and Turk 1982) stress is considered very significant in any educative process much attention is not drawn towards this. Teacher behavior and his performance, classroom interactions, school and classroom climate may consider as the important components of any educative process. It is not easy to ascertain sources of teacher stress, as its ambit is unlimited.

However, several attempts are made to identify the sources that possible, create stress among teachers. Factors prepared by teachers as being troublesome or stressful have included students displine, negative student attitudes towards school, physical violence, is adequate preparation time, lack of clear role definition and heavy workloads".(Bearly, Myette and serna, 1983;Chichen and Koff, 1978;Gollady and Noel 1978;Olanderand Ferrel, 1970).

Further Kaiser and Polezynsky (1982) identified factors within educators themselves as a potential source of excess stress. Quick and Quick (1979) proposed four groups of factors creating work stress. They are 1) Role factors, 2) Job factors, 3) Physical factors and 4) Interpersonal factors. A heap of literature available on job stress identified main sources such as job setting, organizational, situational, lack of control over work, co-workers etc.

Teacher is subjected to stress due to incoherent social life, widening social distance, segregation, lack of social support, corruption, nepotism, unnecessary societal involvement in day-to-day activities, high degree of social indiscipline, deterioration of values, lack of social security etc. Besides the potential stress that occurs outside the school, there are also those associated with the school itself. Teaching as a profession demands continuous growth, but teachers while discharging time for further studies, unable to utilize the training the salaries, lack of opportunity for reading training, less change for further promotion etc. are acting as source of stress on teachers.

Teaching as an occupation, present certain situation where in the teacher has to adjust to unhealthy school atmosphere, lack of recognition, for effective teaching. Teaching the subject is which he is not interested, lack of support for innovative approaches, lack of enthusiasm in staff meeting, monotonous working conditions, difference of opinions with head of the institution etc., are the situations acting as sources of stress.

Student behavior is also a major component in the teaching learning process. Continuous misbehavior or certain students, non-acceptance of teacher's authority indiscipline in the class, lack of interest on outsides. Threat from the students, lack of attention in the class, unable to estimate the student, lack of positive responses from the student etc., are some of the significant sources of stress on teachers. Thus, student as a group can be a significant source of teacher stress. Similarly lack of group cohesiveness in school, lack of social support and interpersonal conflicts create teacher stress.

So far, extra organizational, organizational and group stressors are discussed; teacher is the ultimate consumer of stress due to previously mentioned stressors. Thus individual dispositions such as role conflict and ambiguity at organizational and group levels, causes stress. Teachers have to play multiple roles and these often make conflicting expectation. In the present education system heavy expectation are there on teachers. Hence, teachers are supposed to undertake high magnitude of work. Now teachers are experiencing stress as they are supposed to teach more periods a day without rest between periods, excess correction work, undertaking institutional work like censes lack of time for completing syllabus, conduct of co-curricular and extracurricular activities etc.

Effects of Teacher Stress

As job stress effect organizational performance, teacher stress impedes teacher performance in teaching. Infect it is assumed that mild stress can even enhance performance but high level of stress can create physical, Psychological and behavioral problems among teacher. There are several research studies, which observed that, a high level of stress accompanied by physical illness such as high blood pressures, ulcers and even cancer. Similarly high level of stress may be accompanied by psychological problems such as anger, anxiety, depression, nervousness, irritability, tension and boredom. Excessive stress may also result in behavioral problems such as sleeplessness, under eating or over eating, increased smoking and drinking and drug abuse. Many researches of teacher studies have established some strong correlates of teacher stress. From these researches, it has found that teacher stress related to job dissatisfaction (Rudd and Wiseman 1962; Krysacon and Suteliff 1979). Absenteeism, (Bridger 1980; Kaiser and Polezynsky 1982); greater intention to leave profession (Kryiacon and Suteliff 1979), Physical Distress (Coats and Thoresen, 1979) and teacher performance (Kkryiacon and Sutcliffe 1977-79, Pettegrew and Wolf 1982, Kaiser and Polezynsky 1982, Soloman 1960).

However, teaching competency has been recognized as important component of teaching learning process, relatively little effort is made to define the term. A peep in into the literature of teacher effectiveness as one finds many related terms such as teaching success; successful teacher, teaching efficiency, teacher performance, teacher competency etc. "As one looks through heap of investigations in this field" Writes Barr (1961), "One finds various terms used to designate or describe the successful teacher. Frequently the word 'efficiency' is used one will not that the terms are sometimes applied to teacher as in teacher efficiency and sometimes in the teacher behavior as in the teaching efficiency.

Donald M. Medley (1982) States that the teacher competency as those of knowledge, abilities and beliefs on teacher processes and brings to the teaching situation. Teaching competency differs from teacher performance and teacher effectiveness in that it is a stable characteristic of the teacher that does not change appreciably when the teacher moves from one situation to another. By this, it is evident that the knowledge of subject matter, teaching skills, beliefs and feelings of teacher may be considered as the components of teaching competent that a competent teacher is supposed to process.

Biddle (1964) advocates that "disagreement and ambiguity with respect to the description of teaching competence are to be expected and cannot entirely be avoided because competent teaching as undoubtedly a relative matter. Some investigators to refer to training process, properties of teachers, behavior exhibited by teacher and effects produced by teachers, have used the term competence. The same variable have been termed by other investigators as effectiveness, criteria of competency, ability in reach and a host of other terms-teacher success, teacher effectiveness, teacher efficiency, teacher performance, teacher competency etc., are used synonymously by investigators.

Researchers study teacher effectiveness in three component, presage, process and product. Here the presage component refers to thought processes, training aspect and personality factors of the teachers. The process component effects produced by teachers, the same variable have been termed by other investigators as effectiveness, criteria of competency, ability in reach and a host of other terms-teacher success, teacher effectiveness, teacher efficiency, teacher performance, teacher competency etc., are used synonymously by investigators.

Ryan (1960) States, "What constitutes effective teaching?" What are the distinguishing characteristics of competent teacher? are provocative and running questions unfortunately, no universally acceptable definite answers can be given to these complex queries-embarrassing as it may be for professional educators to recognize relatively little progress has been made."

Similarly, Biddle and Ellena accepted in 1966 that nobody knows what a competent teacher was. They said, "Probably no aspect of education has been discussed with greater frequency with as much deep concern or by more educators and citizens. The teacher effectiveness-How to define it, how to identify it, how to measure it, how to evaluate it, and how to detect and remove obstacles to its achievement-finding about the competence of teachers are inconclusive and peace meal and little is presently known for certain about teacher excellence. Researchers study teacher effectiveness in three components; presage, process and product. Here the presage component refers to thought processes, training aspects and personality factors of the teachers. The process component to the teacher's action or classroom practices and the product component refer to the quality of the products i.e. students predicted.

Jangira (1979) states, "teacher's effectiveness has been considered into its three separate components for convenience of presentation. It should be taken that these components are watertight compartment. It also fallow that there are no clear-cut lines to distinguish one component from the other.

Teacher Competency and Stress

The study is about teacher competency in relation to stress. Teacher competency, in general sense impedes, when teacher suffers from stress. In this chapter, a discussion is made about teacher competency, stress, and the development of this type of study in the world.

Teacher Competency

One of the most difficult problems in educational research is that of recognizing teacher competency of discriminating between more and less effective teachers. The role of the classroom teacher in educational is central. The teacher is, after all, the point at contact between the educational system and the pupil. The impact of any educational programme or innovation on the pupil operates through the pupil's teacher. It is therefore quite accurate to say that a school's competence depends on the competence of its teachers. Maximizing teacher competence is a major goal of education. "Teacher competency" refers to the behavior of a teacher while teaching a class (both inside and outside the classroom).Teacher performance differs from teacher competence. It is defined in terms of teacher behavior, of what the teacher does, teacher performance resembles teacher competence in that it is a product of interaction between certain teacher characteristics and the teaching situation-teacher performance is often used as a basis from which teacher competence can be inferred.

"Teacher competence" refers to the set of knowledge, abilities and beliefs a teacher process and bring to the teaching situation Teacher competence differs from teacher performance and teacher effectiveness in that it is a stable characteristic of the teacher that does not change appreciably when the teacher moves from one situation to another. It resembles teacher performance in that it has also been proposed as a basis from which teacher effectiveness can be inferred.

Early Research: The first recorded study of teacher competence (Kratz, 1896), one of the earliest pieces of educational research of any kind to appear, set a design precedent that was to be followed for many years. A large group of elementary school pupils was asked to try to remember the best teacher each of them had ever encountered to write down what made that teacher different from others. Their descriptions were then collated and compared and from them was derived a list of characteristics that supposedly distinguished effective teachers from in effective ones. For the next half-century of so this kind of study was repeact6e again and again with groups chosen in various ways; sometime the task was performed by pupils currently attending schools sometimes by persons considered to be exports, educators, or teacher educators. Perhaps the most extensive and sophisticated example of this was the monumental common wealth teachers training study. (Charters of Waples 1929), which is used exhaustive and meticulous procedures to produce a number of lists of lengths. Typical of the characteristics listed were the following, which were the top six on a list of twenty-five.

1. Adaptability
2. Considerateness
3. Enthusiasm
4. Good judgment
5. Honesty
6. Magnetism

Pupil learning is a direct outcome of pupil learning experiences; learning is after all, something that pupils do not something teachers do. When a teacher "teacher' what she or he really does is try to provide certain learning experiences for the pupils that all expected to bring about desired learning out-comes.

Whatever the nature of the teachers performance, different pupils will have different learning experiences and will make different amounts of gain. Since the unit of study in the process-product model of the class, not the pupil, learning outcomes must be measured in terms of class mean gain before they can be correlated with teacher performance, and variations in gain made by different pupils with the same class must be related as errors that attitude the correlations obtains.

Dissatisfaction, Stress and Burnout

Do schools personnel have high moral and are they satisfied in their work setting? Newspaper headlines that emphasize teacher strikes, teacher burnout and stress on school employees suggest that many teachers are not satisfied. A number of studies conducted throughout the 1970s and into the 111980s indicate a gradual reduction in teacher satisfaction (for example, Fuller and Miskel (1972) found that about 89 percent of the teachers participating in this study were satisfied or very satisfied with their job. However, Bentzen, Williams and Heckman (1980), in an investigation conducted in the late 1970s, reported that slightly more than 75 percent of the teachers were satisfied with their jobs. In the later study, important difference in job satisfaction was discovered at the various levels of teaching, with elementary teachers expressing more satisfaction with their jobs than secondary teachers do. A nationwide poll of teachers conducted by the National Educational Association (NBA) in 1980 ("Teachers opinion poll: job satisfaction "1980) found that 35 percent of all public schoolteachers were dissatisfied with their current jobs. Two-fifths of the teacher said they would probably not become teachers if they had it to do all over again; one teacher in ten was planning to leave teaching as soon as possible, and another two teachers in ten were undecided about how long they would remain in teaching. These studies suggest a moderate trend in the direction of increasing dissatisfaction on the part of teachers-although a majority of school personnel continues to express satisfaction with this work.

Symptoms and Causes of Stress

Symptoms of teacher dissatisfaction and low morale vary. They include questioning and criticizing of school goals and polices, lack of enthusiasm for teaching rejection or lack of follow- up on administrative directives (Cook, 1979), absenteeism (Educational Research Service, 1980) and fragmentation, that is, a general feeling of being pulled in different directions (Klugman, Cartes &Israel, 1979). Some of these symptoms are also reported in a study by Staplenton, Craft and Frankiewicz (1979).

These researches found a positive relationship between teacher job satisfaction and teacher brink man ship, which they defined as teacher behavior that attempts to challenge the authority structure of the school while attempting to avoid its negative sanctions.

The causes of teacher stress and burnout are not easy to as certain nor are they easily distinguishable from the symptoms, although there is no shortage of suggested causes. With regard to teacher stress, quick and quick (1979) believe that four group of factors create work stress. 1) Role factors 2) job factors 3) physical factors and 4) interpersonal factors. They recommended a number of techniques for reducing the stress related by the various factors. The New York State United Teachers Organization that the most important factors contributing to stress is the effect of disruptive children, incompetent administrators are identifies as the second most important cause of stress ("Urban teachers report more stress", 1980).

In the New York stud, urban teachers reported more stress than did sub urban or rural teachers. Cichon and Koff, (1980) found in their research on Chicago teachers that the more important causes of teacher stress are problems of disruption and threats to the teacher's, physical professional and personal well being. In this connection, in NEA survey of its membership in 1980("teacher opinion poll attacks on teacher",1980)estimated that 1,13,000 of the country's 21,84,000 public school teachers were physically attacked by students during a recent twelve month period. Suggested causes of teaches burnout are usually believed to those associated with stress (block, 1978;weiskopt,1980).In a personal account of teacher burnout, Bardol (1979) has described several symptoms and perceived causes.

A number of investigations into the causes of teacher dissatisfaction have been conducted. An NEA survey ("teacher opinion poll; job satisfaction", 1980), found that a majority of teachers felt that the following factors, listed in order of frequency of identification had agentive of feet on their job satisfaction. 1. Public attitudes toward the school.2.treatment of education by the media.3.Student attitudes toward learning. 4. Salary and 5. Status of teachers in the community. In addition, 49 per cent of the teachers indicated that student behavior had negative effect upon their job satisfaction.

Ford (1979) believe that variables faculty workloads may be related to teacher dissatisfaction between class size and teacher satisfaction is investigated (Glass, et al., 1979,Pages and price (1980)discovered in their study of 130 teachers that the factors contributing most to job dissatisfaction are in order of important.1.lack of planning time. 2. Tedious paper and clerical work 3.On out of tough and autocratic administration.4. Disruptive and unmotivated student's 5.Non teaching activities, such as faculty meeting and "time wasting" workshop 6.Uncooperative parents 7.Lack of autonomy to prescribe curriculum 8.Feeling of failure and 9.Low occupational prestige.

Thus, a brief discussion and outline is presented in the chapter about matters relating to teacher competency and stress. Thus, this kind of analysis gave the investigator. Some clues on the subject on the hand.

II

Reviev of the Related Literature

The investigator reviewed the available related literature pertaining to teacher stress and teaching competency for the present study and presented as follows.

1. Studies related to Teacher stress.
2. Studies related to Teaching competency.

Moholick's (1969), Mastach And Jacksons (1980)

Studies Related To Teacher Stress

A study of meaning in life, Stress and Burnout in Teachers of Secondary Schools in Calcutta.

Objects of the Study

1. To study if teachers varied in the degree of overall meaning in life and if they showed a trend low or high meaning.
2. To identify important sources of meaning in the personal and professional life of teachers and to investigate if teachers varied in the degree of meaning derived from these sources.

3. To find out the relationship, if any among the different measures of meaning in life.
4. To identify the main sources of stress in teaching and to investigate if teachers varied in the extent of experienced stress.
5. To study if teachers varied in the extent of perceived.
6. To study the relationship between stress and burnout meaning

The tools used for data collection were Moholick's (1969) purpose in life Test, Mastach and Jackson (1981) inventory for study of burnout and a scale and interview schedules prepared by the investigator for measurement of stress and other background variables. The sample comprised 345 teachers from 15 secondary schools and an in service teachers Population of three teacher training institutions in Calcutta. Survey and case study techniques were followed in the conduct of the study. Descriptive and non-parametric statistical techniques were used for analysis of data.

Findings the Study

1. Meaningfulness of life of the teachers was quite high according to their own perception.
2. Meaning in professional life was derived primarily from psychic reward obtained from task related outcomes and relationship with the student.
3. All the measures of meaning in life namely self reported meaning in life, source of meaning in life and sources of meaning in teaching had a political relationship with meaning of life.
4. The relationship between stress studied through test and stress reported by teachers was highly significant.
5. Age difference was significant with regard to stress of teachers.
6. The sample teachers had a lower degree of burnout.
7. Sex difference was significant on the burnout variable.
8. Stress was positively related to burnout with regard to emotional exhaustion and depersonalization.

9. There was negative relationship between meaning in life and stress variables measured by tests as well as self – reporting items.

10. A comparatively low level of meaning in life was identified among the sample teachers.

Studies Related to Teaching Competency

L.S.Verne. M. R.,L.V.C.U.1985

A study of Some of the Personality Component of Creative Student Teachers In Relation To Their Competence Towards Teaching.

The study was designed to compare high, medium and low creative student teachers on three dimensions of creativity and total creativity in terms of certain personality components sex, Teaching competence and achievement levels. The sample consisted of 210 B.Ed., students randomly select from our educational instructions in Lucknow. Data regarding creative were collected with the help of tolerance Test of creative thinking. For assessment personality characteristics, the multivariate personality inventory and 16PF were administered to the student teachers. A teacher effectiveness scale was administered to get an idea about their effectiveness as teachers and division scored by them in practice teaching was taken as the criterion of their performance as teachers.

Main Findings of the Study

(1) The F ratio for the effect of fluency was significant for dominance-reserved vs. outgoing, humble vs assertive and tough-minded vs. tender minded.

(2) The F ratio for the main effects of flexibility were significant for ego ideal, dominance, sober vs. happy-go-luck and group-dependent vs. self-sufficient.

(3) The F ratio for the effect of originality was significant for self-confidence humble vs. assertive and sober vs. happy-go-lucky.

(4) The F ratio for the effect of total creativity were significant for empathy, self confidence, reserved vs. outgoing sober vs. happy-go-lucky and taught minded vs. tender minded.

(5) The F ratio for the interaction of sex and total creativity was significant for neuroticism, self confidence and reserved vs. outgoing

(6) Personality factors distinguishing the low total creativity group from the medium total creativity group were self-confidence, thought minded vs. tender minded and sober vs. happy-go-luck.

Natarajan.s. Madras-u

A competency based Program in Teacher Education Curriculum:

The major objectives of these investigations were;

1. To study the relative efficiency of competency based teacher education in the pre-service education program of secondary school teachers.
2. To identify factors influencing competency achievement such as social status, economic status and level of education and.
3. To find out the relationship between an individual's self-esteem and competency achievement.

Major Findings of the Study

1. Competency-based instruction proved suitable for teaching selected units in institutions, planning and administration.
2. The seminar method seemed to be an effective method as it compared favourable with the competency-based approach.
3. The lecture method was effective as a group method.
4. Directed self-study did not compare well with other methods.
5. There was a significant relation between self-esteem and acquisition of competencies.

6. Attitude towards teaching methods had a favorable correlation with acquisition of competencies.

7. The study proved that teacher education programme could be made more effective through a competency-based approach.

Bhalwankara.G.

Sndt College of Education-pune-1984

Sie Maharastra Financed

A Study of Reliability and Validity of the Process-Process Appraising Scale of Teacher of Effectiveness.

The Major Objectives of the Study:

1. To determine the reliability of the process-process appraising scale of teacher.

2. To determine criterion related to and the content validity of the PASTE.

3. To determine the relationship between various component scores of PASTE teacher effectiveness scores on PASTE.

4. To study the effect of increase or decrease in number of components of PASTE on reliability and

5. To determine the relationship between presage variables and teacher effectiveness scores of student teacher.

The Major Findings of the Study

1. The reliability of PASTE by four-way analysis of variance was 0.72; the reliability of PASTE was quite satisfactory.

2. PASTE had satisfactory content and criterion related validity.

3. All the components correlated positively with the total teacher 3effectiveness score some skills were significant related to total teacher effectiveness.

Singh.r.s.,Gor.-1987

A Study of Teacher's Effectiveness and Its Correlates At Higher Secondary Stage In Eastern.

Major Objectives of the Study

1. To compare teacher effectiveness of Male and Female teachers of Urban and Rural area.
2. To compare their intelligence, socio-economic status, attitude towards teaching profession and adjustment.
3. To find out the relationship between teacher effectiveness and
4. To determine the combined effect of the correlates on teacher effectiveness.

The sample comprised 330 teachers of Urban and Rural areas from 22 intermediate colleges of Varanasi, Gorekhpur and Jaunpur districts. The tools used were teacher attitude inventory. Teacher adjustment inventory, SES Scale, Samoohik, Mansik Yogyata, Prakash (1/61) and teaching effectiveness rating scale.

The Major Findings

1. No significant difference in the mean scores of male and female teachers in their effectiveness was observed.
2. The difference in the mean intelligence scores of male and female teachers was not significant.
3. It was revealed that the rural female teachers had secured comparatively better scores than the rural male teachers in teacher effectiveness.
4. The difference in the mean scores of urban male and female teachers was found to be non-significant on the SES scale.
5. There was no-significant difference in the mean scores of male and female teachers belonging to rural and urban area in their attitude towards teaching.

6. There was no-significant difference in the mean scores of adjustment of male and female teachers.
7. The scores of male and female teachers in teaching effectiveness appeared to be correlated significantly with only two variables-intelligence and attitudes towards the teaching profession.
8. A low relationship between intelligence and socio-economic status was observed. It was however not sigrificant.
9. The teacher effectiveness scores of rural male and female teachers appeared to significantly relate with intelligence, socio-economic status and adjustment.
10. Intelligence showed a moderate and significant relationship with socio-economic status and adjustment of the urban teachers irrespective of sex.

Sushila Singhal; Stress in Education Indian Experience, Rawat publication, New Delhi, 2004, pp. 294-334.

The Major Findings

The personal profiles of teachers are not much important, as most of them show mild to moderate levels of stress and burnout, yet the older and those having higher educational qualifications seem to be more stress prone. Those having higher socio-economic status are more involved with students and feel more responsible, but become less idealistic over the tears. In the regular as well as in special schools, teachers experience different levels of stress. So do the males and females, and the more vs. less experienced teache-s. The negative perceptions of work-setting can induce negative feelings in teachers resulting in subsequent stress and burnout. Female teachers tend to perceive the work-setting as more positive than males. The special schoolteachers rate their work load higher; their contacts with students more frequent and intense feel more socially isolated and have more role conflicts. More experienced teachers have fewer interpersonal interactions, yet lower social isolation and fewer conflicts in regular as well as special schools. The work-setting of regular schools emerges as the necessary condition, and the stress as the sufficient condition for the onset of burnout. All teachers experience moderate levels of burnout, indicating something more can activate it to be a matter of concern. Males and females both experience it evenly. Teachers in the middle range of experience are more susceptible to stress and burnout than those with a few years or long experience. Lack of proper training is a good predictor of burnout in special school teachers. The work overload, inadequate orientation few interpersonal interactions, and more role conflicts are associated with greater self-interest. Higher social isolation leads to reduced work goals. Those facing more role conflicts tend to become emotionally detached. The improvements in work-setting need to be initiated to suit the needs of the teachers so that they can efficaciously deliver instruction to their pupils and derive satisfaction from their performance.

III

Methods of Investigation

The present study is titled "A study of the Factors Influencing Teachers Stress among the School Teachers in Chittoor".

Need for the Study

Accomplishment of educational goals and the objectives of teaching is possible only with teachers those who are competent in teaching and free from any type of stress. Teacher stress directly or indirectly influences the competency of teachers in teaching. So the teacher who is subjected to stress may not be possible to teach properly which in term competency in teaching.

Theoretically, the teacher stress may be heard to perform teaching in a competent way. But in practice how far teacher stress is influencing on teaching competency and to what extent teacher stress and teaching competency are related-are the questions waiting for answer. Hence, this study has taken up to find cut how teacher stress and teaching competency are inter-related to each other in the context of high school education.

The present investigator has surveyed the available researches on teacher stress and teaching competency and presented in chapter-111.

Design is the heart of research. The following aspects have been discussed in detail, which are concerned with the design of the present study. The present chapter is set apart for making a brief discussion of the objectives of the study, the research procedure includes the operational definitions of the different terms used the various hypotheses that were framed for verification in the present study and the rationale of these hypotheses. The selection of sample includes the sampling techniques used, the reasons for selection of a particular sampling technique and the selection of the sample according to different variables. The selection of suitable tool for collection of data and the procedure followed in administering the tool to collect the data required for the present study.

Problem of the Sudy

In the view of the previous chapter, the investigator titled the problem in the following manner.

"A study of factors Influencing Teacher's Stress among the School Teachers in Chittoor"

Objectives of the Study

1. To test the teacher stress and teaching competency scales to be use by the teacher himself.
2. To find out the relationship between teacher stress and teaching competency.
3. To find out the effect of demographical variables in respect of teacher stress.
4. To find out the effect of demographical variables in respect of teaching competency.

Item Analysis

For the purpose of determining the degree to which each item is effective in discriminating between high and low teaching competency and item analysis of the data obtained from above sample is undertaken by taking two extreme groups (High and Low) All the fifty two responses of the 200 subjects are scored and scores are arranged in an order from highest score to lowest score. Then the upper 27 per cent of the responses and lower 27per cent of the responses are taken into consideration for measuring significance of difference of means to know the item validity. A.M.S. and S.D.S for the 46 items of upper half and lower half are calculated for all the 46 items between upper and lower half using the following formula.

If the value of the critical ratio 0 the item is greater than 1. 96 (significant at 0.05 level of significant). Then the item is found valid and accepted. If the value of critical ratio of item is less than 1.96 then the item is found invalid and rejected.

Re-testing of Teacher Stress Scale

In the present study, the investigator adopted the Rama's teacher stress self-rating five-point scale developed and standardized by. Dr. Krishnan Raju (1994) because it is more appropriate to measure the teacher stress related to the areas of 1.Professional growth, 2. Work load 3). Occupational Hazards 4).Student behavior 5). Family 6), Societal

The present investigator re-tested this scale on a tryout sample of 200teachers to minimize the error in the tool.

There are 46 items under six different areas of teacher stress scale of Dr. Krishnan Raju. The distribution or 52 items is as fallows. The items are given in appendix-2.

1. Items under professional growth area of teacher stress are 8 i.e., from 1to 8.
2. Items under workload area of teacher stress are 9 i.e., from 9 to 17.
3. Items under occupational Hazards area are of teacher stress are 9 i.e., 18 to26.

4. Items under student behavior area of teacher stress are 9 i.e., 27 to 35.
5. Items under family area of teacher stress are 8 i.e., 36 to43.
6. Items under society area of teacher stress are 3 i.e., 3.

Table-1

SHOWING THE NUMBER OF ITEMS AND PERCENTAGE OF ITEMS IN TEACHERS STRESS.

	Professional Growth	Work Load	Occupational Hazards	Student Behavior	Family	Societal	Total
No.of Que %	8 16.9	9 15.2	9 16.9	9 .9	8 16.9	3 16.9	46 99.7

Adminisrration

This tool I administered to a try out samples of 200 teachers of Chittoor. Instructions to the teachers are given on the title page of the scale. Care is taken to reduce bias in rating. This is done by clearly stating the purpose of study.

Scoring

The responses are scored according to the key. The scoring procedure, which was followed in the teacher competency scale, is followed to this teacher stress also. Total number of items is 46. The maximum is 230 and the minimum possible score is 46 the high score indicates high teacher stress; the low score indicates low teacher stress.

Item Analysis

For the purpose of determining the degree to which each item is effective in discriminating high, low stress of teacher an item analysis of the data obtained from the above sample is under taken by taking two extreme groups (High and low) All the 46 responses of the 200subjects are scored and total scores are arranged in an order from highest score to lowest score. Then the upper 27per cent of the total response and lower 27 per cent of total responses are taken into consideration. For measuring significance of the items retained after item analysis for the final student in teacher difference of means to know item validity A.M.S and SDS for all the 46 items of the upper half and lower half are calculated. Critical ratio is then calculated for all the items between upper and lower halves. If the value of critical for ratio of the items is greater than 1.96 (significant at 0.05 level of significance). Then the item is found valid and accepted. If the value of the critical ratio of the item is less than 1.96 then the item is found as invalid and rejected. The scale with all the accepted items used for final study is given in appendix 4.

Collection of Data

After retesting the two tools of the study, fresh and final scales are prepared for the final study with personal data pose. There two standardized tools of the resent study are administered to 200teacher of different schools in Chittioor of A.P. for collecting the data the investigator visited each school and administered the scales to the teachers personally. They are advised to put their name, sex, qualification, designation, experience etc. against the place provided in the personal data sheet of each scale.

Instructions are given in the first page of each scale. The investigator requested the teacher to fallow the instruction while responding the tools. Most of the teachers filled the tools on the spot and returned to the investigator. These two tools collected and scored according to the scoring procedure explained in the development and standardization of tools.

Sample

The sample selected for the present investigation consist 200 teachers of different Schools in Chittoor of A.P. The age of the teachers up to 35 and above 35 years, both male and female teachers are found in the sample. Teachers having 2 slabs experience i.e. above15 years, below 15 years are found in the sample. Teachers of two cadres of P.G. and graduate teachers. Another sample Government teacher. Thus, it is found to be a satisfactory sample and the sample is believed to be adequate to test the hypothesis. The sample distribution of the study is shown in below

AGE IN YEARS	ABOVE 35	BELOW 35
		121 79
SEX	MALE	FEMALE
	88	112
GENERAL	GRADUATES	P.G
QUALIFICATION	100	100
TEACHING	ABOVE 35	BELOW 35
EXPERIENCE	84	116
MANAGEMENT	GOVT.	PRIVATE
	99	101

Analysis of Data

The following statistical techniques are used to analyze the data.

Mean and standard deviations of all the distributions are calculated.

To find out the relationship between teaching competency and Teacher stress "r" values are computed.

Co-efficiency of co-relation for the entire dimension was also calculated.

Critical ratios are calculated for testing the subsidiary hypothesis.

Hypotheses of the Study

1. There is no significant difference between Above 35 years age of teachers and Below 35 years age of teacher towards teacher stress.
2. There is no significant difference between Male and Female teachers towards teacher stress.
3. There is no significant difference between Graduate teachers and post Graduate Teachers towards teacher stress.

4. There is no significant difference between Above 15 tears, and Below 15 years teaching experience towards teacher stress.
5. There is no significant difference between Government School Teachers and Private school Teachers towards teacher stress.
6. There is no significant difference between Male and Female Teachers towards teacher stress in Professional growth.
7. There is no significant difference between Male and Female Teachers towards teacher stress in Work Load.
8. There is no significant difference between Male and Female Teachers towards teacher stress in Occupational Hazards.
9. There is no significant difference between Male and Female Teachers towards teacher stress in Student Behavior.
10. There is no significant difference between Male and Female Teachers towards teacher stress in Family.
11. There is no significant difference between Graduate teachers and Post Graduate Teachers towards teacher stress in Professional Growth
12. There is no significant difference between Graduate teachers and Post Graduate Teachers towards teacher stress in Work Load
13. There is no significant difference between Graduate teachers and Post Graduate Teachers towards teacher stress in Occupational Hazards.
14. There is no significant difference between Graduate teachers and Post Graduate Teachers towards teacher stress in Student Behavior
15. There is no significant difference between Graduate teachers and Post Graduate Teachers towards teacher stress in Family.

Limitations of the Study

1. The study is limited to only teachers of different primary and secondary schools in Chittoor of A.P.

2. Of the three criteria of teaching competency, only two criteria i.e. presage and process are covered in this study.
3. To measure the teaching competency and teacher stress teacher self -rating scales are used in this study.
4. Of many dimensions of teaching competency, planning presentation, closing evaluation, and managerial dimensions are considered in this study.
5. Of many dimensions of teacher stress professional growth, work load, Occupational hazards, Students behavior, family and societal dimensions are considered in this study

Procedure

In order to test the Hypothesis the investigator planned and executed in three steps

(1) Measurement of teacher stress with the help of standardized teacher stress,

(2) .Measurement of teaching competency with the help of Rama's teaching competency scale.

(3) Using appropriate statistical procedures to find out relationship between teacher stress and teaching competency.

Re-testing of Rama's Teacher Stress Scale

In the present study, the investigator adopted the Rama's teacher stress self rating five point scale developed and standardized by Prof. R. Rama (2004) because it is more appropriate to measure the teacher stress related to the areas of

1. Professional Growth 2. Workload 3. Occupational Hazards 4. Student Behavior 5. Family 6. Societal.

1. There are 46 items under 6 different areas of teacher stress scale of Prof. R. Rama.

2. Items under professional growth area of teacher stress are 8 i.e., from 1to 8.

3. Items under Work Load area of teacher stress are 9 i.e., from 9 to 17.
4. Items under Occupational Hazards area of teacher stress are 9 i.e., from18 to 26.
5. Items under Student Behavior area of teacher stress are 9 i.e., from 27 to 35.
6. Items under Family area of teacher stress are 8 i.e., from 36 to 43.
7. Items under Societal area of teacher stress are 3 i.e., from 44 to 46.

Table - 2

VARIABLE WISE DISTRIBUTION OF THE SAMPLE

Variable	Categories	Size	Grand Total
Sex	Male	85	
	Female	115	200
Age	Above 35	129	
	Below 35	71	200
Qualification	Graduate	92	
	Post-Graduate	108	200
Management	Government	99	
	Private	101	200
Teaching	Above 15	92	
Experience	Below 15	108	200

Selection of the Tool

A research tool plays a major role in any worthwhile research as it is the sole factor is determining the sound data and in arriving at perfect conclusions about the problem or study on hand, which ultimately, helps in providing suitable remedial measures to the problem concerned.

The progress of making depends upon well-conducted research programme. Well conducted research programmes postulate sufficient, reliable and valid facts such facts are obtained through a systematic procedure, which involves various devices. Each rehear tool is appropriate in a given situation to accomplish a particular purpose. It may be stressed that these tools may be used in combination. They supplement the work of each other.

John Best observes, "Like the tools in the carpenter box, each research tool is appropriate in a given situation to accomplish a particular purpose". Each data gathering -device has both merits and Hazards of limitations.

Different tools are used to collect various kinds of information for different purposes. The investigator should familiarize themselves with nature, merits and limitations of these tools and should attempt to learn how to construct and use them effectively.

The following are some of the tools generally employed for the purpose of research.

(a) Inquiry forms:

1. Questionnaire
2. Schedule
3. Check-list
4. Rating scale
5. Score card
6. Attitude scale

b) Observation

c) Interview

d) Sociometry

e). Psychological tests:

1.Achivement test
2. Aptitude test
3. Intelligence test
4. Interest Inventory
5. Personality measures

Inequity forms are class of data gathering devices which make use of properly prepared Performa or forms for enquiring into and securing information about certain phenomena under study. Out of number of such inequity forms, perhaps the most used and the most abused of tools is the questionnaire.

Keeping in view the desirability and suitability for the collection of the data, the investigator adapted the questionnaire in case of the present investigation.

Administration of the Tool

The investigator personally went to each institution and has taken permission from the respective head of the institutions and personally administered to 200 teachers in the various schools. The investigator first explained to the teachers about the importance of the investigation and attitude of teachers towards teacher stress in relation to teaching competency in school teachers. As stated earlier, the present investigation is intended to the attitudes of schoolteachers.

Analisis of the Data

The following statistical techniques are followed to analyze of the data.

1. Mean and Standard Deviation of all the distributions are calculated.
2. To find out the relationship between teacher stress and teaching competency 'r' values are computed.

The analyze and interpretation of the present data is presented in proceeding Chapter

Scoring Procedure

The responses are scored in stress according to key, for all the items scores from five to one for the five responses i.e. N. S. (No stress), Mi. S (Mild stress), Mo. S (Moderate Stress), M. S.(More

Stress), S. S. (Sevier Stress) total No. of items 46 in teacher stress scale.

Table-3: THE WEIGHTAGE GIVEN TO RESPONSES

KIND OF RESPONSES	MARKS
No Stress (N.S)	5
Mild Stress (Mi. S.)	4
Moderate Stress (Mo. S.)	3
More Stress (M. S.)	2
Sevier Stress (S. S.)	1

Stitistical Techniques Used

The above-mentioned hypotheses, which were framed keeping the variables like age, sex, teaching experience, medium of teaching, Qualification Type of management were taken into consideration. The collected data analyzed and the results are interpreted and statistical aspects like means, standard deviation and critical ratios are taken as the statistical techniques to study and analyze the variables. Co-efficient of co-relation with the help of scatter diagram was made use of to study the reliability of the test scores. The technique of the significance of the difference between means is used. Here technique only large samples in different categories considered for comparison so that use was made only of the formula for large samples. It was further assumed that the means were uncorrelated.

Where

A.M =Arithmetic mean

A.A.M = Assumed arithmetic mean

S.D = Standard deviation

C.R = Critical Ratio

1,2 = Standard deviation of two samples

M1, m2 = Means of the two samples

N1,N2 = The size of the two sample

IV

Analysis and Interpretation of the Data

Introduction

Data analysis is the heart of any social science research. Using questionnaire or any inventory the researcher collects the information. Until and unless, it is proposed through statistical treatment, it serves no purpose. The researcher using the standardized procedure that tool so constructed collected data from various variables. The he collected information is given numerical scoring and scores are tabulated. The mean, median, mode, quartile deviation, standard deviation, kurtosis etc. are also obtained. Basing on the responses of the individuals the researcher tabulated the item of the tool according to their scoring order presented findings and calculations. Finally, the researcher presented suggestions for the teacher stress in relation to teaching competency scope for further research.

Analysis

The analysis and interpretation of data involves the objectives material in the processions of the research and his subjective and desires to derive from the data, the inherent meaning in their relation to the problem. To avoid making conclusions are interpretations from insufficient are invalid data, the final analysis must be anticipated in detailed when plans are being made for collecting information.

J. C. Agarwal, has explained thus:"However values, reliable and adequate the data may be, it does not serve any worthwhile purpose unless it is carefully edited. Systematically analyzed intelligently interpreted and rationally concluded".

Analysis of data means studying the tabulated material in order to determine inherent facts of meaning. It involves breaking down existing complex factors into smaller parts and putting the together in new arrangements for purposes interpretation.

The Following are the Methods Most Commonly Used In Statistical Analysis

1. Calculating frequency distribution (usually in percentage) of items under study.
2. Testing the data for morality of distribution-Skewness and Kurtosis.
3. Calculating methods of central tendency -Mean, Median, Mode and establishing norms.
4. Calculating percentile and percentile ranks.
5. Calculating measures of dispersion -Standard deviation, Mean deviation, Quartile deviation and Range.
6. Calculating measures of relationship-Coefficient of correlation reliability and validity.
7. Graphical representation of data -Frequency Polygon curve, Hectograph, Cumulative frequency, Polygon and Ogive etc.

In the process of analysis of the data, the investigators usually make used of us many of the above simply statistical devises as necessary for purpose of their study. There are some other complicated devices of statistical analysis which researches use in particular experimental or complex casual comparative studies investigation.

Interpretation

"The process of interpretation is essentially one of the stating what the results (findings) show, what do they means What is their significance What is the answer to original problem Interpretation is thus by no means a much of process. Its uses of scientific examination of the results of one's analysis in the light of all the limitations of the data gathering, Interpretation means the application of deductive and inductive logic to the research process.

Interpretation is the most important step in the total procedure of research, it is purely subjective and many errors are made at their stage. An adequate knowledge not only of techniques of research, but also of one's field of study and a capacity to do carefully and critical thinking are very essential to safe guard against misinterpretation of facts collected.

The analysis and interpretation of the data represent the application of deductive and inductive logic to the research process. Interpretation calls for a critical examination of the result of one's analysis in the light of all the limitation of the data gathering and his subjective attitude to avoid subjectively, one must be critical on one's own thinking.

Good, Barr and Scats the following characteristics of good generalizations.

1. Education generalization should be conceivable and in agreement with facts.
2. They should not conflict with the known laws of nature of previously established generalization.
3. They should be stated in the simplest possib e terms.
4. They should be amenable to deductive reasoning.

In this part the result of present study are analyzed and interpreted. The results are presented and all the hypotheses are tested and verified in the present study, the results are analyzed and presented in three parts.

1. The first part deals with related to significant relationship between the teacher stress and teaching competency.
2. The second part deals with testing the hypotheses pertaining to teacher stress.
3. The third part deals with testing the hypotheses pertaining to teaching competency.

Testing of Hypotheses-1

There is no significant difference between above 35 years age of teachers and blow 35 years age of teachers towards teachers stress.

To test the validity of the above hypothesis, the following calculations are made. Table showing the significant difference between above 35 years age of teachers and below 35 years age of teacher in respect of teachers stress.

TABLE -4

AGE	N	MEAN	SD	't' VALUE
1.00	129	161.66	35.70	0.56
2.00	71	158.87	29.49	@

From the above table the calculated 't' value is 0.56 found to be less than the table value (1.96) at 0.05 level. Hence, the hypothesis-1 is accepted. Hence, there is no significance difference between above 35 years age of teachers and below 35 years age of teachers towards teacher stress.

Testing of Hypotheses - 2

There is no significant difference between male and female teachers towards teacher stress. To test the validity of the above hypothesis, the following calculations are made. The table showing the significant differences between male and female teachers in respect of teacher stress.

TABLE -5

SEX	N	MEAN	SD	't' VALUE
1.00	85	28.41	6.02	1.54
2.00	115	29.78	6.33	@

From the above table the calculated 't' value is 1.54 found to be less than the table value (1.96) at 0.05 level. Hence, the hypothesis-2 is accepted. Hence, there is no significance difference between male and female teacher towards teacher stress.

Testing of Hypotheses - 3

There is no significant difference between graduate teachers and post-graduate teachers towards teacher stress. To test the validity of the above hypothesis, the following calculations are made. The table showing the significant differences between graduate teachers and post-graduate teachers in respect of teacher stress.

TABLE -6

EDUCATIONAL QUALIFICATION	N	MEAN	SD	't' VALUE
1.00	92	164.22	37.00	1.386
2.00	108	157.63	30.20	@

From the above table the calculated 't' value is 1.386 found to be greater than the table value (1.96) at 0.05 level. Hence, the hypothesis-3 is accepted. Hence, there no is significance difference between graduate teacher and post-graduate teachers towards teacher stress.

Testing of Hypotheses - 6

There is no significant difference between male and female teachers towards teacher stress in professional growth. To test the validity of the above hypothesis, the following calculations are made. The table showing the significant differences between male and female teachers in respect of teacher stress in professional growth.

TABLE -9

SEX	N	MEAN	SD	't' VALUE
1.00	85	28.41	6.02	01.544
2.00	115	29.78	6.33	@

From the above table the calculated 't' value is 01.544 found to be less than the table value (1.96) at 0.05 level. Hence, the hypothesis-6 is accepted. Hence, there is no significance difference between male and female teacher towards teacher stress in professional growth.

Testing Of Hypotheses - 7

There is no significant difference between male and female teachers towards teacher stress in work load. To test the validity of the above hypothesis, the following calculations are made. The table showing the significant differences between male and female teachers in respect of teacher stress in work load.

TABLE -10

SEX	N	MEAN	SD	't' VALUE
1.00	85	30.20	8.22	0.939
2.00	115	31.32	8.44	@

From the above table the calculated't' value is -.939 found to be greater than the table value (1.96) at 0.05 level. Hence, the hypothesis-7 is accepted. Hence, there is no significance difference between male and female teacher towards teacher stress in workload.

Testing of Hypotheses - 8

There is no significant difference between male and female teachers towards teacher stress in occupational hazards. To test the validity of the above hypothesis, the following calculations are made. The table showing the significant differences between male and female teachers in respect of teacher stress in occupational hazards.

TABLE -11

SEX	N	MEAN	SD	't' VALUE
1.00	85	31.44	7.34	0.685
2.00	115	32.20	7.91	@

From the above table the calculated 't' value is 0.685 found to be greater than the table value (1.96) at 0.05 level. Hence, the hypothesis-8 is accepted. Hence, there is no significance difference between male and female teacher towards teacher stress in occupational hazards.

Testing Of Hypotheses - 9

There is no significant difference between male and female teachers towards teacher stress in student behaviour. To test the validity of the above hypothesis, the following calculations are made. The table showing the significant differences between male and female teachers in respect of teacher stress in student behaviour.

TABLE -12

SEX	N	MEAN	SD	't' VALUE
1.00	85	30.87	8.51	1.386
2.00	115	29.26	7.81	@

From the above table the calculated 't' value is 1.386 found to be greater than the table value (1.96) at 0.05 level. Hence, the hypothesis-9 is accepted. Hence, there is no significance difference between male and female teacher towards teacher stress in student behaviour.

Testing of Hypotheses - 10

There is no significant difference between male and female teachers towards teacher stress in family. To test the validity of the above hypothesis, the following calculations are made. The table showing the significant differences between male and female teachers in respect of teacher stress in family.

TABLE -13

SEX	N	MEAN	SD	't' VALUE
1.00	85	28.01	7.266	1.305
2.00	115	29.417	7.72	@

From the above table the calculated 't' value is 1.305 found to be greater than the table value (1.96) at 0.05 level. Hence, the hypothesis-10 is accepted. Hence, there is no significance difference between male and female teacher towards teacher stress in family.

Testing of Hypotheses - 11

There is no significant difference between graduate teachers and post-graduate teachers towards stress in professional growth.

To test the validity of the above hypothesis, the following calculations are made. The table showing the significant differences between graduate teachers and post-graduate teachers in respect of teacher stress in professional growth.

TABLE -14

EDUCATIONAL QUALIFICATION	N	MEAN	SD	't' VALUE
1.00	92	29.81	6.70	1.291
2.00	108	28.67	5.77	@

From the above table the calculated 't' value is 1.291 found to be greater than the table value (1.96) at 0.05 level. Hence, the hypothesis-11 is accepted. Hence, there is no significance difference between graduate teacher and post-graduate teachers towards teacher stress in professional growth.

Testing of Hypotheses - 12

There is no significant difference between graduate teachers and post-graduate teachers towards stress in workload. To test the validity of the above hypothesis, the following calculations are made. The table showing the significant differences between graduate teachers and post-graduate teachers in respect of teacher stress in workload.

TABLE -15

EDUCATIONAL QUALIFICATION	N	MEAN	SD	't' VALUE
1.00	92	32.4348	8.3827	2.518
2.00	108	29.4907	8.1166	*

From the above table the calculated 't' value is 2.518 found to be less than the table value (1.96) at 0.05 level. Hence, the hypothesis-12 is rejected. Hence, there is significance difference between graduate teacher and post-graduate teachers towards teacher stress in workload.

Testing of Hypotheses - 14

There is no significant difference between graduate teachers and post-graduate teachers towards stress in student behaviour.

To test the validity of the above hypothesis, the following calculations are made. The table showing the significant differences between graduate teachers and post-graduate teachers in respect of teacher stress in student behaviour.

TABLE -17

EDUCATIONAL QUALIFICATION	N	MEAN	SD	't' VALUE
1.00	92	30.0109	8.7549	0.105
2.00	108	29.8889	7.6162	@

From the above table the calculated 't' value is 0 105 found to be greater than the table value (1.96) at 0.05 level. Hence, the hypothesis-14 is accepted. Hence, there is no significance difference between graduate teacher and post-graduate teachers towards teacher stress in student behaviour.

Testing Of Hypotheses - 15

There is no significant difference between graduate teachers and post-graduate teachers towards stress in family. To test the validity of the above hypothesis, the following calculations are made. The table showing the significant differences between graduate teachers and post-graduate teachers in respect of teacher stress in family.

TABLE -18

EDUCATIONAL QUALIFICATION	N	MEAN	SD	't' VALUE
1.00	92	29.27	7.68	0.781
2.00	108	28.43	7.44	@

From the above table the calculated 't' value is 0.781 found to be greater than the table value (1.96) at 0.05 level. Hence, the hypothesis-15 is accepted. Hence, there is no significance difference between graduate teacher and post-graduate teachers towards teacher stress in family.

V

Summary and Conclusion

It is high time to identify the problem of the teacher in particular his competency and his mental agony to make the teaching learning process useful to the present day condition. In the modern days teacher is loaded with so many sophisticated technological trends that were place in the modern human beings also confronted with many perplexing problems caused due to perpetually changing world resulting in frustration, Conflict, Anxiety, Stress and so on. Coleman in n1982 also observed that, "The 17th century has been called the age of enlightenment, the 18th century the age of reason, the 19th century the age of progress and the 20th century the age of anxiety". This emphasizes that a meaningful and satisfying way of life has become difficult in this age of anxiety the teacher of today is not exempted from the above age of anxiety.

Teaching is a sensitive weapon to achieve the expected educational goals through effective teaching learning process. The effective teaching is possible only with the teacher, those who are mentally sound. We should make the teacher away from the Anxiety, Stress and so on. So as to utilize all his teaching competencies to make the teaching learning processes in an effective way.

The modern research studies observed that the teacher performance and teacher behavior are strongly affected by stress. ARYACDU and SUTCLIFFE (1977) stated that," The stress with the teaching profession may affect the school as an organization, teacher performance, the physical and emotional well being of the teacher".

The modern research studies observed that the teacher performance and teacher behavior are strongly affected by stress. ARYACDU and SUTCLIFRE (1977) stated the, "The stress with the teaching profession may affect the school as an organization, teacher performance, the physical and emotional well being of the teacher".

Meaning of Stress

Stress is a condition stream on one's emotions, thought processes and physical conditions. When it is excessive, it can pretend once ability to cope with environment. (Hans Selye, 1976) "Stress is the general term applied to the pressures; employs developed various symptoms of stress as, "an adjective demand placed on the organism".

Stress has been defined following Lazarus's model, as a state of imbalance when the demands made on the person in different areas of life exceed her / his capabilities and resources (Lazarus and Folkman , 1984)

Stress has been defined following Lazarus (1974) as a state arising from imbalance between the demands made and the coping resources at one's disposal.

Stress has been defined as a state of imbalance between one's personal resources and the environmental demands, and manifested in the form of a number of psychosomatic factor, such as Somatization, Obsessive-Compulsive interpersonal sensitivity, Depression and Anxiety.

Teacher Stress

Job stress is most common psychological phenomena that are prevalent among people who are in different jobs and professions. The stress studies are initially directed toward industrial organizations within the private sector. Researchers have come to believe that stress may be especially prevalent among human service profession, particularly the teaching profession, (Kjyiacou and Suteliffe 1977-78; Pettegrew and Wolf 1982, Cherniss 1980: and Coorper and Marshall 1980). As a teaching is a human service profession, stress within the teaching profession is considerable and may have far-reaching consequences on the entire education system. Teaching is complex process were in teacher is expected to exhibit many skills. This makes a teacher to experiences stress in the profession.

Further, Pettergrew and Wolf (1982) opined that 'Teacher stress has a nationwide concern and relatively new area of empirical research".

Factors prepared by teachers as being troublesome or stressful have included students discipline, negative attitudes towards school, physical violence, is adequate preparation time, lack of clear role definition and heavy workloads". (Bearly, Myette and Serma, 1983; Chichen and Koff, 1978; Olander and Ferrel, 1970).

Teacher is subjected to stress due to incoherent social life, widening social distance, segregation, lack of societal support, corruption, nepotism, unnecessary societal involvement in day-to-day activities, high degree of social indiscipline, deterioration of values, lack of social security etc.

Effects of Teacher Stress

As job stress effect organizational performance teacher stress impedes teacher performance in teaching. Infect it is assumed that mild stress can even enhance performance but high level of stress can create physical, Psychological and behavioral problems among teacher. There are several research studies, which observed that, a high level of stress accompanied by physical illness such as high blood pressures, ulcers and even cancer. Similarly high level of stress may be accompanied by psychological problems such as anger, anxiety, depression, nervousness, irritability, tension and boredom. Excessive stress may also result in behavioral problems such as sleeplessness, under eating or over eating, increased smoking and drinking and drug abuse. Many researches of teacher

Teacher competency and Stress-a Briefoutline

The study is about teacher competency in relation to stress. Teacher competence, in general scene, impedes when teacher suffer from stress. In this chapter, a discussion is made about teacher competency, stress, and the development of this type of study in the world.

"Teacher competency" refers to the set of knowledge, abilities and beliefs a teacher possess and bring to the teaching situation. Teacher competence differs from teacher performance and teacher effectiveness in that it is a stable characteristic of the teacher that does not change appreciably when the teacher moves from one situation to another. It resembles teacher performance in that it has also been proposed as a basis from which teach effectiveness can be inferred.

Need for the Study

Accomplishment of educational goals and the objectives of teaching is possible only with the teacher those who are competent in teaching and free from any type of stress. Teacher stress directly or indirectly influences the competency of teacher in teaching. So the teacher who is subjected to stress may not be possible to teach properly which in term Indus is competency in teaching. Theoretically, this teacher stress may be heard to perform teaching in a competent way. But in practice how for teacher stress is influencing on teaching competency and to what extent teacher stress and teaching competency are related-are the questions waiting for answer. Hence, this study has taken up to find out how teacher stress teaching competency are inter related to each other in the context of high school education.

Objectives of the Study

1. To test the teacher stress and teaching competency scales to be use by the teacher himself.

2. To find out the relationship between teacher stress and teaching competency.
3. To find out the effect of demographical variables in respect of teacher stress.
4. To find out the effect of demographical variables in respect of teaching competency.

Hypotheses of the Study

1. There is no significant difference between Above 35 years age of teachers and Below 35 years age of teachers towards teacher stress.
2. There is no significant difference between Male and Female Teachers towards teacher stress.
3. There is no significant difference between Graduate teachers and Post Graduate Teachers towards teacher stress.
4. There is no significant difference between Above 15 tears, and Below 15 years teaching experience towards teacher stress.
5. There is no significant difference between Government School Teachers and Private school Teachers towards teacher stress.
6. There is no significant difference between Male and Female Teachers towards teacher stress in Professional growth.
7. There is no significant difference between Male and Female Teachers towards teacher stress in Work Load.
8. There is no significant difference between Male and Female Teachers towards teacher stress in Occupational Hazards.
9. There is no significant difference between Male and Female Teachers towards teacher stress in Student Behavior.
10. There is no significant difference between Male and Female Teachers towards teacher stress in Family.
11. There is no significant difference between Graduate teachers and Post Graduate Teachers towards teacher stress in Professional Growth

12. There is no significant difference between Graduate teachers and Post Graduate Teachers towards teacher stress in Work Load

13. There is no significant difference between Graduate teachers and Post Graduate Teachers towards teacher stress in Occupational Hazards.

14. There is no significant difference between Graduate teachers and Post Graduate Teachers towards teacher stress in.Student Behavior

15. There is no significant difference between Graduate teachers and Post Graduate Teachers towards teacher stress in Family.

Limitations of the Study

1. The study is limited to only teachers of different schools in Chittoor of A.P.
2. Of the three criteria of teaching competency, only two criteria i.e. presage and process are covered in this study.
3. To measure the teaching competency and teacher stress teacher self -rating scales are used in this study.
4. Of many dimensions of teaching competency, planning presentation, closing evaluation, and managerial dimensions are considered in this study.
5. Of many dimensions of teacher stress professional growth, work load, Occupational hazards, Students behavior, family and societal dimensions are considered in this study

Conclusions

From the present study only one factor that is Educational Qualification as significant impact on teachers stress. The male teachers Mean value is 32.4348, which is more than Female teachers mean value (29.4907). The other factors are viz.,

1. There is no significance difference between Above 35 year's age of teachers and below 35 years age of teachers towards teacher stress.
2. There is no significance difference between Male and Female teachers towards teacher stress.
3. There is no significance difference between Graduate teachers and Post-Graduate teachers towards teacher stress.
4. There is no significance difference between Experience of above 15 years and below 15 years towards teacher stress.
5. There is no significance difference between Govt. school teachers and private school teachers towards teacher stress.
6. There is no significance difference between Male and Female teachers towards teacher stress in professional growth.
7. There is no significance difference between Male and Female teachers towards teacher stress in Work Load.
8. There is no significance difference between Male and Female teachers towards teacher stress in Occupational Hazards.
9. There is no significance difference between Male and Female teachers towards teacher stress in Student behavior.
10. There is no significance difference between Male and Female teachers towards teacher stress in Family.
11. There is no significance difference between Graduate teachers and Post-Graduate teachers towards teacher stress in Professional Growth.
12. There is significance difference between Graduate teachers and Post-Graduate teachers towards teacher stress in Work Load.
13. There is no significance difference between Graduate teachers and Post-Graduate teachers towards teacher stress in Occupational Hazards.

14. There is no significance difference between Graduate teachers and Post-Graduate teachers towards teacher stress in Student behavior.

15. There is no significance difference between Graduate teachers and Post-Graduate teachers towards teacher stress in Family.

Hence, there is no significant impact on teachers stress. Teachers would give more importance for the quality of education. It is necessary to encourage teachers to study for the further education. The role of Government is also important to motivate the teachers towards higher education.

Suggestions

EXERCISE: Physical exercise is accepted as the best antidote to stress. It keeps the body healthy, makes one emotionally strong, and eases nervous tension. It keeps the mind, body and action coordinated.

RELAXATION: Relaxation response is an innate physiological change elicited by some psychological means. Evidence indicates that the immune function in the body improves by relaxation training, and its regular practice can help maintain the cool. These can include hobbies like reading, listening to music, etc.

VALUE EDUCATION: Intervention for change in social and practical values can help them think and act rationally and proactively.

MEDITATION: It is a continuous scream of effortless concentration, on a single point, over an extended period. It is suggested that the concentration should be maintained unbroken. Psychologists have argued that meditation leads to better emotional and physical health.

YOGA: A stress management programme in the Indian setting may combine some elements of Gita and Yoga in the preventive plans. Srivastava (1981) concluded that persons coping more effectively with stress have more positive orientation to life in general, and employ a valuable mix of coping and defense response. Yoga is a holistic science, which gives to the person tools and techniques to expand conscious awareness into the unconscious In order to become aware of the patterns and tendencies that cause stress.

1. It is to be suggested that teachers effects teaching competency.
2. The stress creators harm the teacher effectiveness and teaching competency
3. The government or Private management of the institution should improve the conditions for better teaching by reducing the stress factors.
4. The main stress creators like lack of promotional opportunities lack of professional growth are to be tackled to improve the teaching competency.
5. Unless stress creators are reduced qualitative improvement teaching, learning process cannot be improved.

Suggestions For Further Study

1. The study may be extended to higher and primary education.
2. To measure the teaching competency presage, process and product variables may be compared.
3. Stress and psychological well-being Among Tribal and Non-Tribal primary school teachers.
4. Stress and burnout among teachers in Regular and special schools.
5. Stress and coping among college students.
6. Stress and Coping among Adolescents.
7. Relationship between teaching competency and teacher motivation may be studied.
8. Relationship between teacher stress and teacher adjustment may be studied.

9. An extensive study is needed for teacher stress and teaching competency.

Bibliography

1. Bailkeri, K. N. (1983): Effect of self- Instructional Remedial Micro Teaching course on the Instructional Competency of in service secondary school mathematics teachers.
2. Bhalwankar, A. G. (1984): A study of Reliability and Validity of the process appraising scale of teacher effectiveness.
3. Balachandran, E. S. (1981): Teaching effectiveness and student evaluation of Teaching, Ph.D., Education, Madras University.
4. Coates, T. I. and Thoresen (1976 spring): Teacher anxiety, A review with recommendation, Review of educational research 49(2), pp.159-184.
5. Cooper, C. Marshal, J. (1976): Occupational sources of stress. A review of the literature relating to coronary heart disease and mental ill health Journal of occupational Psychology, pp.11-28.
6. Cox, T. Mackay, C. J. Cox, S. Watts, C. and Brockley (1978): Stress and wellbeing in schoolteachers psycho-physiological response to occupational stress. Paper presented to the Economic Society Conference, Nottingham University England.
7. Dohrenwend, D. et. al (1981): Stress in the community a report to the president's commission on the accidents at three-mile land. Annual of the New York Academy of Sciences 365, 159-174.
8. Dac, R.C. Passi, B K. and Singh, A. (1982): Effectiveness of different strategies of integration of teaching skills in developing general teaching competency of student's teachers department of teacher education, NCERT.
9. Davis, H. (1964): Evaluation of current practices in evaluating teacher competency, in B. J. Biddle and J. Ellance (Eds).

Contemporary research on teacher effectiveness, New York, Holt, Rinehart and Winston.

10. Donald, M. Medley (1982): Teacher Effectiveness" Encyclopedia of Educational Research, Education Harold. E. Mitzel, Vol. 4. Mac millan publishing &Co., New York.

11. Fimian, M. J. and Santoro, T.M. (1983): sources and manifestations of occupational stress and reported by full item special education teachers. Exceptional children, pp. 540-543.

12. Gupta, N. and Beehr, T.A. (1973): "Job stress and employee behavior", Organization behaviors and human performance, pp. 373-387.

13. Girdano, D.E. and Everly, G. S. (1979): Controlling stress and tension, Englewood cliffs, N.J. Prinetice hall.

14. Greenwood, G.E. Olejuik, S. F. and Parkoy, F. W. (1990): Relationship between four teacher efficiency belief patterns and selected teacher characteristics. Journal of research and development in education,23 (2), 102-106.

15. Gupta, S. (1981): A comparative study of Socio-Economic background problems and professional behavior of men women teachers in co-education Institutions at different levels in the state of Haryana, Ph.D., Education, Kurnool University.

16. Gupta, U. (1981): job involvement and need patterns of primary school teachers in relation to teaching effectiveness Ph.D. Education, All Universities.

17. Hodge, J. and Marker (1978): assuring teacher stress; Beneficial task for administrator, American secondary Education, 8(4).

18. Joseph schwrzwaldet at stress reaction of school age children to the Bombardment by send missiles journal of Abnormal Psychology 1993, Vol. 102, No.3, 404-410.

19. Kaiser, J.S. and Polezynski, J. J. (1982): Educational stress sources, reaction, preventions. Poe body journal of education 10.

20. Kessler, R. C. Price, R.H. and Wortman, C. B. (1985): social factors in phycho pathology, stress support and coping process, annual review of psychology 36, 531-572.

21. Kryiacane and Suteliffe, J. (1977): Teacher Stress; A review educational review 29.

22. Kryiacau, C. and Sutclifee, J. (1978): Teacher stress; Prevalence, Source and Symptoms, British journal of educational psychology 48.

23. Lazarus, S. Folkman (1984): Stress appraisal and coping, New York springer publishing company.

24. Lislie Sovoy (1990): "Source of stress on trainee lectures for further and higher education". Journal for Higher education summer (1990).

25. Vene, M.R. (1985): A study of some of the personality components of creative student teacher in relation to their competency towards teaching.

26. Yogendra Kumar and Rattan Lai (1980): Use of micro-teaching in improving general teaching competency of in service teachers.

27. Arnett, J.J. (1999): Adolescent storm and stress, Reconsidered. American Psychologist, pp. 317-326.

28. Folkman, S. and Lazarus, R. S.(1985): If it changes it must be a prosess: Study of emotion and coping during three stages of a college examination. Journal of personality and social psychology, 48, 150-170.

29. Lazarus, R. S. (1993): Coping theory and research: Past, present and future. Psychosomatic Medicine, pp.234-247.